Subjectivity and Selfhood

Subjectivity and Selfhood

Investigating the First-Person Perspective

Dan Zahavi

A Bradford Book
The MIT Press
Cambridge, Massachusetts
London, England

First MIT Press paperback edition, 2008
© 2005 Massachusetts Institute of Technology

MIT Press books may be purchased at special quantity discounts for business or sales promotional use. For information, please email special_sales@mitpress.mit.edu or write to Special Sales Department, The MIT Press, 55 Hayward Street, Cambridge, MA 02142.

This book was set in Sabon by SNP Best-set Typesetter Ltd., Hong Kong.
Printed and bound in the United States of America.

Library of Congress Cataloging-in-Publication Data

Zahavi, Dan.
Subjectivity and selfhood: investigating the first-person perspective / Dan Zahavi.
    p.   cm.
"A Bradford book."
Includes bibliographical references (p.   ) and index.
ISBN 978-0-262-24050-5 (hc : alk. paper)—978-0-262-74034-0 (pb : alk. paper)
1. Self (Philosophy). 2. Consciousness. 3. Subjectivity. 4. Self-knowledge, Theory of.
I. Title.
BD438.5.Z34   2006   126—dc22   2005047918

10 9 8 7 6 5 4

Contents

Acknowledgments

This book is the result of prolonged interest in and work on the nature of consciousness, self-consciousness, selfhood, and intersubjectivity. Much of its foundational research has taken place in an interdisciplinary setting at the Center for Subjectivity Research, a Center of Excellence located at the University of Copenhagen and funded by the Danish National Research Foundation.

I have learned much from my discussions with the following people, many of whom have also read and commented on parts of the manuscript: Rudolf Bernet, John Brough, Jonathan Cole, Steven Crowell, Ingolf Dalferth, John Drummond, Shaun Gallagher, Arne Grøn, Thor Grünbaum, Jim Hart, Lisa Käll, Uriah Kriegel, Dieter Lohmar, Alva Noë, Søren Overgaard, Josef Parnas, Michael Quante, Philippe Rochat, David Rosenthal, Charles Siewert, Galen Strawson, and Evan Thompson.

I have had the opportunity to present material from the following text during lectures at various universities, including Rutgers, Stony Brook, Oxford, Warwick, CREA (Paris), Stockholm, Marburg, Boston College, Leuven, McGill, Köln, University College Dublin, Chicago, Boston University, New School University, Geneva, Helsinki, Würzburg, Kyoto, Tokyo, Kent, Jyväskylä, and Heidelberg. I have profited, in every instance, from the ensuing discussions and comments I have received.

I am very grateful to the Danish National Research Foundation, whose generous funding permitted me to write this book. I offer a special thanks to Institutionen San Cataldo for granting me a wonderful month at their monastery in Italy that allowed me to develop its composition.

Finally, I would like to thank Kristina Mommens, whose diligent proofreading of the manuscript provided countless grammatical and linguistic improvements.

Introduction

What is a self? Does it exist in reality or is it a mere social construct—or perhaps a neurologically induced illusion? If something like a self exists, what role does it play in our conscious life, and how and when does it emerge in the development of the infant? What might such psychopathological and neuropsychiatric disorders as schizophrenia or autism reveal about the fragility of self-identity and self-coherence? As this brief list of questions indicates, the contemporary discussion of the self is highly interdisciplinary in nature (see, e.g., Gallagher and Shear 1999; Zahavi 2000; Kircher and David 2003).

The legitimacy of the concept of self has recently been questioned by both neuroscientists and philosophers. Some have argued that the self is nothing but an illusion created by an interplay of various subsystems and modules in the brain (Dennett 1991; Wegner 2002; Metzinger 2003a). Others have claimed that the concept of self is a Eurocentric invention with limited historical relevance (Berrios and Marková 2003). In contrast, the hypothesis to be defended in the following chapters is that the notion of self is crucial for a proper understanding of consciousness, and consequently it is indispensable to a variety of disciplines such as philosophy of mind, social philosophy, psychiatry, developmental psychology, and cognitive neuroscience.

It would, of course, be something of an exaggeration to claim that the concept of self is unequivocal and that there is widespread consensus about what, exactly, it means to be a self. Quite to the contrary, the concept is currently used in a manifold of rival senses and it is a simple fact that the concept connotes different things in different disciplines—sometimes radically different things. What is urgently needed is a clarification of the relationship between these sometimes conflicting, sometimes complementary notions and aspects of selfhood. Moreover, such a taxonomic clarification is essential in order to evaluate the merits of the "no-self" doctrine, that is, the claim that the self is nothing but a fiction.

Such an investigation may also help clarify the perennial question concerning the relation between self and other. To what extent does selfhood involve interpersonal relations? Is the self necessarily embodied and embedded in a physical, social, and historical environment? Some have argued that the constitution of the self is a social process, that we are selves not by individual right, but in virtue of our relation to others and that we achieve self-awareness by adopting the perspective of the other toward ourselves. Who one is depends on the values, ideals, and goals one has: it is a question of what has significance and meaning, and this, of course, is conditioned by the linguistic community to which one belongs. Thus, it has been said that one cannot be a self on one's own, but only together with others. Others have denied that selfhood and self-experience emerge in the course of a (long) developmental process. While recognizing that the maturation of the self is a complex social process, they have also insisted that the sense of self is an integral and fundamental part of conscious life, which the infant is already in possession of from birth onward.

In order to shed light on these issues, I intend to investigate the relation between experience, self-awareness, and selfhood. What is the relation between (phenomenal) consciousness and the self? Are experiences always experiences for someone? Is it a conceptual and experiential truth that any episode of experiencing necessarily involves a *subject of experience*? Must we evoke a subject of experience in order to account for the unity and continuity of experience, or are experiences rather anonymous mental events that simply occur without being states or properties of anybody? What is the relation between self-awareness and the self? When we speak of self-awareness, do we then necessarily also speak of a self? Is there always a self involved in self-awareness, or is it possible to speak of self-awareness without assuming the existence of anybody being self-aware? Is *self*-awareness always to be understood as awareness of *a self*, or can it rather be understood simply as the awareness that a specific experience has of *itself*? Finally, what is the relation between consciousness and self-awareness? Is self-awareness the exception rather than the rule, insofar as consciousness is concerned? Is it something that occurs only occasionally in the life of the mind, or is it rather the case that conscious mental states differ from nonconscious mental states precisely by involving self-awareness, that is, is self-awareness a defining feature of all conscious states?

My claim is that none of the three notions can be properly understood in isolation. If we wish to understand what it means to be a *self*, we will have to examine the structure of *experience* and *self-awareness*, and vice versa. To put it differently, the claim I wish to make is that the investigations of self, self-awareness, and experience must be integrated if they are to be successful.

This approach is not without precedent. Many phenomenologists have engaged the question of self by focusing on its experiential givenness and by taking the first-person perspective seriously. They have typically taken an investigation of self-awareness to be crucial for an understanding of what it means to be a self; that is, they have typically argued that no account of self that failed to explain the experiential accessibility of the self to itself could be successful.

But why should one take the first-person perspective seriously, and why should one pay any attention to what phenomenology might have to say on the issue of selfhood and subjectivity? Is it not—as has recently been claimed—a discredited research program that has been intellectually bankrupt for at least fifty years?[1] Although this might have been a prevalent view in mainstream cognitive science and analytical philosophy of mind, the current situation is slightly more blurred. It is true that many scientists have, until recently, considered the study of phenomenal consciousness to be inherently unreliable owing to its subjective nature and thus unsuitable for scientific research. As Damasio writes, "studying consciousness was simply not the thing to do before you made tenure, and even after you did it was looked upon with suspicion" (Damasio 1999, 7). Some even went so far as to deny the existence of phenomenal consciousness (e.g. Rey 1991, 692). Within the last decade or so, however, a profound change has taken place, one occasionally described in terms of an ongoing "consciousness boom." Many new journals devoted to the study of consciousness have been established, and currently many scientists regard questions pertaining to the nature of phenomenal consciousness, the structure of the first-person perspective, and the status of the self to be among the few remaining major unsolved problems of modern science.

After a (too) long period of behaviorism and functionalism, it has consequently become rather obvious that the problem of subjectivity will not simply go away. A satisfying account of consciousness cannot make do with a mere functional analysis of intentional behavior, but must necessarily take the first-personal or subjective dimension of consciousness seriously. Much consciousness research is still aimed at locating and identifying particular neural correlates of consciousness. Yet there is also a growing realization that we will not get very far in giving an account of the relationship between consciousness and the brain unless we have a clear conception of what it is that we are trying to relate. To put it another way, any assessment of the possibility of reducing consciousness to neuronal structures and any appraisal of whether a *naturalization* of consciousness is possible will require a detailed analysis and description of the experiential aspects of consciousness. As Nagel once pointed out, a necessary requirement for any coherent reductionism is that the entity to be reduced is properly understood (Nagel 1974, 437).

Given the recent interest in the subjective or phenomenal dimension of consciousness, it is no wonder that many analytical philosophers have started to emphasize the importance of *phenomenology*. An example is Owen Flanagan, who in his 1992 book *Consciousness Reconsidered* argues for what he calls the *natural method*. If we wish to undertake a serious investigation of consciousness we cannot make do with neuroscientific or psychological (i.e., functional) analyses alone; we also need to give phenomenology its due (Flanagan 1992, 11). Thus, when studying consciousness rather than, say, deep-sea ecology, we must take phenomenological considerations into account since an important and nonnegligible feature of consciousness is the way in which it is experienced by the subject. Similar claims can be found in the recent work of Searle, Block, McGinn, Chalmers, Strawson, and Baars, among many others.

At first glance, this might indeed seem to indicate that there has been a change of attitude, that the customary hostility is a thing of the past, and that analytical philosophers and cognitive scientists are currently appreciative of the philosophical resources found in phenomenology. Things are not that simple, however. Although a small number of prominent figures in consciousness research have recently started to take philosophical phenomenology seriously, the vast majority of (Anglophone) philosophers and cognitive scientists are not using the term in its technical sense when they talk of phenomenology, but are still simply referring to a first-person description of what the "what it is like" of experience is really like. In fact, there has been a widespread tendency to identify phenomenology with some kind of introspectionism. Phenomenology is not, however, just another name for a kind of psychological self-observation; rather it is the name of a philosophical approach specifically interested in consciousness and experience inaugurated by Husserl and further developed and transformed by, among many others, Scheler, Heidegger, Gurwitsch, Sartre, Merleau-Ponty, Lévinas, Henry, and Ricoeur.

Philosophical phenomenology can offer much more to contemporary consciousness research than a simple compilation of introspective evidence.[2] Not only does it address issues and provide analyses that are crucial for an understanding of the true complexity of consciousness and which are nevertheless frequently absent from the current debate, but it can also offer a conceptual framework for understanding subjectivity that might be of considerably more value than some of the models currently in vogue in cognitive science. By ignoring the tradition and the resources therein, contemporary consciousness research risks missing out on important insights that, in the best of circumstances, will end up being rediscovered decades or centuries later (see, e.g., Zahavi 2002a, 2004a).

To put it bluntly, given some of the recent developments in cognitive science and analytical philosophy of mind along with the upsurge of theoretical and empirical interest in the subjective or phenomenal dimension of consciousness, it is simply counterproductive to continue to ignore the analyses of consciousness that phenomenology can provide. The fact that subjectivity has always been of central concern for phenomenologists, and that they have devoted so much time to a scrutiny of the first-person perspective, the structures of experience, time-consciousness, body-awareness, self-awareness, intentionality, and so forth, makes them obvious interlocutors.

The present book is an attempt to redeem some of these promissory notes. It will explore and present a number of phenomenological analyses pertaining to the nature of consciousness, self, and self-experience, but with an eye to contemporary discussions in consciousness research. This approach is motivated not only by the belief that consciousness research can profit from insights to be found in phenomenology; but also by the firm conviction that phenomenology needs to engage in a more critical dialogue with other philosophical and empirical positions than is currently the case. It is precisely by confronting, discussing, and criticizing alternative approaches that phenomenology can demonstrate its vitality and contemporary relevance. Of course this is not to deny that phenomenology has its own quite legitimate agenda; but the very attempt to engage in such a dialogue with analytical philosophy of mind, developmental psychology, or psychopathology might force phenomenology to become more problem oriented and thereby counteract what is currently one of its greatest weaknesses: its preoccupation with exegesis.[3]

Chapter 1

The first chapter will provide a preliminary outline of a phenomenological account of the relation between consciousness and self-awareness. The main focus will be on Sartre's concept of pre-reflective self-awareness and on his claim that the experiential dimension is as such characterized by a primitive or minimal type of self-awareness. Sartre's view will first be contrasted with a number of competing definitions of self-awareness found in developmental psychology, social philosophy, and philosophy of language. It will then be compared in detail to a prevalent version of the higher-order theory of consciousness, according to which the difference between a conscious and a nonconscious mental state rests on the presence or absence of a relevant meta-mental state. Despite a superficial similarity, it will be shown that Sartre's theory differs from the higher-order theory by its firm commitment to a one-level account of consciousness. The chapter will conclude by discussing whether higher-order theories can adequately account for the first-person perspective, or whether their attempt to do so gives rise to an infinite regress.

After setting the scene in the introductory chapter, the phenomenological analyses of the relation between self, consciousness, and self-consciousness will be discussed in more detail in the next three chapters. The focus, in particular, will be on Husserl's initial analysis of consciousness in *Logische Untersuchungen* (chapter 2), on his later analysis of time-consciousness (chapter 3), and on Heidegger's discussion of whether reflection can provide us with reliable access to the experiential dimension (chapter 4).

Chapter 2

The second chapter will take up two issues that are discussed in the beginning of Husserl's Fifth Logical Investigation (1901), and which will be crucial to the argument in the chapters to follow. The first issue concerns whether consciousness contains an ego, or in other words, whether every episode of experiencing necessarily involves a *subject of experience*. The second asks how we aware of our own occurrent experiences; how are they given to us? Husserl's answer to the first question constitutes a defense of a non-egological theory of consciousness that in many ways anticipates Sartre's arguments in *La transcendance de l'ego*. His reply to the second question takes the form of a critical response to Brentano's position in *Psychologie vom empirischen Standpunkt*. I will analyze Sartre's and Brentano's positions and show that Husserl, contrary to what has been the prevalent interpretation, advocated a concept of pre-reflective self-awareness already in *Logische Untersuchungen*.

Chapter 3

Husserl's discussion of self, consciousness, and self-awareness in *Logische Untersuchungen* was not the culmination, however, but only the beginning of his lifelong struggle with these issues. The third chapter will investigate the considerably more complex and sophisticated account that can be found in Husserl's later writings on inner time-consciousness (1905–1910, 1917–1918). It is in these lectures and research manuscripts that Husserl attempted to analyze the inner structure of pre-reflective self-awareness in terms of the temporal schema *protention–primal presentation–retention*. One of the questions to be discussed is whether our experiences are given as objects in inner time-consciousness prior to reflection, or whether pre-reflective self-awareness is by nature nonobjectifying.

Chapter 4

Phenomenology is generally assumed to employ a reflective methodology. But does reflection provide us with a reliable and trustworthy access to subjectivity, or does it rather objectify and distort that which it makes appear? Natorp discussed this question in his *Allgemeine Psychologie* (1912), and the conclusion he reached was highly anti-phenomenological. In the fourth chapter, I give a presentation of Natorp's neo-Kantian criticism followed by a discussion of Heidegger's subsequent response to it. This response can be found in Heidegger's early Freiburg lectures (1919–1922), and apart from addressing the concerns of Natorp, it provides a clear exposé of Heidegger's early views on self and experience. One of the implications of the analysis is that "reflection" is a polysemical term and that it is necessary to distinguish between different types of reflection. This is a view shared by Sartre, Husserl, and Merleau-Ponty. Although all of the latter rejected the view that reflection necessarily distorts lived experience (they occasionally compare reflection to attention), they nevertheless insisted that reflection does occasion a kind of self-alteration. Indeed, some forms of reflection might even be characterized as a kind of self-alienation. They involve the adoption of the perspective of the other on oneself. The chapter concludes by discussing the tenability of the customary distinction between two types of phenomenology, a reflective and a hermeneutical.

Chapter 5

After the detailed analyses in chapters 2–4, the central fifth chapter of the book will contain an extensive discussion of subjectivity and selfhood. The chapter will begin by discussing some classical and contemporary arguments in favor of a non-egological theory of consciousness and will then turn to a detailed analysis of two different notions of self: (1) the self as a narrative construction and (2) the self as an experiential dimension. The narrative approach, advocated by Ricoeur, MacIntyre, and Dennett, among others, conceives of the self as the product of a narratively structured life, thereby stressing the socially and linguistically constructed character of the self; the experiential approach, primarily defended by Husserl and Henry, insists that an investigation of the self must necessarily involve the first-person perspective and ultimately conceives of the self as the *invariant* dimension of first-personal givenness within the multitude of changing experiences. After considering some of the limitations of the narrative approach, in particular the concern that by declaring the self a construction, it might be committed to a version of the no-self doctrine and, after analyzing the structure of first-personal givenness and phenomenal consciousness in detail, thereby adding new facets to the previous discussion in chapter 1, I will argue that the two notions of self are complementary. At the same time, I argue that the experiential notion of a core or minimal self is both more fundamental than and a presupposition of the narrative self. The chapter concludes by discussing some of the empirical implications of this conclusion, in particular its relevance for our understanding of the disorders of self encountered in neurological and psychiatric afflictions.

The references in chapter 4 and 5 to intersubjectively mediated forms of self-awareness and self-understanding lead to a focused discussion of the relation between the experience of self and the experience of others in the final two chapters of the book.

Chapter 6

The sixth chapter will provide a systematic outline of the different phenomenological approaches to intersubjectivity (Scheler, Heidegger, Merleau-Ponty, Husserl, and Sartre), thereby allowing for a more nuanced perspective on the link between selfhood and otherness. The point of departure will be Scheler's criticism of the argument from analogy. It will quickly become clear that a proper understanding of our experience of others must entail a proper understanding of the relation between experience and expressive behavior. Our understanding of how we come to experience others as minded bodies must include a correct appreciation of how we come to experience ourselves as embodied minds. This observation, however, which will be crucial to the discussion of the theory of mind in chapter 7, is, only the beginning. Much more is at stake in the phenomenological analyses than simply a "solution" to the "traditional" problem of other minds. Intersubjectivity does not merely concern concrete face-to-face encounters between individuals. It is also something that is at play in perception, in the use of tools, in the expression of various emotions, and in different types of self-experience and self-apprehension. Ultimately, the phenomenologists will argue that a treatment of intersubjectivity requires a simultaneous analysis of the relationship between subjectivity and world. It is not satisfactory to simply insert intersubjectivity somewhere within an already established metaphysical framework; rather, the three dimensions "self," "others," and "world" reciprocally illuminate one another and can be fully understood only in their interconnection.

Chapter 7

The concluding seventh chapter will address the problem of selfhood and self-awareness by discussing the validity of the theory-theory of mind, that is, the validity of the claim that the experience of minded beings (be it oneself or others) requires a theory of mind. This claim has found wide resonance in a number of empirical disciplines, not the least in the study of autism. Is it true, however, that self-awareness and intersubjectivity—the experience of self and of others—are theoretical, inferential, and quasi-scientific in nature? Is it true that mental states are unobservable and are theoretically postulated explanatory devices introduced in order to help us predict and explain behavioral data? Drawing on insights and results obtained in the previous chapters (in particular the discussions of higher-order theories, of pre-reflective self-awareness, of self-disorders in schizophrenia, and of embodied intersubjectivity) and supplementing these with empirical findings from contemporary developmental psychology concerning infantile experience of self and other, I will argue here that the theory-theory of mind is mistaken when it claims that theoretical knowledge constitutes the core of what we call upon when we understand ourselves and others.

Self-Awareness and Phenomenal Consciousness

One should not overestimate the homogeneity of the phenomenological tradition; like any other tradition, it spans many differences. Although phenomenologists might disagree on important questions concerning method and focus, and even about the status and existence of self, they are in nearly unanimous agreement when it comes to the relation between consciousness and self-consciousness. Literally all the major figures in phenomenology defend the view that the experiential dimension is characterized by a tacit self-consciousness.

In *Erste Philosophie II*, for instance, Husserl wrote that the experiential stream is characterized by a *"Für-sich-selbst-erscheinens,"* that is, by a self-appearance or self-manifestation (Hua 8/189, 412).[1] Throughout his writings, he argued that self-consciousness, rather than being something that occurs only during exceptional circumstances, namely whenever we pay attention to our conscious life, is a feature characterizing subjectivity as such, no matter what worldly entities it might otherwise be conscious of and occupied with. As he put it in *Zur Phänomenologie der Intersubjektivität II*, "To be a subject is to be in the mode of being aware of oneself" (Hua 14/151).

We find similar ideas in Heidegger. Heidegger argued that the self is present and implicated in all of its intentional comportments. Thus, the intentional directedness toward worldly entities is not to be understood as an intentional experience that gains a reference to the self only afterward, as if it would first have to turn its attention back upon itself with the help of a subsequent (reflective) experience. Rather, the co-disclosure of the self belongs to intentionality as such (Heidegger GA 24: 225; GA 27: 208).[2] Heidegger also wrote that every worldly experiencing involves a certain component of self-acquaintance and self-familiarity, and that every experiencing is characterized by the fact that "I am always somehow acquainted with myself"

(Heidegger GA 58: 251). Adopting a more traditional terminology in his lecture course *Einleitung in die Philosophie* from 1928–29 he stated, "Every consciousness is also self-consciousness" (Heidegger GA 27: 135).

Sartre, probably the best-known defender of a phenomenological theory of self-consciousness, considered consciousness to be essentially characterized by intentionality. He also claimed, however, that each intentional experience is characterized by self-consciousness. Thus, Sartre took self-consciousness to constitute a necessary condition for being conscious of something. To perceive a withering oak, a dance performance, or a red pillow consciously without being aware of it, that is, without having access to or being acquainted with the experience in question was, for Sartre, a manifest absurdity (Sartre 1943, 18, 20, 28; 1948, 62). This line of thought is elaborated in the important introduction to *L'être et le néant*, where he claimed that an ontological analysis of intentionality leads to self-consciousness since the *mode of being* of intentional consciousness is to be *for-itself* (*pour-soi*), that is, self-conscious. An experience does not simply exist; it exists for itself, that is, it is given for itself, and this self-givenness is not simply a quality added to the experience, a mere varnish, but it rather constitutes the very mode of being of the experience. As Sartre wrote: "This self-consciousness we ought to consider not as a new consciousness, but as *the only mode of existence which is possible for a consciousness of something*" (Sartre 1943, 20 [1956, liv]).

These claims should not be misunderstood. The phenomenologists are not advocating strong theses concerning total and infallible self-knowledge; rather they are calling attention to the constitutive link between experiential phenomena and first-personal givenness or accessibility. They are emphasizing the importance of considering the first-person perspective when elucidating phenomenal consciousness. When speaking of a first-person perspective it is important to be clear about the distinction between having such a perspective and being able to articulate it linguistically (eventually to be labeled as a weak and strong first-person perspective, respectively). Whereas the latter obviously presupposes mastery of the first-person pronoun, the former is simply a question of having first-personal access to one's own experiential life. Although both capabilities deserve to be investigated, phenomenologists have mainly been accentuating the significance of the former.[3] They would consequently concur with the observation by Shoemaker that "it is essential for a philosophical understanding of the mental that we appreciate that there *is* a first person perspective on it, a distinctive way mental states present themselves to the subjects whose states they are, and that an essential part of the philosophical task is to give an account of mind which makes intelligible the perspective mental subjects have on their own mental lives" (Shoemaker 1996, 157). Whereas others must rely on what I say and do in order to know what I think or feel, first-person ascriptions of psychological states are immediate in the sense of not being based on observational or inferential evidence. Rather, they are based on a "direct acquaintance" with the mental states themselves.

The claim concerning immediacy is a claim concerning the character of first-person *access*, and has little to do with epistemic claims concerning infallibility or incorrigibility. Thus, in cases of careless self-description, for instance, first-person beliefs can certainly be corrected by others or be overridden by external evidence. Furthermore, not all self-knowledge is of the immediate kind. Much is, as Moran puts it, hard-won knowledge based on the same kinds of considerations that are available to others (Moran 2001, xxx). However, all of this does not change the fact that a satisfying theory of consciousness has to account for the first-personal access to our own consciousness that each of us enjoy.[4]

I Varieties of Self-Awareness

What has first-person accessibility to do with self-awareness? The term "self-awareness" is notoriously ambiguous; the philosophical, psychological, and neuroscientific literatures are filled with competing, conflicting, and complementary definitions. Let us take a quick look at some of the main candidates.

• In philosophy, many have sought to link self-awareness to the ability to think "I"-thoughts. A recent defense of such an approach can be found in Baker, who has argued that all sentient beings are subjects of experience, that they all have perspectival attitudes and that they all experience the world from their own egocentric perspective. In doing so they show that they are in possession of what Baker calls *weak first-person phenomena* (Baker 2000, 60, 67). Merely having a subjective point of view, however, is not enough for having self-awareness. In order to be in possession of self-awareness, which Baker considers a *strong first-person phenomenon*, one must be able to think of oneself *as* oneself. It is not enough to have desires and beliefs, it is not enough to have a perspectival attitude, nor is it enough to be able to distinguish between self and nonself; one must also be able to *conceptualize* this distinction. Baker consequently argues that self-awareness presupposes the possession of a first-person *concept*. One is self-conscious only from the moment one can *conceive* of oneself *as* oneself and has the linguistic ability to use the first-person pronoun to refer to oneself (Baker 2000, 67–68; see also Block 1997, 389). Given this definition, self-awareness is obviously taken to be something that emerges in the course of a developmental process and depends on the eventual acquisition of concepts and language.

• Another popular and related philosophical move has been to argue that self-consciousness, in the proper sense of the term, requires consciousness of a self. In other words, for a creature to be self-conscious it is not sufficient that the creature in question be able to self-ascribe experiences on an individual basis without recognizing the identity of that to which the experiences are ascribed. Rather the creature must be capable of thinking of the self-ascribed experiences as belonging to one and the same self. Thus, genuine self-consciousness requires that the creature is capable of being conscious of its own identity as the subject, bearer, or owner of different experiences (cf. Cassam 1997, 117–119).

• If we shift terrain and move into social psychology, we will frequently encounter the claim, famously defended by Mead, that self-consciousness is a matter of becoming an object to oneself in virtue of one's social relations to others, that is, that self-consciousness is constituted by adopting the perspective of the other toward oneself (Mead 1962, 164, 172). According to this account, self-awareness is per se a social phenomenon. It is not something you can acquire on your own. As Mead wrote: "Consciousness, as frequently used, simply has reference to the field of experience, but self-consciousness refers to the ability to call out in ourselves a set of definite responses which belong to the others of the group. Consciousness and self-consciousness are not on the same level. A man alone has, fortunately or unfortunately, access to his own toothache, but that is not what we mean by self-consciousness" (Mead 1962, 163; see also 171–172).

• Within developmental psychology, the so-called mirror-recognition task has occasionally been heralded as the decisive test for self-consciousness. Hence, it has been argued that self-awareness is present only from the moment when the child (at around eighteen months) is capable of recognizing itself in the mirror (see Lewis 2003, 281–282).

▪ Some, however, have raised the stakes even further and have argued that self-consciousness presupposes possession of a theory of mind. Roughly, the idea is that self-consciousness requires the ability to be aware of experiences *as* experiences, which in turn requires possession of a concept of experience. However, this concept cannot stand alone. It gets its significance from being embedded in a network of theoretical concepts. In particular, to think of experiences *as* experiences requires one to have the conception of objects or states of affairs that are capable of being experienced and of existing unexperienced. This has made some argue that children do not gain self-awareness until around the age of four, and that one can test the presence of self-awareness by using classical theory of mind tasks, such as the false-belief task or the appearance–reality task (see chapter 7 below).

There are kernels of truth in all of these definitions in the sense that they all capture various important aspects of the phenomenon; yet none of them have much to do with the minimalist take on self-awareness found in phenomenology. Using present-day terminology, the phenomenological line of thought can be construed as follows: Self-consciousness is not merely something that comes about the moment one scrutinizes one's experiences attentively (let alone something that only comes about the moment one recognizes one's own mirror image, refers to oneself using the first-person pronoun, or is in possession of identifying knowledge of one's own life story). Rather, self-consciousness comes in many forms and degrees. It makes perfect sense to speak of self-consciousness whenever I am not simply conscious of an external object—a chair, a chestnut tree, or a rising sun—but acquainted with my experience of the object as well, for in such a case my consciousness reveals itself to me. Thus, the basic distinction to be made is the distinction between the case where an object is given (object-consciousness) and the case wherein consciousness itself is given (self-consciousness). In its most primitive and fundamental form, self-consciousness is taken to be a question of having first-personal access to one's own consciousness; it is a question of the first-personal givenness or manifestation of experiential life.

Most people are prepared to concede that there is necessarily something "it is like" for a subject to undergo an experience (to taste ice cream, to feel joy, to remember a walk in the Alps). However, insofar as there is something it is like for the subject to have the experience, the subject must in some way have access to and be acquainted with the experience. Moreover, although conscious experiences differ from one another—what it is like to smell crushed mint leaves is different from what it is like to see a sunset or to hear Lalo's *Symphonie Espagnole*—they also share certain features. One commonality is the quality of *mineness*, the fact that the experiences are characterized by first-personal givenness. That is, the experience is given (at least tacitly) as *my* experience, as an experience *I* am undergoing or living through. Given this outlook, it is natural to argue that self-awareness is of pertinence for an understanding of phenomenal consciousness. In fact, phenomenal consciousness must be interpreted precisely as entailing a minimal or thin form of self-awareness. On this account, any experience that lacks self-awareness is nonconscious (cf. Zahavi 1999, 2002a, 2003a).[5]

In analytical philosophy of mind, an analogous view has been defended by Flanagan, who not only argues that consciousness involves self-consciousness in the weak sense that there is something it is like for the subject to have the experience, but who has also spoken of the low-level self-consciousness involved in experiencing my experiences as mine (Flanagan 1992, 194). Arguing along similar lines, Kriegel has more recently claimed that peripheral self-consciousness is an integral moment of phenomenal consciousness. As he writes, "It is impossible to think or experience something consciously without thinking or experiencing it self-consciously, i.e., without being peripherally aware of thinking or experiencing it" (Kriegel 2004, 200). Thus, in his view, unless a mental state is self-conscious, there will be nothing it is like to undergo the state, and it therefore cannot be a phenomenally conscious state (Kriegel 2003, 103–106).[6]

Let me forestall a possible objection, namely that such a minimal definition of self-awareness is entirely too broad and includes too much. That is, since it does not match our everyday or folk-psychological notion of self-awareness, which tends to view it as the ability to recognize or identify ourselves in a thematic way, the present use of the term is inappropriate. However, I do not think this objection carries much weight. First, from a conceptual point of view, there are no intrinsic problems whatsoever in using the term "self-awareness" to designate a situation where consciousness is aware of or given to itself. Second, many of the classical philosophical theories of self-awareness, as well as the more recent contributions by such thinkers as Brentano, Husserl, Sartre, Henry, Henrich, and Frank, among others, have been discussions of precisely this broad notion (see Zahavi 1999).

One of the characteristic features of the phenomenological discussion of self-awareness is that it (for good reasons) combines two topics that have frequently been kept apart by analytical philosophers. On the one hand, the phenomenological analysis can be seen as a contribution to the understanding of *first-person reference* and *perspective*. Just like Castañeda, Perry, Nagel, Cassam, and others in the analytic tradition, the phenomenologists argue that the types of self-reference available from a first-person perspective and those available from a third-person perspective are different. They have typically claimed that first-personal self-reference owes its uniqueness to the fact that we are acquainted with our own subjectivity in a way that differs radically from the way in which we are acquainted with objects. On the other hand, however, the phenomenological discussion of self-awareness is equally concerned with the question (also raised by Dretske, Carruthers, Tye, Rosenthal, and many others) of what makes a mental state conscious, that is, what it is that makes it manifest itself subjectively.

II Higher-Order Theories of Consciousness

The claim that there is a close link between consciousness and self-consciousness is less exceptional than might be expected. In fact, it could even be argued that such a claim is part of current orthodoxy, since higher-order theories typically take the difference between conscious and nonconscious mental states to rest upon the presence or absence of a relevant meta-mental state (see Armstrong 1968; Rosenthal 1986; Lycan 1987; Carruthers 1996a). In order to appraise this proposal let us distinguish between two uses of the term "conscious," a transitive and an intransitive use. On the one hand, we can speak of our being conscious of something, be it x, y, or z. On the other we can speak of our being conscious *simpliciter* (rather than nonconscious). According to the higher-order theories, what makes a mental state (intransitively) conscious is the fact that it is taken as an object by a relevant higher-order state. It is the occurrence of the higher-order representation that makes us conscious of the first-order mental state. In short, a conscious state is a state we are conscious of, or as Rosenthal puts it, "the mental state's being intransitively conscious simply consists in one's being transitively conscious of it" (Rosenthal 1997, 739). Thus, intransitive consciousness is taken to be a nonintrinsic, relational property (Rosenthal 1997, 736–737), that is, a property that a mental state has only insofar as it stands in relevant relation to something else. There have generally been two ways of interpreting this: Either we become aware of being in the first-order mental state by means of some higher-order perception or monitoring (Armstrong 1968; Lycan 1997), or we become aware of it by means of some higher-order thought, that is, the state is conscious just in case we have a roughly contemporaneous thought to the effect *that* we are in that very state (Rosenthal 1993a, 199). Thus, the basic divide between the higher-order perception (HOP) and the higher-order thought (HOT) models has been precisely on the issue of whether the conscious-making meta-mental states are perception-like or thought-like in nature.[7] In both cases, however, consciousness has been taken to be a question of the mind directing its intentional aim upon its own states and operations. Self-directedness has been taken to be constitutive of (intransitive) consciousness; to put it differently, higher-order theories have typically explained (intransitive) consciousness in terms of self-awareness.[8] As Van Gulick puts it, it is "the addition of the relevant meta-intentional self-awareness that transforms a nonconscious mental state into a conscious one" (Van Gulick 2000, 276).

One can find a clear articulation of this link between self-awareness and a higher-order account of consciousness in Carruthers's book *Language, Thought, and Consciousness*. According to Carruthers, the aim of a theory of consciousness is to explain what it is for mental states to be conscious as opposed to nonconscious (Carruthers 1996a, 148). This is a different question from the question of what it is for an organism or creature to be conscious (i.e., awake) as opposed to nonconscious (i.e., asleep), and it is also a different question from that of what it is for an organism to be conscious rather than nonconscious of events or objects in the world. Carruthers admits that it might be argued that what he is really after is a theory of self-consciousness rather than simply a theory of consciousness. For his view, a conscious mental state is one of which the agent is aware, and to that extent it is something that involves self-consciousness. The only reason he prefers to think of his own theory as a theory of consciousness rather than as a theory of self-consciousness is because a reference to self-consciousness could suggest that the subject of a mental state would have to be in possession of a developed conception of self, that is, a conception of the self as an enduring agent with a determinate past and an open-ended future, in order for the mental state to be conscious. Since Carruthers finds it highly likely that there are organisms capable of having conscious mental states while having only the most tenuous conception of themselves as continuing subjects of thought and experience, he regards it as being quite legitimate to talk of creatures with conscious mental states who nevertheless lack self-consciousness (Carruthers 1996a, 149).

It soon turns out, however, that Carruthers fails to comply with his own admonition. As he points out a bit later in the book, the subjective feel of experience presupposes a capacity for higher-order awareness, and, as he then continues, "such self-awareness is a conceptually necessary condition for an organism to be a subject of phenomenal feelings, or for there to be anything that its experiences are like" (Carruthers 1996a, 152; see also 154). To speak of what an experience is like, or of its phenomenal feel, is an attempt to characterize those aspects of experience that are subjective. But to speak of the subjective aspects of experience is to speak of aspects that are available to the subject. What this means, according to Carruthers, is that for mental states to be conscious is for the subject of those states to be capable of discriminating between them. They must be states of which the subject is aware, and this obviously involves a certain amount of self-awareness; in fact, it requires *reflective* self-awareness (Carruthers 1996a, 155, 157). To be more precise, for a creature to be capable of discriminating between its mental states is for the creature to be capable of reflecting on, thinking about, and hence conceptualizing its own mental states. This is why Carruthers ultimately argues that only creatures in possession of a *theory of mind* are capable of enjoying conscious experiences or of having mental states with phenomenal feels (Carruthers 1996a, 158). As he puts it:

[I]n order to think about your own thoughts, or your own experiences, you have to possess the *concepts* of thought and experience. And these get their life and significance from being embedded in a folk-psychological theory of the structure and functioning of the mind. So in the case of any creature to whom it is implausible to attribute a theory of mind—and I assume that this includes most animals and young children—it will be equally implausible to suppose that they engage in conscious thinking. . . . If animals (or most animals) lack higher-order thoughts, then by the same token they will lack conscious experiences. For there will be just as little reason to believe that they are capable of thinking about their own experiences, as such. If true, this conclusion may have profound implications for our moral attitudes towards animals and animal suffering. (Carruthers 1996a, 221; see also Carruthers 2000, 194)

Carruthers consequently holds the view that animals (and children under the age of three) lack phenomenal consciousness, that they lack a dimension of subjectivity. In his view, they are blind to the existence of their own mental states; there is in fact nothing it is like for them to feel pain or pleasure (Carruthers 1998, 216; 2000, 203). Carruthers concedes that most of us believe that it must be like something to be a bat, a cat, or a camel, and that the experiences of these creatures have subjective feels to them, but he considers this commonsense belief to be quite groundless. In his view, the postulation of conscious experience is entirely otiose when it comes to explaining the bat's or cat's behavior, since everything the bat or cat does can be explained perfectly well by attributing beliefs, desires, and perceptions to it. They do not necessarily have to be *conscious* beliefs, desires, or perceptions (Carruthers 1996a, 223).[9]

III A One-Level Account of Consciousness

We will have reason to return to Carruthers's position later on, but for now, what needs to be stressed is simply that one might share the view that there is a close link between consciousness and self-consciousness and still disagree about the nature of the link. Although the phenomenological take might superficially resemble the view of the higher-order theories, we are ultimately confronted with two radically divergent accounts. In contrast to the higher-order theories, the phenomenologists explicitly deny that the self-consciousness that is present the moment I consciously experience something is to be understood in terms of some kind of reflection, or introspection, or higher-order monitoring. It does not involve an additional mental state, but is rather to be understood as an intrinsic feature of the primary experience. That is, in contrast to the higher-order account of consciousness, which claims that consciousness is an extrinsic property of those mental states that have it, a property bestowed upon them from without by some further states, the phenomenologists typically argue that the feature that makes a mental state conscious is located within the state itself; it is an intrinsic property of those mental states that have it.[10]

In the previously quoted central passage from *L'être et le néant*, Sartre emphasized quite explicitly that the self-consciousness in question is *not* a "new" consciousness (Sartre 1943, 20). It is not something added to the experience, an additional mental state, but rather an intrinsic feature of the experience. Thus, when he spoke of self-awareness as a permanent feature of consciousness, Sartre was not referring to what he called reflective self-awareness. Reflection (or higher-order monitoring) is the process whereby consciousness directs its intentional aim at itself, thereby taking itself as its own object. According to Sartre, however, this type of self-awareness is derived; it involves a subject–object split, and any attempt to account for *self*-consciousness in such terms was, for Sartre, bound to fail. It either generates an infinite regress or accepts a nonconscious starting point, and he considered both of these options to be unacceptable (Sartre 1943, 19).

Sartre readily admitted the existence of reflective self-consciousness. We can, for instance, reflect on, and thereby become thematically conscious of, an occurrent perception of a Swiss Army knife. In reflection we can distinguish the reflecting experience and the experience reflected on. The first takes the latter as its object. But for Sartre, the experience reflected on is already self-conscious prior to reflection, and the self-consciousness in question is of a nonreflective and nonpositional kind, that is, it does not have a reflective structure, and it does not posit that which it is aware of as an object (Sartre 1936, 28–29).[11] As Sartre wrote: "[T]here is no infinite regress here, since a consciousness has no need at all of a reflecting consciousness in order to be conscious of itself. It simply does not posit itself as an object" (Sartre 1936, 29 [1957, 45]). Thus, Sartre also spoke of *pre-reflective self-awareness* as an immediate and noncognitive "relation" of the self to itself (Sartre 1943, 19).

If I am engaged in some conscious activity, such as the reading of a story, my attention is neither on myself nor on my activity of reading, but on the story. If my reading is interrupted by someone asking me what I am doing, I immediately reply that I am (and have for some time been) reading; the self-consciousness on the basis of which I answer the question is not something acquired at just that moment, but a consciousness of myself that has been present to me all along. To put it differently, it is because I am pre-reflectively conscious of my experiences that I am usually able to respond immediately, that is, without inference or observation, if somebody asks me what I have been doing, or thinking, or seeing, or feeling immediately prior to the question.

According to Sartre, consciousness has two different modes of existence, a pre-reflective and a reflective. Whereas the former is an immersed non-objectifying self-acquaintance, the latter is a detached objectifying self-awareness that (normally) introduces a phenomenological distinction between the observer and the observed. The former has priority since it can prevail independently of the latter, whereas reflective self-consciousness always presupposes pre-reflective self-consciousness. As Sartre wrote, "reflection has no kind of primacy over the consciousness reflected-on. It is not reflection which reveals the consciousness reflected-on to itself. Quite the contrary, it is the non-reflective consciousness which renders the reflection possible; there is a pre-reflective cogito which is the condition of the Cartesian cogito" (Sartre 1943, 19–20 [1956, liii]). For Sartre, pre-reflective self-consciousness is not an addendum to but a constitutive aspect of the original experience itself. The experience is conscious of itself at the time of its occurrence. If I consciously see, remember, know, think, hope, feel, or will something I am *eo ipso* aware of it.

When Sartre said that every positional consciousness of an object is simultaneously a nonpositional consciousness of itself and insisted on the close link between the experiential phenomena and their first-personal givenness, it is essential to emphasize that this pre-reflective self-consciousness is not to be understood as an intentional or objectifying stance, and consequently is neither to be interpreted as some kind of inner perception, nor more generally as a type of conceptual knowledge (Sartre 1936, 23–24, 66; 1943, 19). He would consequently oppose what Shoemaker has recently called the *perceptual model of self-knowledge.* According to this model, the relation between our mental states and our awareness of these mental states is a causal relation. The existence of the mental states is logically independent of our being aware of them from a first-person perspective, and our awareness of the states is caused by these very states via some kind of reliable mechanism (Shoemaker 1996, 224). According to a classical take on causality, however, cause and effect are distinct existences, and distinct existences are only contingently connected. "Where there is causation, there is contingency: a causal connection that holds might not have held" (Chalmers 1996, 195). In contrast, the link between an experience and its first-personal givenness (our first-personal access to it) is taken to be of a much stronger constitutive variety. Chalmers writes that having an experience is automatically to stand in an intimate epistemic relation to the experience, a relation more primitive than knowledge that might be called "acquaintance" (Chalmers 1996, 197). Sartre would concur. However, this also implies that the self-consciousness in question might very well be accompanied by a fundamental *lack of knowledge*. Although I cannot be unconscious of my present experience, I might very well ignore it in favor of its object, and this is of course the natural attitude. In my daily life, I am absorbed by and preoccupied with projects and objects in the world. Thus, pervasive pre-reflective self-consciousness is definitely not identical with total self-comprehension, but can rather be likened to a precomprehension that allows for a subsequent reflection and thematization. One should consequently distinguish between the claim that our consciousness is characterized by an immediate self-givenness and the claim that consciousness is characterized by total self-knowledge. One can easily accept the first and reject the latter, that is, one can argue in favor of the existence of a pervasive self-consciousness and still take self-comprehension to be an infinite task (Ricoeur 1950, 354–355).

Siewert has recently criticized Sartre's account and has argued that since Sartre on the one hand claimed that all consciousness is consciousness of itself and on the other hand denied that this ubiquitous self-consciousness is reflective, thetic, positional, epistemic, and objectifying, his account is inconsistent, confused, extremely misleading, and totally unclear (Siewert 1998, 360). Is this rather harsh judgment justified? I think not. As Sartre himself pointed out, it is only the necessity of syntax that compelled him to write that we are pre-reflectively aware *of* our experiences and that there is a pre-reflective consciousness *of* self. (In French, the term for self-consciousness—*conscience de soi*—literally means consciousness of self.) Thus, Sartre readily admitted that the use of "of" (or "de") is unfortunate since it suggests that self-consciousness is simply a subtype of object-consciousness, as if the manner in which we are aware *of* ourselves is structurally comparable with the manner in which we are aware *of* apples and clouds. We cannot avoid the "of," but in order to show that it is merely there in order to satisfy a grammatical requirement, Sartre placed it inside parentheses, and frequently spoke of a "*conscience (de) soi*" and of a "*conscience (de) plaisir*," and so on (Sartre 1943, 22; 1948, 62). Thus, Sartre was quite keen to avoid any phrasing that might misleadingly suggest that we, in order to have conscious mental states, must be aware of them as objects.[12]

As already indicated, this view is shared by other phenomenologists. All argue that consciousness and self-consciousness are closely linked. All defend what might be called a one-level account of consciousness. Moreover—and this might come as a surprise to those who believe that one of the central doctrines in phenomenology is the doctrine of intentionality, that is, the claim that all consciousness is intentional, that all consciousness is object-consciousness—they also reject the attempt to construe intransitive consciousness in terms of transitive consciousness, that is, they reject the view that a conscious state is a state *of* which we are intentionally conscious. To put it yet differently, not only do they reject the view that a mental state becomes conscious by being taken as an object by a higher-order state, they also reject the view—generally associated with Brentano—according to which a mental state becomes conscious by taking itself as an object. They consequently deny that the type of self-consciousness entailed by phenomenal consciousness is intentionally structured, that is, a question of a subject–object relation.

What are the actual arguments for these claims? When it comes to defending the existence of a tacit and unthematic self-awareness, the argument is occasionally an indirect argument by elimination and consists in a rejection of the two obvious alternatives. Phenomenologists would first deny that we could consciously experience something without in some way having access to or being acquainted with the experience in question. They would then argue that this first-personal access to one's own experiences amounts to a form of self-awareness. Second, they would reject the suggestion that all conscious states are states we pay attention to, that is, they would argue that there are unnoticed or unattended experiences. By rejecting these two alternatives, the notion of pre-reflective self-awareness wins by default. As for the more specific claims concerning the structure of this pre-reflective self-awareness, in particular the claim that it is nonobjectifying and therefore not the result of any self-directed intentionality, phenomenologists would insist that this claim is based on a correct phenomenological description of our conscious life—in everyday life, I might enjoy a continuous first-personal access to my own consciousness, but I am definitely not aware of my own stream of consciousness as a succession of immanent marginal objects—and that this is the best argument to be found.

I have quite a lot of sympathy with such an answer. However, if one were to look for an additional, more theoretical, argument, what would one then find? One line of reasoning encountered in literally all phenomenologists is the view that the attempt to let (intransitive) consciousness be a result of a reflection (or higher-order monitoring) will generate an infinite regress. This is, on the face of it, a rather old idea. Typically, the regress argument has been understood in the following manner: If all occurrent mental states are conscious in the sense of being taken as objects by occurrent second-order mental states, then these second-order mental states must also be taken as objects by occurrent third-order mental states, and so forth *ad infinitum*.

However, the standard reply to this argument has been that the premise is false and question begging. To put it differently, the easy way to halt the regress is by accepting the existence of nonconscious mental states. Needless to say, this is precisely the position adopted by the defenders of a higher-order theory. For them, the second-order perception or thought does not have to be conscious. This will be the case only if it is accompanied by a (nonconscious) third-order thought or perception (see Rosenthal 1997, 745). However, the phenomenological reply to this "solution" is rather straight-forward. The phenomenologists would concede that it is possible to halt the regress by postulating the existence of nonconscious mental states, but they would maintain that such an appeal to the nonconscious leaves us with a case of explanatory vacuity. That is, they would be quite unconvinced by the claim that the relation between two otherwise nonconscious processes can make one of them conscious; they would find it quite unclear how a state without subjective or phenomenal qualities can be transformed into one with such qualities, that is, into an experience with first-personal givenness or *mineness*, by the mere relational addition of a meta-state having the first-order state as its intentional object.

IV The Problem of Infinite Regress

It is also possible to reconstruct the regress argument in such a fashion that an appeal to the nonconscious will be unable to halt the regress, but this reconstruction is not one that has been explicitly worked out by the phenomenologists themselves.

One of the questions that a higher-order theory must answer is what is it that makes one mental state conscious of another mental state? For Rosenthal, a "higher-order thought, B, is an awareness of the mental-state token, A, simply because A is the intentional object of B" (Rosenthal 1993b, 160). Rosenthal readily admits, however, that the relation between the higher-order state and the first-order state is of a rather special kind. On the one hand, we regard mental states as being conscious only if we are conscious of them in some suitably unmediated way, namely noninferentially; otherwise, a nonconscious mental process would qualify as conscious, simply because we could infer that we would have to be in it (Rosenthal 1997, 737). On the other hand, Rosenthal argues that for a mental state to be conscious, it is not sufficient that we are noninferentially conscious of the state; we also have to be conscious of being *ourselves* in that very mental state: "Only if one's thought is about oneself as such, and not just about someone that happens to be oneself, will the mental state be a conscious state" (Rosenthal 1997, 750; see also 741).[13] To put it another way, it is not enough to explain how a certain state becomes conscious; the theory also has to explain how the state comes to be given as *my* state, as a state that *I* am in. Why? Because this first-personal givenness is an ineliminable part of what it means for a state to be conscious—it pertains to the fact that a conscious mental state feels like something *for somebody*, that is, it concerns the fact that when one is directly and noninferentially conscious of one's own occurrent thoughts, perceptions, or pains, they are characterized by a first-personal givenness that immediately reveals them as one's own—and for a theory of consciousness to leave out this aspect is to leave out something absolutely crucial.

The decisive question, however, is whether the higher-order theories are capable of accounting for this feature in a satisfactory manner. Rosenthal has argued that if one wishes to present a nontrivial and informative account of consciousness one must avoid the claim that consciousness is an intrinsic property of our mental states. To call something intrinsic is, for Rosenthal, to imply that it is something unanalyzable and mysterious and consequently beyond the reach of scientific and theoretical study: "We would insist that being conscious is an intrinsic property of mental states only if we were convinced that it lacked articulated structure, and thus defied explanation" (Rosenthal 1993b, 157). Although Rosenthal acknowledges that there is something intuitively appealing about taking consciousness to be an intrinsic property, he still thinks that this approach must be avoided since it will impede a naturalistic (and reductionistic) account, which seeks to explain consciousness by appeal to nonconscious mental states, and nonconscious mental states by appeal to nonmental states (Rosenthal 1993b, 165; 1997, 735). As Baker has recently pointed out, however, although Rosenthal's account of consciousness requires a first-person perspective—a first-order mental state is conscious by being accompanied by a nonconscious higher-order state that only a being with a first-person perspective could have—his theory simply presupposes this first-person perspective, or in other words, "the first-person perspective that is required for the explanation of conscious states is itself left unexplained" (Baker 2000, 84).

This objection can be elaborated and amplified by means of some of the classical analyses of first-personal self-reference found in the writings of Castañeda, Perry, Shoemaker, and others. These analyses have purported to show that the types of self-reference available from a first-person perspective and from a third-person perspective are very different. I can refer to a publicly available object by way of a proper name, a demonstrative, or a definite description, and occasionally this object happens to be myself. When I refer to myself in this way, that is, when I refer to myself from the third-person perspective, I am referring to myself in exactly the same way that I can refer to others, and that others can refer to me (the only difference being that I am the one doing it, thus making the reference into a self-reference). But this type of objectifying self-reference is neither necessary nor sufficient if one is to be aware of oneself in the proper first-personal manner. For me to know that *I* am perceiving a sunset, it is not sufficient for me to know that Dan Zahavi, or a thirty-seven-year-old Dane, and so on, is perceiving a sunset, since I can be in possession of knowledge that identifies me from a third-person perspective and still fail to realize that I am the person in question. Since there is always a gap between grasping that a certain third-person description applies to a person and grasping that I am that person, and since there is no third-person description such that grasping that it fits a certain person guarantees that I realize that I am that person, first-personal self-reference cannot be regarded as involving the identification of an object by any third-person description (Castañeda 1967). Nor is such third-person identificatory knowledge necessary, since I can be in a state of complete amnesia and be ignorant of all those properties that would identify me from a third-person perspective, and still remain in possession of first-personal self-reference, still remain aware that this ongoing experience is *mine*, and that it is *me* who is undergoing it.

Why is first-personal self-reference different from third-personal self-reference? A natural reply is that first-personal self-reference owes its uniqueness to the fact that we are acquainted with our own subjectivity in a way that differs from the way in which we are acquainted with objects. In first-personal self-reference one is not aware of oneself as an object that happens to be oneself, nor is one aware of oneself as one specific object rather than another. Rather, first-personal self-reference involves a nonobjectifying self-acquaintance. It involves what has alternately been called "self-reference without identification" (Shoemaker 1968) and "non-ascriptive reference to self" (Brook 1994).

But why is it impossible to account for first-personal self-reference in terms of a successful object-identification? Why is self-awareness not a type of object-consciousness? Shoemaker has provided one of the classical arguments (I will later return to some of the others). In order to identify something as oneself one has to hold something true of it that one already knows to be true of oneself. In some cases, this self-knowledge might be grounded on some further identification, but the supposition that *every* item of self-knowledge rests on identification leads to an infinite regress (Shoemaker 1968, 561). This even holds true for self-identification obtained through introspection. That is, it will not do to claim that introspection is distinguished by the fact that its object has a property that immediately identifies it as being me, since no other self could possibly have it, namely the property of being the private and exclusive object of precisely my introspection. This explanation will not do, since I will be unable to identify an introspected self as myself by the fact that it is introspectively observed by me unless I know it is the object of *my* introspection, that is, unless I know that it is in fact *me* who undertakes this introspection, and this knowledge cannot itself be based on identification if one is to avoid an infinite regress (Shoemaker 1968, 562–563).

Any convincing theory of consciousness has to account for the first-personal givenness of our conscious states and has to respect the difference between our consciousness of a foreign object and our consciousness of ourselves. Any convincing theory of consciousness has to be able to explain the distinction between *intentionality*, which is characterized by an epistemic *difference* between the subject and the object of experience, and *self-consciousness*, which implies some form of *identity*. However, this is exactly what the higher-order theory, which seeks to provide an extrinsic and relational account of consciousness, persistently fails to do (see Zahavi 1999).[14] Every higher-order theory operates with a duality: one mental state takes another mental state as its object, and we consequently have to *distinguish* the two. Given that their relation is supposed to account for the *mineness* of the first-order state, that is, for the fact that the conscious mental state is given as *my* state, as a state *I* am in, the process must somehow circumvent the division or difference between the two states and posit some kind of identity, namely that of belonging to the same mind or stream of consciousness.

But how is this supposed to work? Just as I cannot recognize something as mine unless I am already aware of myself, a nonconscious second-order mental state (that per definition lacks consciousness of itself) cannot recognize or identify a first-order mental state as belonging to the same mind as *itself*. To suggest that the second-order state might be furnished with the required self-intimation by being taken as intentional object by a third-order mental state, and a higher-order theory has no other option, would obviously generate an infinite regress (Henrich 1970, 268; 1982, 64; Cramer 1974, 563; Frank 1991a, 498, 529).

Let us, after this introductory overview, dig deeper. In the next three chapters we take a closer look at some of the analyses that are to be found in the writings of Husserl and Heidegger.

The Concept(s) of Consciousness in Early Phenomenology

Logische Untersuchungen (1900–1901) was not Husserl's first published work, yet he considered it to constitute his "breakthrough" in phenomenology (Hua 18/8), and it certainly stands out, not only as one of his most important works, but also as a key text in twentieth-century philosophy.

Any overall appraisal of *Logische Untersuchungen* must take a stand on its relation to Husserl's later phenomenology. Are most of the insights that can be found in *Logische Untersuchungen* superseded by Husserl's later analyses, or did his turn to transcendental philosophy, contrarily, represent a fateful and global decline? When it comes to such a comparison between Husserl's early and later thought, the two most popular topics have undoubtedly been the analysis of intentionality on the one hand, and the very idea of phenomenology (descriptive vs. transcendental phenomenology) on the other. In this chapter, I will discuss another central but somewhat less favored topic, namely Husserl's analysis of *consciousness*. More specifically, I will focus on the first chapter in the Fifth Investigation, which bears the title "Consciousness as the phenomenological subsistence of the ego and consciousness as inner perception," to determine whether the position defended by Husserl in the first edition of *Logische Untersuchungen* is superior to the one he adopted later on.[1]

I Three Concepts of Consciousness

In the first paragraph of the Fifth Investigation, Husserl stated that the concept of consciousness is equivocal and he distinguished three interwoven senses. This tripartition was not intended to be exhaustive, but Husserl considered the senses in question to be of particular relevance for the analyses to follow. To quote his list in full:

1. Consciousness as the entire phenomenological being of the spiritual ego. (Consciousness = the phenomenological ego, as "bundle" or interweaving of psychic experiences.)
2. Consciousness as the inner awareness of one's own psychic experiences.
3. Consciousness as a comprehensive designation for "mental acts" or "intentional experiences" of all sorts. (Hua 19/356 [2001, II/81, translation modified])

What exactly was Husserl saying here? The first notion refers to the unity or totality of experiences. It is this notion that we evoke when we speak, for instance, of the stream of consciousness. Second, Husserl called attention to the fact that we can use consciousness in an intransitive sense as a one-place predicate, that is, we can say of an experience that it is inwardly given to us and thus conscious (rather than nonconscious). This use of the term is related to the issue of self-awareness. Finally, we can speak of consciousness in a transitive sense. We can say of a certain experience that it is conscious *of something*, that is, we can speak of consciousness in the sense of an intentional directedness.

When it comes to an investigation of consciousness, Husserl consequently distinguished three separate issues: (1) The unity/totality of the stream of consciousness, (2) inner consciousness or self-awareness, and (3) intentionality. The task he set himself was to clarify all three and investigate their interrelation. Are they equiprimordial or is one of them more fundamental than the others? As is well known, in *Logische Untersuchungen* Husserl concerned himself mainly with the third issue, that of the notion of intentionality. In fact, a frequent criticism has been that, in this work, Husserl was so preoccupied with intentionality that he severely neglected the other two issues. He did not pay sufficient attention to the temporal structure of the stream of consciousness and he mistakenly thought that self-awareness was nothing but an unusual type of intentionality, specifically a question of directing one's inner objectifying gaze toward the experience in question. Let us see whether this criticism holds true.

II The Stream of Consciousness

Despite Husserl's use of the term "ego" in his initial listing of the different notions of consciousness, his analysis of the stream of consciousness is a defense of a non-egological theory of consciousness. According to Husserl, there is no pure identical ego-pole shared by all experiences and which conditions their unity. Experiences are not states or properties of anybody, but mental events that simply occur. Whereas we can distinguish between an experience of a red sports car and this red sports car itself, we will be unable to locate a third element, a pure ego that is directed at the sports car through the experience.

This is not to say that we cannot speak of an ego at all, but in the Fifth Investigation, Husserl acknowledged only two legitimate uses of the term. Either the ego is simply identical with the empirical person, that is, with the person to whom we assign intersubjectively accessible properties (such as nationality, profession, gender, weight) from a third-person perspective (Hua 19/363, 761), or the term "ego" is used as a synonym for the stream of consciousness (Hua 19/362). In the latter case, the ego is not a distinct and formal principle of identity. It is not the owner or bearer of experiences, but simply the experiences in their totality. Thus, the relation between a single experience and the ego is analyzable in terms of a part–whole relationship.

Husserl's defense of a non-egological model was partly motivated by his aversion to any kind of ego-metaphysics. In the introduction to the second part of *Logische Untersuchungen*, he made it clear that when we engage in a phenomenological description of experiences we should seek to capture them in their essential purity and not as they are empirically apperceived, namely as the experiences of humans or animals. We should not focus on sensory physiology or neurology, that is, on the empirical conditions that must be fulfilled in order for *Homo sapiens* to be conscious; rather, we should aim at analyzing the fundamental structures of consciousness, regardless of whether it belongs to humans, animals, or extraterrestrials. In other words, when investigating the experiential dimension, we should aim at essential descriptions of the experiences, and, according to Husserl, such descriptions will precisely exclude any reference to their empirical bearers (Hua 19/6, 16; Hua 24/118). Husserl consequently spoke favorably of a *"Psychologie ohne Seele"* (Hua 19/371); as he wrote in a letter to Hans Cornelius in 1906: "The phenomenological investigation is not at all interested in egos or in states, experiences, developments belonging to or occurring in egos" (Husserl 1994, 27).

As is well known, Husserl's non-egological position was subsequently taken over by Sartre (see Sartre 1936, 20). What might be less well known is to what large extent Sartre's arguments in *La transcendance de l'ego* can already be found in *Logische Untersuchungen*.[2]

In this early work, Sartre attempted to question the *necessity, possibility,* and *actuality* of the ego. To start with, he took issue with tradition and argued that the ego is *superfluous*. It has often been argued that the mental life would dissipate into a chaos of unstructured and separate sensations if it were not supported by the unifying, synthesizing, and individuating function of a central and atemporal ego. As Sartre pointed out, however, this reasoning misjudges the nature of the stream of consciousness; it does not need an exterior principle of individuation, since it is *per se* individuated. Nor is consciousness in need of any transcendent principle of unification, since it is, as such, a flowing unity. It is exactly qua temporalizing that consciousness unifies itself. Thus, a correct account of time-consciousness will show that the contribution of an ego is unnecessary and it consequently loses its raison d'être (Sartre 1936, 21–23).[3]

Second, Sartre claimed that the ego, for essential reasons, cannot possibly be a part of consciousness. According to Sartre, consciousness is characterized by its fundamental self-givenness or self-manifestation and it consequently has no hidden or concealed parts. The ego, however, is opaque; it is something whose nature has to be unearthed gradually and which always possesses aspects yet to be disclosed. It consequently proves to be of quite a different nature than consciousness and therefore cannot be a part of it.

Sartre's third and final argument was that a correct phenomenological description of lived consciousness will simply not find any ego, whether understood as an inhabitant in or possessor of consciousness. One occasionally says of a person who is absorbed in something that he has forgotten himself. This way of speaking contains a truth. When I am absorbed in reading a story, I have a consciousness of the narrative and a pre-reflective self-awareness of the reading but, according to Sartre, I do not have any awareness of an ego. In keeping with Sartre, pre-reflective consciousness has no egological structure. As long as we are absorbed in the experience, *living* it, no ego will appear. The ego emerges only when we adopt a distancing and objectifying attitude to the experience in question, that is, when we *reflect* upon it. Even then, however, we are not dealing with an I-consciousness, since the reflecting pole remains non-egological, but merely with a consciousness *of* I. As Sartre put it, the appearing ego is the object and not the subject of reflection. When I engage in a reflective exploration of this object, I will be examining it as if it were the ego of an other. In other words, I will assume the perspective of an other on myself (Sartre 1936, 65, 69). It is in this sense that the ego is transcendent (cf. the title of Sartre's book), and it is exactly for this reason that Sartre, in an attempt to bypass the problem of solipsism, denied that my ego is something about which I enjoy a special certitude: "My I, in effect, is *no more certain for consciousness than the I of other men*. It is only more intimate" (Sartre 1936, 85 [1957, 104]).

If we now return to Husserl's analysis, we will find some striking parallels. Husserl argued, as already mentioned, that the phenomenologically purified ego—in contrast to the empirical ego or personality, which Husserl took to be just as empirical an object as a house or a tree (Hua 19/363)—is nothing but the totality of a complex of experiences. He even spoke of the ego as a "bundle of experiences" (Hua 19/390). Thus, the phenomenological ego is not something that floats above manifold experiences; rather, it is simply identical with their *unified* whole. Moreover, even though the experiences are unified, this unification is not due to the synthesizing contribution of the ego; on the contrary, such a contribution is *superfluous* since the unification has already taken place in accordance with intraexperiential laws.[4] To put it differently, the stream of experiences is self-unifying. To understand its unity, we do not need to look at anything above, beyond, or external to the stream itself. Since the ego, properly speaking, is the result of this unification, it cannot be something that precedes or conditions it (Hua 19/364).

In his paragraphs 8 and 12, Husserl followed up on this point and claimed that as long as we simply live through the experience in question, as long as we are absorbed in the perception of an event taking place before our eyes, or immersed in a daydream, or the reading of a story, or in the carrying out of a mathematical proof, we will encounter no identical ego-pole (Hua 19/390). As Husserl remarked after having briefly accounted for Natorp's arguments for the existence of a pure ego: "I must frankly confess, however, that I am quite unable to find this ego, this primitive, necessary centre of relations" (Hua 19/374 [2001, II/92]). Despite this very Humean assertion, Husserl did not claim that we never experience an ego; we do and in a twofold manner, depending on whether we are speaking of the ego qua empirical person or qua totality of experiences:

• In the first case, Husserl pointed out that our empirical ego stands in relation to numerous other objects. To take a simple example, when I am sitting on a chair, there is a quite tangible relation between the chair and myself. If we reflect on this relation, our reflection will, in fact, contain a reference to an ego (Hua 19/374). It would be quite natural to say, "I am sitting on a chair." The ego in question is not some elusive formal entity, but simply myself in flesh and blood. It is on the basis of this observation that Husserl made the following somewhat reckless claim: "Self-perception of the empirical ego is, however, a daily business, which involves no difficulty for understanding. We perceive the ego, just as we perceive an external thing" (Hua 19/375 [2001, II/93]).

• As for the second case, Husserl remarked that if we identify the ego with the stream of consciousness, it will then, to some extent, be true to say that there is an ego involved whenever we are conscious of an object. Although such a reference to an ego (qua stream of consciousness) might be almost unavoidable whenever we reflect on an intentional experience and try to describe it—after all, it seems so much more natural to say "I am thinking of the election" than "there is a thinking of the election"—it would be wrong to claim that there is actually an ego present in the experience; for how could the whole possibly be contained in one of its parts? That we nevertheless tend to experience an ego in these cases testifies to the transforming nature of reflection. When we reflect on an experience, we are no longer simply living it through. We transcend it, and by doing that, so to speak, we situate the experience in an egological context (Hua 19/391). Husserl consequently made the same claim as Sartre (yet 35 years earlier): Our experience of an ego is the result of a *reflective operation*.

Thus far, Husserl had been analyzing the first notion of consciousness, but at this point in his argumentation, he posed the following question: How do we know that there is at all something like a stream of consciousness; how do we know that there is something like an experience? Is our claim based on an inference to best explanation, or rather on some kind of more direct acquaintance? Husserl's answer was, of course, the latter: It is phenomenologically legitimate to speak of a stream of consciousness precisely because our experiences are given to us, precisely because we have access to them and can reflect on them. To put it differently, the second notion of consciousness concerned with the conscious givenness of experience is methodologically prior to the first notion of consciousness (Hua 19/367). It is by expanding the focus from a single conscious experience to include all those experiences that are retained and remembered that we can eventually reach the notion of a stream of consciousness and of a totality of experiences. Let us, with this in mind, turn to the second notion of consciousness.

III Inner Consciousness and Self-Awareness

What did Husserl have to say about experiential givenness in the Fifth Investigation? If we look at the central paragraph entitled " 'Inner' consciousness as inner perception," Husserl's view appears to have been roughly something like the following: Inner consciousness (our awareness of our own mental life) is a kind of inner perception that might accompany our occurrent experiences by taking them as its objects (Hua 19/365). Husserl's use of the term "inner consciousness" contains a clear reference to Brentano, and so, in order to better appreciate Husserl's take on the issue, let us briefly consider Brentano's position.

After his famous analysis of intentionality in book II, chapter I of *Psychologie vom empirischen Standpunkt* (1874), Brentano turned to the problem of self-awareness or, as he called it, *inner consciousness (inneres Bewußtsein)*. According to Brentano, the term "conscious" can be used in a twofold sense. In one sense, we can say of an experience that it is conscious of an object. In the other, we can say of an object that it is conscious insofar as it is that of which one is aware. All experiences are characterized by their being conscious of something. The question is whether they are also conscious in the second sense, that is, whether one is also aware of them, or whether one must deny this and consequently admit the existence of nonconscious (or unconscious) psychical phenomena (Brentano 1874, 142–143).

One of the traditional arguments in defense of the existence of *nonconscious* mental states insists that only the nonconscious can save us from a vicious infinite regress. *If* all occurrent mental states were conscious, in the sense of being taken as objects by an inner consciousness, and this inner consciousness were itself conceived of as a new occurrent mental state, it itself would also have to be taken as an object by a further inner consciousness, and so forth *ad infinitum*. Furthermore, as Brentano pointed out, this would not be the only problem. If, say, the perception of a sunset were really the object of a higher-order awareness, the sunset would be given as an object twice; first as an object for the perception and second as an object of the higher-order state. In the third-order awareness of the second-order awareness of the perception of the sunset we would have the sunset as object thrice, whereas the original perception would be given twice as object, and so forth. Thus, the regress would be of an exceedingly vicious kind, implying, in addition to the simple infinite iteration, a simultaneous complication of its single members. Since this consequence is absurd, that is, since it is absurd that even as simple an experience as the perception of a sunset should involve an infinitely complex series of conscious states, one is obliged to end the regress by accepting the existence of nonconscious intentional states (Brentano 1874, 171).

In *Psychologie vom empirischen Standpunkt*, however, Brentano rejected this "solution" since he claimed that it has an implication that is just as absurd as the position it seeks to avoid, namely, that consciousness can be accounted for in terms of the nonconscious. Nevertheless, Brentano obviously also wanted to avoid the infinite regress. How did he manage to pull off this trick? Brentano denied one of the crucial premises and argued that the inner consciousness in question, rather than being a new mental state, is simply an internal feature of the primary experience. Thus, for a mental state to be conscious is for the state to be intentionally directed at itself. A mental state is conscious, not by being taken as an object by a further mental state, but by taking itself as object, and in keeping with Brentano, this prevents any infinite regress from getting off the ground.[5]

While hearing a sound, I am aware of hearing it. What, according to Brentano, is the structure of my consciousness in this case? I have a perception of the sound and an awareness of the perception and, consequently, two objects: The sound and the perception. Contrary to appearance, however, I do not have two different mental states. As Brentano pointed out, the perception of the sound is united so intrinsically and intimately with the awareness of the perception of the sound that they constitute only one single psychical phenomenon. Their apparent separation is due to a mere conceptual differentiation:

In the same mental phenomenon in which the sound is present to our minds we simultaneously apprehend the mental phenomenon itself. What is more, we apprehend it in accordance with its dual nature insofar as it has the sound as content within it, and insofar as it has itself as content at the same time. We can say that the sound is the *primary object* of the *act* of hearing, and that the act of hearing itself is the *secondary object*. (Brentano 1874, 179–180 [1973, 127–128])

Brentano consequently claimed that every intentional experience has a double object, a primary and a secondary. If I am watching a sunset, I have a mental state that is directed both at the sunset and at itself. The primary and thematic object is the sunset; the secondary and unthematic object is the perception. Moreover, it is important to emphasize that the focus of attention is on the primary object and that our awareness of the mental state itself is normally secondary and incidental. In fact, according to Brentano, the experience is, in principle, incapable of observing itself thematically; it cannot take itself as its own primary object. Only in recollection, where one psychical act can take a preceding act as its primary object, can we pay attention to our own mental life (Brentano 1874, 41, 181).

How did Husserl appraise Brentano's theory? Rather negatively, in fact. Husserl denied that there was any evidence in support of the claim concerning the existence of a constant and continuous inner perception, and he consequently rejected Brentano's theory as a piece of construction (Hua 19/367, 759).[6]

Where does this leave us with regard to Husserl's own position? It is tempting to conclude as follows: According to Husserl, our experiences are consciously given the moment they are objectified by an inner perception; an inner perception that Husserl incidentally also characterized with the use of the term "reflection" (Hua 19/669). In contrast to Brentano, however, Husserl did not believe such an inner perception to be always present. On the contrary, it accompanies our experiences only under unusual circumstances, namely whenever we turn our intentional gaze away from the worldly objects and toward our experiences, that is, whenever we reflect. In short, Husserl might be seen as having advocated a so-called reflection-theoretical account of self-awareness, which can be construed as the traditional precursor to the higher-order theories of present day.

By and large, this has been the dominant interpretation of Husserl's position in *Logische Untersuchungen*, and more imprudent scholars have even claimed that it also remains true for Husserl's later work. In *Selbstbewußtsein und Selbstbestimmung*, for instance, Tugendhat argues that Husserl, in *Logische Untersuchungen*, understood self-awareness in terms of an inner perception, that is, as a subject–object relation between two different experiences (a perceiving and a perceived) and that, as he then adds, Husserl never succeeded in explaining why such a relation should result in self-awareness (Tugendhat 1979, 15, 17, 52–53).

At first glance, this interpretation seems to have a solid textual basis. As a result, one of the standard objections against Husserl appears warranted: Because of his preoccupation with *intentionality*, Husserl took object-consciousness as the paradigm of every kind of awareness and therefore settled with a model of self-awareness based on the subject–object dichotomy with its entailed difference between the intending and the intended. Consequently, Husserl never discovered the existence of a pre-reflective self-awareness, but remained committed to the view that self-awareness is a question of reflection or higher-order monitoring (see Gloy 1998, 300).

On closer inspection, however, one can find a number of statements scattered throughout *Logische Untersuchungen* that run counter to this interpretation. Again according to the standard interpretation of the central fifth paragraph in the Fifth Investigation, Husserl was supposed to be arguing that an occurrent experience becomes conscious when it is taken as an object by a higher-order act, namely by an inner perception. (Husserl used the expression "act" as terminus technicus for an intentional experience.) But how does this agree with the following passages? In the First Investigation, Husserl wrote that sensations are originally simply lived through (*erlebt*) as moments of the experience; they are not objectified or taken as objects. This happens only in a subsequent psychological reflection (Hua 19/80). This assertion is then followed up in the Second Investigation, where we find the following significant remark:

That an appropriate train of sensations or images is *experienced*, and is in this sense conscious, does not and cannot mean that this is the *object* of an act of consciousness, in the sense that a perception, a presentation or a judgment is directed upon it. (Hua 19/165 [2001, I/273])

Obviously, the central word is the term "conscious." Husserl denied that sensations are a phenomenological naught. On the contrary, they are conscious, that is, experientially given, when they are lived through and, as he pointed out, this givenness does not come about as the result of an objectification or because the sensations are taken as objects by an (inner) perception. The sensations are given, not as objects, but precisely as subjective experiences. The very same line of thought can be found in the Fifth Investigation. There Husserl wrote that the intentional experiences themselves are lived through, but he denied that they appear in an objectified manner; they are neither seen nor heard. They are conscious without being intentional objects (Hua 19/395, 19/399). This is not to deny that we can, in fact, direct our attention toward our experiences and thereby take them as objects of an inner perception (Hua 19/424), but this occurs only at the moment we reflect on them.

In the light of these statements, the conclusion is easy to draw. In contrast to Brentano, Husserl did not seek to identify the (self-)givenness of our experiences with the givenness of objects. He did not believe that our experiences are conscious by being taken as secondary *objects*. As he explicitly stated in the Sixth Investigation: "Experiential being is not object being [*Erlebtsein ist nicht Gegenständlichsein*]" (Hua 19/669 [2001, II/279, translation modified]).

Contrary to what Gloy is claiming, Husserl did indeed realize that the structure of object-intentionality falls short when it comes to an understanding of experiential self-givenness. Husserl's account in the key fifth paragraph, which deals with the issue of inner consciousness and inner perception, should not make us overlook that he elsewhere in *Logische Untersuchungen* employed the highly relevant distinction between perceiving (*Wahrnehmen*) and experiencing (*Erleben*). Prior to reflection, one perceives the perceptual object, but one experiences, literally "lives through," the intentional act. Although I am not intentionally directed toward the act (this happens only in the subsequent reflection, where the act is thematized), it is not unconscious but conscious, that is, pre-reflectively self-given.

The central question then is whether Husserl's account in the fifth paragraph simply contradicts his other statements or whether it is possible to reinterpret it in a manner that removes the contradiction. We have a choice between the two following interpretations.

• Husserl equated self-awareness with reflective (or introspective) self-awareness, but he denied that this self-awareness is constantly present.[7]
• Husserl distinguished two types of experiential self-givenness, a reflective and a pre-reflective. What he was denying in the fifth paragraph is simply the claim that we are always and incessantly conscious of our own experiences as objects. However, this does not prevent the experiences from being conscious in a pre-reflective and nonobjectifying manner, which is exactly what he is claiming elsewhere in the text.

Obviously, I believe the second interpretation to be the correct one; it removes the contradiction and presents us with a better theory.

Husserl presented his own account as being in opposition to the view defended by Brentano. One remaining question, though, is whether Husserl's criticism of Brentano is fair. Husserl's criticism can be interpreted in two ways. One option is that Husserl was taking Brentano to have claimed that we are constantly thematically aware of our occurrent experiences. If this reading were correct, Husserl would have been right in rejecting the thesis, but wrong in ascribing it to Brentano. As we have already seen, Brentano explicitly warned against taking inner consciousness as a kind of thematic observation (see Brentano 1874, 181). The other possibility is that Husserl is criticizing Brentano for having held the view that we are constantly objectifying our own experiences. This criticism would be right on target.

As we have seen, Brentano argued that the feature that makes a mental state conscious is intrinsic to that very state. It is not bestowed upon it from without by some further state. Thus, Brentano seemed firmly committed to a one-level account of consciousness. However, as Thomasson has recently pointed out, the question is whether Brentano really succeeded in staying clear of the pitfalls of the higher-order view. Is it consistent to defend a one-level account while at the same time claiming that each conscious state involves not only a primary awareness of its object but also a secondary awareness of itself, or does the latter claim show Brentano's supposedly one-level theory to be a higher-order theory in disguise (Thomasson 2000, 190–192, 199)?

According to Thomasson, it is misleading to speak as if consciousness involves an awareness *of* our mental states. To speak in such a manner suggests that, in order to have conscious mental states, we must be aware of them as objects (Thomasson 2000, 200). In fact, it could be argued that Brentano's claim that every conscious intentional state takes two objects, a primary (external) object, and a secondary (internal) object, remains committed to a higher-order take on consciousness; it simply postulates it as being implicitly contained in every conscious state. "It wants," as Thomas puts it, "the benefits of a first order account of consciousness while illegitimately smuggling in a second order (higher-order) view as well" (Thomas 2003, 169).

Is there a better way to capture Brentano's core insight? Thomasson's own simple but ingenious suggestion is that we should adopt an adverbialist interpretation of the secondary awareness. We should construe the secondary awareness as a property of the primary act, and the best way to do so is by thinking of consciousness in adverbial terms. Rather than saying that our conscious mental states are in possession of a secondary awareness of themselves, that there is a perception of an object and additionally an awareness of the perception, it is better to say that we simply see, hear, or feel *consciously* (Thomasson 2000, 203). The decisive advantage of this phrasing is that it avoids interpreting the secondary awareness as a form of object-consciousness. This temptation will remain as long as we keep talking about conscious states as states *of* which we are conscious. But what is gained by adding the adverb "consciously"? As Thomasson points out, the difference between those mental states that remain nonconscious and those that make us consciously aware of (external) objects is that in the latter case objects seem certain ways to us. The difference between a nonconscious perception of a sunset, and a conscious perception of the sunset, is that there is something it is like to perceive a sunset consciously. So although my attention is on the object, the experience itself remains conscious, not in the sense that I am aware *of* it, but in the sense that there is something it is like to be in that state (Thomasson 2000, 203–204).

In my view, Thomasson's adverbialist take has some decisive advantages over Brentano's view. In fact, the question is whether we are still moving within a broadly conceived Brentanian framework or whether we are instead faced with a new theory. Thomasson herself admits that the view she is proposing might look as if it is rather far removed from Brentano, precisely because she is discarding his idea of an "inner consciousness." However, as she then argues, the idea of an inner consciousness based on an awareness of our own mental states as objects was never central to Brentano to start with. What is crucial to the Brentanian model is the idea that consciousness is a dependent aspect of the mental state that possesses it, rather than something that is conferred upon it by a higher-order state, and it is precisely this Brentanian idea that Thomasson is attempting to develop (Thomasson 2000, 204).

I disagree with this appraisal. In my view, the distinction between the primary and the secondary object of consciousness is an integral feature of Brentano's theory, as well as the idea that mental states are either nonconscious or given as objects. If one jettisons these ideas, as one rightly should, one will also take leave of the Brentanian framework. Even more important, there is as little reason to designate every one-level account of consciousness as Brentanian or neo-Brentanian as there is to call every nonreductionistic theory of intentionality Brentanian or neo-Brentanian. This might perhaps have been defensible if Brentano's theory had been the only one-level game in town. However, this is clearly not the case, since a number of phenomenologists defend a one-level account of consciousness much more unequivocally than Brentano. These phenomenologists share the view of Brentano that self-awareness, or inner consciousness, differs from ordinary object-consciousness; the issue of controversy is over whether self-awareness is an extraordinary object-consciousness or not an object-consciousness at all. In contrast to Brentano, Husserl and the other phenomenologists believe the latter more radical move is required.

IV Some Shortcomings

We now return to the earlier question of whether or not Husserl's account of the non-egological character of the stream of consciousness and the nature of self-awareness is persuasive. More specifically, does his treatment of these issues in *Logische Untersuchungen* compare to or surpass the analyses we find in his later works? To put it in one word: No.

Let us first return to Husserl's account of self-awareness. This account is less problematic than is usually believed and although it is very much on the right track, it remains severely underdetermined and can by no means compete with the analyses that were subsequently developed in volumes like *Ding und Raum, Ideen II, Erste Philosophie II,* and *Analysen zur passiven Synthesis,* not to mention *Vorlesungen zur Phänomenologie des inneren Zeitbewußtseins.* In the following chapters, I will take a closer look at some of these analyses, but let me now list a few of the aspects that were later introduced, but which remain absent in the account found in *Logische Untersuchungen*:

- An analysis of the temporal structure of self-awareness
- An investigation of the lived body and of a variety of bodily forms of self-awareness
- A detailed analysis of different types of reflection
- An analysis of the intersubjective modalities of self-awareness

Aside from the fact that Husserl's later theory of self-awareness is far more articulate and draws on many further aspects than his treatment in *Logische Untersuchungen,* there is also another significant development. Husserl was initially prepared to concede that the issue of self-awareness had primacy over an investigation of the stream of consciousness, but he did not make a similar claim when it came to the relation between self-awareness and intentionality. On the contrary, in *Logische Untersuchungen,* Husserl unequivocally gave priority to the topic of intentionality. In later works, however, Husserl came to recognize that an elucidation of self-awareness was of at least as crucial importance to phenomenology as was the analysis of intentionality. Not only did his own methodology make such extensive use of reflection that a detailed examination of reflective self-awareness was required, but Husserl also realized that his analysis of intentionality would lack a proper foundation as long as the problem concerning the self-givenness of consciousness remained unaccounted for. It would be impossible to account convincingly for the appearance of objects without elucidating the first-personal givenness of consciousness. After all, appearing objects always appear *for somebody*. To put it more appropriately in first-person terms, the objects I perceive consciously do not only appear, they appear *for me*. Phenomenology would consequently be incapable of truly clarifying the structures of the dimension of phenomenality as long as it did not first tackle the issue of first-personal givenness head on.

Whereas a criticism of Husserl's account of self-awareness in *Logische Untersuchungen* might be rather uncontroversial, a criticism of his non-egological position might be more contentious. Although Husserl's rather cursory description of the stream of consciousness is no match for what we find in his lectures on inner time-consciousness, some might still positively assess his rejection of the pure ego. The matter is further complicated by the fact that Husserl operated with a number of notions of ego, and with a variety of different egological levels.[8]

One way to approach the issue is to ask what it was that eventually made Husserl change his mind. Why did he write in the second edition of *Logische Untersuchungen* that he was no longer opposed to the doctrine of a "pure" ego and that he had, in the meantime, managed to find it, by learning not to ignore it due to his aversion to different corrupt forms of ego-metaphysics (Hua 19/364, 374)?

As Marbach has shown, one of Husserl's principal reasons for this change was the difficulties his original theory encountered when it came to tackling the problem of *intersubjectivity* (Marbach 1974, 77, 90). A condition of possibility for investigating intersubjectivity is that one operates with a conception of subjectivity that allows one to demarcate one consciousness from another, thereby allowing for plurality. As long as Husserl held on to a non-egological theory, which operated with anonymous experiences belonging to nobody (Hua 16/40), and which took the unity of consciousness to be nothing but the sum total of all contiguous experiences, he was faced with difficulties of the following kind.

If we imagine a situation wherein I am upset by the unexpected scorn of a colleague, we would say that I am upset, not by my own scorn, but by the scorn of another. In my encounter with the colleague's scorn, I am acquainted with myself and I am conscious of somebody else; I am conscious of two different subjects. What is it that permits me to distinguish between my own experience (of distress) and the other's experience (of scorn)? Whereas my own experience is given to me in a distinct first-personal mode of presentation, this is obviously not the case with the scorn of my colleague; in fact, the first-personal givenness of the other's experience is, in principle, inaccessible to me. This is why it is given as the experience of an other. As Husserl would later observe: Had I had the same access to the consciousness of the other as I have to my own, the other would cease being an other and would instead become a part of myself (Hua 1/139; 15/12; 9/416). As Shoemaker has more recently argued, it belongs to the essence of mind that each mind has special access to its own contents; each person has a unique access to his or her own mental states. This special access is constitutive of mental unity (whether there are pathological exceptions to this will be discussed later). Thus, it is a noncontingent fact that the special access one has to one's mental states is access that one can have only to one's own mental states (Shoemaker 1996, 194; see also Hua 9/415). As long as one opts for a non-egological theory of consciousness, one will have a difficult time doing justice to this insight. As Marbach puts it:

The analysis of phenomenological experience brings to bear a crucial distinction: I have conscious experiences that I designate as "my own," and I have conscious experiences *of* conscious experiences that are *not* "my own" but rather "alien" ones. In order for clarity to prevail, one can no longer speak of "nobody's" experiences. (Marbach 1974, 100)

When Husserl realized this, he abandoned his non-egological theory. Every experience belongs to a subject, that is, either to me or to somebody else; it cannot belong to nobody. To put it another way, the ego embraced in the second edition of the *Logische Untersuchungen* is not the ego rejected in the first edition. What Husserl came to realize was that there are more than two legitimate ways to speak of an ego. The ego does not need to be conceived of as something standing apart from or above the experience, nor does one need to conceive of the relation between ego and experience as an external relation of ownership. It is also possible to describe the first-personal givenness of an experience, that is, its very self-givenness or self-manifestation, as the most basic sense of self.

A position that equates the first-personal mode of givenness with a certain basic sense of self (see chapter 5 below) is clearly preferable to the one Husserl adopted in *Logische Untersuchungen*. Not only is Husserl's more mature position more mindful of the importance of the first-person perspective, it also enables one to broach the question of intersubjectivity in a more satisfactory manner. Finally, whereas the non-egological conception of self-awareness that Husserl defended in *Logische Untersuchungen* was faced with the difficulty of accounting for a self-awareness that could bridge the difference between individual experiences and across temporal distance, that is, the problem of being able to account only for the self-awareness of a single, isolated experience, these issues are explicitly treated in Husserl's later theory.

In the beginning of this chapter, I posed the following question: Is Husserl's investigation of consciousness in *Logische Untersuchungen* superior to the account he offers later on, or is it rather the case that most of the insights that can be found in *Logische Untersuchungen* are superseded by Husserl's later analyses? Some interpreters have claimed that there is no relevant difference between Husserl's view on consciousness (particularly his conception of self-awareness) in *Logische Untersuchungen* and in his later works, and they, therefore, consider that a criticism of Husserl's account in *Logische Untersuchungen* can serve as a refutation of his account *tout court*. Another group of scholars is so opposed to Husserl's transcendental turn (which they take to constitute a betrayal of the very phenomenological enterprise) that they either condemn or ignore all of Husserl's later writings and instead praise *Logische Untersuchungen* as his phenomenological masterpiece. As should have become clear from the preceding analysis, I take exception to both views. Obviously one should be very careful with any hasty generalization; however, when it comes to an understanding of consciousness, Husserl's treatment in *Logische Untersuchungen* remains a firm beginning and is not yet the culmination.[9]

3 | The Structure of Time-Consciousness

In his 1925 lecture course *Prolegomena zur Geschichte des Zeitbegriffs*, Heidegger wrote that Husserl operated with too narrow a concept of being. As a result of his exclusive interest in intentionality, Husserl identified the being of consciousness with the being of objects and thereby failed to uncover the unique mode of being that characterized intentional subjectivity. Heidegger consequently stated that a more radical phenomenology was called for. He proposed that phenomenology must return to the original givenness of subjectivity and not merely consider it, as Husserl did, as a (potential) *object* of *reflection* (Heidegger GA 20: 143, 152; see also Sartre 1948, 55).

More recently, Tugendhat, Henrich, Frank, and Gloy, who all argue that Husserl's analysis of self-awareness remained committed to a reflection-theoretical account, have voiced similar criticisms. As Frank puts it: "In any case, Husserl does not know any other concept of self-awareness than the reflective one" (Frank 1984, 300; see also Henrich 1966, 231). In fact, Frank even claims that Husserl not only failed to provide a convincing analysis of self-awareness, but that he did not even understand the problem itself (Frank 1986, 45).

A common feature of these critical interpretations has been their narrow textual basis. They largely restrict themselves to Husserl's position in only two of his published works, *Logische Untersuchungen* (1900–1901) and *Ideen zu einer reinen Phänomenologie und phänomenologischen Philosophie I* (1913). Occasionally, material is also drawn from *Zur Phänomenologie des inneren Zeitbewusstseins* (1893–1917), but very rarely is any further material considered, from either the posthumously published volumes of *Husserliana* or any of the still unpublished research-manuscripts found in the Husserl-Archives in Leuven.

If there is anything that recent Husserl scholarship has demonstrated, it is that it is virtually impossible to acquire a satisfactory understanding of Husserl's views if one restricts oneself to the writings that were published during his lifetime. This is the case not only when it comes to topics such as the problem of intersubjectivity, the role of the body, or the structure of temporality, but also when it comes to the question of self-awareness.

Whereas in the previous chapter I questioned the traditional rendition of Husserl's position in *Logische Untersuchungen*, I will in this chapter draw on posthumously published material to demonstrate that the standard interpretation must be rejected. Not only is the notion of pre-reflective self-awareness present in Husserl's later works; it is also subjected there to an illuminating analysis that emphasizes its temporal structure.

I Subjectivity of Experience

What did Husserl have to offer on the subject of self-awareness? Let me begin by showing that he, in a manner not unlike Sartre, took self-awareness to be an essential feature of subjectivity and that he considered reflection to be a founded and derived form of self-awareness. Rather than being something that occurs only during exceptional circumstances, specifically whenever we pay attention to our conscious life, self-awareness is, for Husserl, a characterizing feature of subjectivity, regardless of what worldly entities it might otherwise be conscious of and occupied with.

To be a subject is to be in the mode of being aware of oneself. (Hua 14/151; cf. Hua 13/462, Hua 8/412)

An absolute existent is existent in the form of an intentional life—which, no matter what else it may be intrinsically conscious of, is, at the same time, consciousness of itself. Precisely for that reason (as we can see when we consider more profoundly) it has at all times an essential ability to *reflect* on itself, on all its structures that stand out for it—an essential ability to make itself thematic and produce judgments, and evidences, relating to itself. (Hua 17/279–280 [1969, 273])

For the latter [the life of consciousness] is not only a lived-experiencing continually streaming along; at the same time, as it streams along it is also immediately the consciousness of this streaming. This consciousness is self-perceiving, although it is a thematically executed awareness on the part of the ego only in exceptional circumstances. Belonging to the latter is a reflection that is possible at any time. This perceiving that presents all lived-experiencing to consciousness is the so-called inner consciousness or inner perceiving. (Hua 11/320)

Husserl's interest in self-awareness was motivated by his interest in the question of how consciousness is given to itself, how it manifests itself. As he wrote in the beginning of the recently published *Bernauer Manuskripte über das Zeitbewusstsein*, consciousness exists, it exists as a stream, and it appears to itself as a stream. The enduring question is how the stream of consciousness is capable of being conscious of itself; how is it possible and comprehensible that the very being of the stream is a form of self-consciousness (Hua 33/44, 46)? Husserl took first-personal givenness to be something that essentially characterizes experiential life. It is something the experiences cannot lack without ceasing to be experiences. At its most primitive, self-consciousness is simply a question of having first-personal access to one's own consciousness; it is a question of the first-personal givenness or manifestation of experiential life.

Granted that I am having first-personal access to the experience in question when I consciously perceive a cairn or an almond tree, the central question, of course, is *how* this access comes about. Is it the result of a reflection? Husserl's answer was no. For him, the act of reflection, say, a thematic awareness of an occurrent hearing of Charles Mingus's *Pithecanthropus Erectus*, is founded in a twofold sense. It presents us not with a self-enclosed subjectivity, but with a self-transcending subjectivity directed at an object, and it consequently presupposes the preceding act of object-intentionality (Hua 15/78, 8/157). Moreover, as an explicit self-awareness, it also relies on a prior tacit self-awareness. In Husserl's own words:

The term lived-experience [*Erlebnis*] expresses just this [quality of] being experiential [*Erlebtsein*], that is having conscious awareness in inner consciousness, which at any time makes it pregiven to the I. (Hua 8/45)

[E]very experience is "consciousness," and consciousness is consciousness *of . . .* But every experience is *itself experienced* [*erlebt*], and *to that extent* also "conscious" [*bewußt*]. (Hua 10/291; translation slightly modified; ellipsis in original)

Every act is consciousness of something, but there is also consciousness of every act. Every act is "sensed," is immanently "perceived" (inner consciousness), although naturally not posited, meant (to perceive here does not mean to grasp something and to be turned towards it in an act of meaning). . . . To be sure, this seems to lead back to an infinite regress. For is not the inner consciousness, the perceiving of the act (of judging, of perceiving something external, of rejoicing, and so forth), again an act and therefore itself something internally perceived, and so on? On the contrary, we must say: Every "experience" in the strict sense is internally perceived. But the internal perceiving is not an "experience" in the same sense. It is not itself again internally perceived. (Hua 10/126–127; translation slightly modified)

When I consciously perceive something, say, a drawing of Rembrandt, I am directed at and preoccupied with the drawing. Whenever I am consciously directed at the drawing, I am also self-aware, but I am not thematically conscious of myself. When I do thematize myself in reflection, the very act of thematization remains unthematic.

> Thus we always have the separation between the I and *cogito* as functioning but not grasped (functioning subjectivity), and the possibly thematized, direct or self-grasped I and its *cogito*, or more simply, it is necessary to distinguish between the functioning subjectivity and the objective subjectivity (the objectified, thematically experienced, presented, thought, predicated subjectivity), and whenever I take myself or something else as an object, I am always necessarily unthematically cogiven as a functioning I, accessible to myself through reflection, which, on its part, is a new unthematic activity of the functioning I. (Hua 14/431; see also Hua 14/29, 29/183–184)

When subjectivity functions, it is self-aware but it is not thematically conscious of itself, and it therefore lives, as Husserl put it, in *anonymity*. Thus, contrary to what might perhaps be expected, for Husserl the terms "anonymous" and "anonymity" are not meant to designate the absence of self-awareness. For an experience to be anonymous is for the experience in question to lack thematic self-awareness; it is not for it to lack first-personal givenness altogether. Thus, Husserl explicitly spoke of the unthematic and anonymous life of consciousness as being *mitbewußt*, that is, co-conscious (Hua 7/262).

As far as the interpretation of Henrich, Gloy, Tugendhat, and Frank is concerned, it must be acknowledged that Husserl occasionally wrote that we do not *perceive* our own subjectivity prior to reflection, but live in a state of self-oblivion and self-forfeiture (*Selbstverlorenheit*). When he then added, however, that we only *know* of our acts reflectively, that is, that we only gain *knowledge* of our conscious life through reflection (Hua 8/88; 9/306–307), it becomes clear that he was using the term "perception" to denote a thematic examination. Husserl did not deny the existence of a tacit self-awareness, but he did reject the claim that this self-awareness could provide us with more than awareness; it cannot give us (conceptual) *knowledge* of subjectivity. As he put it in a text from 1917:

> The actual life and lived-experiencing is of course always conscious, but it is not therefore always thematically experienced and known. For that a new pulse of actual life is necessary, a so-called reflective or immanently directed experience. (Hua 25/89)

It is admittedly possible to unearth passages where Husserl did, in fact, describe the tacit self-awareness as a type of *inner perception* (Hua 8/471; 10/126), but a closer examination of these texts does not substantiate the claim that Husserl was trying to reduce self-awareness to a type of object-intentionality. Husserl's choice of term is taken from his classical investigation of the hierarchy of foundation existing between different types of intentional experiences. According to Husserl, different types of intentionality can be ranked according to their ability to give us the intentional object as directly, originally, and optimally as possible. If we compare my perception of a flowering apple tree with my recollection or imagination of a flowering apple tree, we are in all three cases directed toward a flowering apple tree and not toward mental pictures or copies of an apple tree; however, there are still crucial differences between the ways in which the flowering apple tree appears in these three acts. There is a difference between the intention that intends the apple tree in an empty manner and the intention that is fulfilled by the perceptually given apple tree. Only perception gives us the flowering apple tree *in propria persona*, in its bodily presence (Hua 19/434, 646; 3/90–91). In recollection or fantasy, we lack that kind of presence. It is this particular feature of perceptual givenness that Husserl drew on in his discussion of tacit self-awareness. This is brought to light in a passage from *Erste Philosophie II*, where he wrote that the life of the subject is a life in the form of original self-awareness. He then equated this self-awareness with an *innermost* perception, but added that it is a perception not in the sense of being an active self-apprehension, but in the sense of being an *originary* self-appearance (Hua 8/188).

In two of the passages quoted above, from *Analysen zur passiven Synthesis* and *Vorlesungen zur Phänomenologie des inneren Zeitbewusstseins* respectively, Husserl speaks alternately of tacit self-awareness as both an inner perception and an inner consciousness. As will gradually become clear, Husserl ultimately opted for the latter expression. Much misunderstanding might have been avoided if he had always distinguished as clearly between the two as he did in *Ideen II*, where he equated "inner perception" with reflection, and "inner consciousness" with a nonthematic kind of self-awareness that precedes reflection (Hua 4/118).

According to Husserl, our acts are tacitly self-aware, but they are also accessible for reflection. They can be reflected upon and thereby brought to our *attention* (Hua 4/248). An examination of the particular intentional structure of this process can substantiate the thesis concerning the founded status of reflection. In his analysis of the different layers of intentionality, Husserl pointed to the important distinction between activity and passivity. We can find acts in which the subject is actively taking a position, that is, acts in which the subject is comparing, differentiating, judging, valuing, wishing, or willing something; however, according to Husserl, whenever a subject is active, it is also passive, since to be active is to react to something (Hua 4/213, 337). Every kind of active position-taking presupposes a preceding *affection* (Hua 14/44). If we follow Husserl a step further in his analysis, he distinguishes between *receptivity* and *affectivity*: Receptivity is taken to be the first, lowest, and most primitive level of intentional activity, and consists in responding to, or paying attention to, that which is affecting us passively. Thus, receptivity in the sense of a mere "I notice" presupposes a prior affection; that which is now brought into focus was already affecting and stimulating the subject unnoticed (Hua 11/64, 84).

Reflective self-awareness is often taken to be a thematic, articulated, and intensified self-awareness and is normally initiated in order to bring the primary intentional act into focus. In order to explain the occurrence of reflection, however, it is necessary that that which is to be disclosed and thematized is (unthematically) present; otherwise, there would be nothing to motivate and call forth the act of reflection. As Husserl pointed out, it is in the nature of reflection to grasp something that was already given prior to the grasping. Reflection is characterized by disclosing, not by producing its theme:

> When I say "I," I grasp myself in a simple reflection. But this self-experience [*Selbsterfahrung*] is like every experience [*Erfahrung*], and in particular every perception, a mere directing myself towards something that was already there for me, that was already conscious, but not thematically experienced, not noticed. (Hua 15/492–493)

> Whenever I reflect, I find myself "in relation" to something, as affected or active. That which I am related to is experientially conscious—it is already there for me as a "lived-experience" in order for me to be able to relate myself to it. (Husserl Ms. C 10 13a)[1]

In short, reflection is not an act *sui generic*; it does not appear out of nowhere, but presupposes, like all intentional activity, a *motivation*. According to Husserl, to be motivated is to be *affected* by something, and then to respond to it (Hua 4/217). That which motivates reflection is—in a term that we will later have reason to return to—a prior *self-affection*. I can thematize myself because I am already passively self-aware; I can grasp myself because I am already affected by myself (Hua 6/111; 15/78, 120).

When I start reflecting, that which motivates the reflection and is then grasped has already been going on for a while. The reflected experience did not commence the moment I started paying attention to it and is given, not only as still existing, but also and mainly as having already been. It is the *same* act, which is now given reflectively and as enduring in time, that is, as a temporal act (Hua 3/95, 162–164). When reflection sets in, it initially grasps something that has just elapsed, namely the motivating phase of the act reflected upon. The reason this phase can still be thematized by the subsequent reflection is that it does not disappear, but is retained in the *retention*; thus Husserl could claim that retention is a condition of possibility for reflection. It is owing to the retention that consciousness can be made into an object (Hua 10/119), or to rephrase it, reflection can take place only if a *temporal horizon* has been established.

II Temporality

I have just mentioned that Husserl took reflection to depend on *temporality*. In fact, it is precisely in his theory of *inner time-consciousness* that one will find his most elaborate account of the structure of pre-reflective self-awareness. Let us now turn to that theory, and thereby to a nest of problems that has often, and rightly, been characterized as being among the most important and difficult ones in all phenomenology (Hua 10/276, 334).[2]

In *Ideen I*, Husserl confined himself to an analysis of the relation between constituted objects and constituting consciousness. He accounted for the way in which the givenness of objects are conditioned by subjectivity, yet apart from stressing that experiences are not given in the same (perspectival) manner as objects, he had not pursued the question concerning the givenness of subjectivity itself any further. Such a silence was *phenomenologically* unacceptable. Any analysis of the conditioned appearance of objects would necessarily lack a foundation as long as the givenness of the subjective condition was itself left in the dark.[3] Husserl was well aware of this, and he explicitly admitted that in *Ideen I* he left out the most important problems, namely those pertaining to inner time-consciousness (Hua 3/182).

The reason Husserl attributed such immense importance to his analysis of temporality, considering it, as he did, to constitute the bedrock of phenomenology, is precisely because it is not a mere investigation of the temporal givenness of objects. It is not just a clarification of how it is possible to be conscious of objects with temporal extensions—objects such as melodies, which cannot appear all at once, but only unfold over time—rather, it is also an account of the *temporal self-givenness* of consciousness itself.

In his *Vorlesungen zur Phänomenologie des inneren Zeitbewußtseins*, Husserl asks how it is possible for us to be conscious of temporal objects. His well-known thesis is that a perception of a temporal object, as well as the perception of succession and change, would be impossible if consciousness provided us only with access to the pure now-phase of the object and if the stream of consciousness itself was a series of unconnected points of experiencing, like a line of pearls. Had our perception been restricted to being conscious of that which exists right now, it would have been impossible to *perceive* anything with temporal extension and duration, for a succession of isolated, punctual, conscious states does not, as such, enable us to experience succession and duration. Since we are obviously conscious of succession and duration, we must acknowledge that our consciousness, one way or the other, can encompass more than that which is given right now. Although we can be co-conscious of that which has just been, and that which is about to occur, the crucial question remains: *how* can we be conscious of that which is no longer, or not yet, present to our consciousness? Some have suggested that imagination or memory might play a crucial role. There is, however, an obvious difference between seeing a movement (that necessarily extends in time) or hearing a melody, and remembering or imagining either. Husserl's own alternative is to insist on the *width of presence*.

According to Husserl, the basic unit of temporality is not a "knife-edge" present, but a "duration-block," that is, a temporal field that comprises all three temporal modes of present, past, and future. There are three technical terms to describe this temporal form of consciousness. There is (1) what is known as a *primal impression* or *primal presentation*, which is the moment that is narrowly directed toward the now-phase of the object.[4] The primal presentation never appears in isolation and is an abstract component that, by itself, cannot provide us with awareness of a temporal object. It is accompanied by (2) a *retention*, which is the component that provides us with a consciousness of the just-elapsed phase of the object, that is, it allows us to be aware of the phase as it sinks into the past, and by (3) a *protention*, the component that, in a more or less indefinite way, intends the phase of the object about to occur. The role of the protention is evident in our implicit and unreflective anticipation of what is about to happen as experience progresses. The concrete and full structure of all lived experience is consequently *protention–primal presentation–retention*. Although the specific experiential contents of this structure change progressively from moment to moment, at any one given moment this threefold structure is present (synchronically) as a unified whole:

> In this way, it becomes evident that concrete perception as original consciousness (original givenness) of a temporally extended object is structured internally as itself a streaming system of momentary perceptions (so-called primal impressions). But each such momentary perception is the nuclear phase of a continuity, a continuity of momentary gradated retentions on the one side, and a horizon of what is coming on the other side: a horizon of "protention," which is disclosed to be characterized as a constantly gradated coming. (Hua 9/202)

To illustrate, let us take the case of hearing the beginning of a spoken sentence, say, "Joe, come home now! Or I will take. . . ." When hearing the last word "take," I am no longer hearing the previous words, but I must retain their sense if the sentence is to be meaningful to me. Correspondingly, when hearing the last word, I will have some anticipatory sense of where the sentence is heading. This is why I would be surprised if the sentence just ended with the word "take," or if it was continued with the words "the blue raincoat out of the closet."

What is the dynamic structure of this temporal process? If, for reasons of simplicity, we focus on the role of retention and take as our example Husserl's own preferred case of a melody or string of tones such as C–D–E, the orthodox Husserlian account is as follows. When the tone C is first heard, it is intended by the primal presentation. When it is succeeded by the tone D, the tone D is given in the primal presentation, whereas the tone C is now retained by the retention, and when the E sounds, it replaces the tone D in the primal presentation, whereas the tone D is now retained by the retention, and so on. The retention, however, is not simply a consciousness of the tone that has just passed. Every time a new tone is intended in a primal presentation, the entire retentional sequence is modified. When the tone C is succeeded by the tone D, our presentational consciousness of the tone D will be accompanied by a retention of the tone C (D(c)). When the tone D is replaced by the tone E, our presentational consciousness of the tone E will be accompanied not only by a retention of the tone D, but also by a retention of the tone retained in the tone D ($E(d_{(c)})$), and so forth (Hua 10/81, 100).

Husserl's model was intended to account for the facts that we experience continuity and that our experience itself is continuous. It could be objected, however, that his theory furnishes each occurrent episode of consciousness with an exceedingly complex structure, since it will supposedly contain retentional traces of every conscious state preceding it. But as Husserl pointed out, as time passes the past objects and experiences quickly lose their differentiation and distinctive qualities; they recede into the background, become vague, and are finally lost in the night of the unconscious (Hua 11/169–171).

Retention and protention should be distinguished from proper (thematic) *recollection* and *expectation*. There is an obvious difference between retaining and protending the tones that have just sounded and are about to sound, and remembering a past holiday or looking forward to the next vacation. Whereas the two latter performances are full-blown intentional experiences that presuppose the work of the retention and the protention, the protention and retention are dependent moments of any occurrent experience. They do not provide us with additional intentional objects, but with a consciousness of the temporal horizon of the present object. Whereas recollection and expectation are, at least to some extent,[5] subject to our will, that is, whereas they are intentional acts that we can initiate ourselves, we cannot stop having retentions and protentions. They are passive processes that take place without our active contribution.

What does all of this have to do with self-consciousness? Husserl's analysis of the structure of inner time-consciousness serves a double purpose. It is meant to explain not only how we can be aware of objects with temporal extension, but also how we can be aware of our own fluctuating stream of experiences. In short, it is not sufficient to understand how we are able to be conscious of temporal objects; we also need to understand how we are able to be aware of the very experiences that intend these temporal objects. Our perceptual objects are temporal, but what about our very perceptions of these objects? Are they also subjugated to the strict laws of temporal constitution? Are they also temporal unities, which arise, endure, and perish? Husserl often speaks of the experiences themselves as being constituted in the structure of protention–primal presentation–retention; they are only given, only self-aware, within this framework (Hua 11/233, 293; 4/102). But how is this temporal self-awareness to be understood? One can find different (and conflicting) accounts in Husserl's writings. Let us look at some of them.

III The Internal Object Account

In Husserl's recently published *Bernauer Manuskripte über das Zeitbewusstsein* (originally written in 1917–1918) one can find texts wherein he defended what might be called an *internal object* account, that is, he argued that inner time-consciousness makes us aware of the intentional experiences as immanent temporal objects. In text number six, for instance, which carries the title "Acts as objects in the 'phenomenological time,'" Husserl argued that one should distinguish between the perception of a tone, on the one hand, and the original or inner consciousness in which the perception is constituted as a temporal unity on the other. Every perception is what Husserl called an act-object (*Aktgegenständlichkeit*). Every perception is itself something that is constituted as an object in original time-consciousness (Hua 33/107–109). Similar statements can be found elsewhere in the volume. In text number seven, Husserl wrote that it is a necessary fact that every experience in the course of streaming life is constituted as an immanent temporal object (Hua 33/128). In text number 18, he wrote that every concrete experience is a unity of becoming and is constituted as an object in inner consciousness. Experiences are, in fact, simply objects in inner consciousness—objects in which further objects are constituted (Hua 33/318).[6]

In a note from 1929, Husserl's last assistant, Eugen Fink, wrote that Husserl, in his intended revision of the *Bernau Manuscripts*, planned to work out what he took to be their most important advances via-à-vis his original (and more well known) lectures on time-consciousness from 1905 to 1910 and that this included a "restitution of the Brentanian–Aristotelian doctrine" (Quoted in Bruzina 1993, 360). It is, in fact, quite easy to identify these Brentanian elements in the *Bernau Manuscripts*; whether they also constitute an advance vis-à-vis Husserl's earlier reflections is, however, a different question. First, Husserl did briefly consider the possibility of avoiding an infinite regress of foundation by means of the unconscious, but just like Brentano (cf. page 38 above), he ultimately rejected this solution (Hua 33/200). Second, Husserl frequently seems to simply have accepted Brentano's alternative: mental states are either nonconscious or given as conscious objects, and there is no third possibility. Finally, and most revealing, on several occasions Husserl employed Brentano's distinction between the primary and the secondary objects of consciousness:

Consciousness is not merely object-consciousness, consciousness of its "primary" object, but also "inner" consciousness, consciousness of itself and its intentional process. Next to its primary objects, it has its "secondary" objects. (Hua 33/42)

On both sides, we have mediate intentionality, and to every mediate intentionality there belongs the double "directedness" of intentionality, the directedness toward the primary object and toward the secondary object, i.e., toward the "acts" and the primary objects in "the how of their givenness." On both sides, this does not lead to any infinite intentional regress. (Hua 33/10; see also 33/206)

Husserl's positive appraisal in the *Bernau Manuscripts* differs rather strikingly from his original assessment of Brentano's theory. As we saw in chapter 2, Husserl denied in *Logische Untersuchungen* that there is any evidence in support of the claim concerning the existence of a *constant* and *ceaseless* inner perception, and he consequently rejected Brentano's theory as a mere piece of construction (Hua 19/367, 759). Husserl, in his early work, quite explicitly and unequivocally discarded the attempt to equate the givenness of our experiences with the givenness of objects. Whereas he there obviously distanced himself from the view that our experiences are conscious by being taken as secondary objects, he regrettably seems to have forgotten these insights in central texts from the Bernau period.

In my view, the position outlined in text number six (and elsewhere) is fundamentally mistaken. Before I proceed to present one of Husserl's alternative and more convincing accounts, let me briefly outline why I believe the *internal object* account is wrong and why I think this is something Husserl himself has amply demonstrated.

It is relatively, but not completely, uncontroversial to concede that we, under certain circumstances, are aware of our own experiences as immanent objects, namely whenever we reflect. If I reflect on my occurrent perception of my laptop and reflectively try to discern and articulate the different structures of this perception, I do seem to be confronted with a rather peculiar immanent object. In the *Bernau Manuscripts*, Husserl called these objects of reflection "noetic objects" (Hua 33/449). The crucial question, however, is whether our experiences are also given as *objects* in inner time-consciousness prior to reflection. Is their primal givenness an object-manifestation? This is what the *internal object* account claims; but is it true? Not only do I think it is wrong from a purely descriptive point of view—in my everyday life, I am absorbed by and preoccupied with projects and objects in the world, I am not aware of my own stream of consciousness as a succession of immanent *objects*—but I also think that such a view is conceptually and theoretically misleading.

When we consciously experience something, are we then self-aware? As we have already seen, Husserl's answer is affirmative. When I consciously perceive an object, the perceptual experience itself is, at least tacitly, *given* as *my* experience. When I consciously taste freshly brewed coffee, touch an ice cube, see a dragonfly, or feel pain or dizziness, the experiences in question are characterized by a first-personal givenness that immediately reveals them as my own. First-personal experience presents me with an immediate access to myself, and it is therefore legitimate to speak of an implicit (and minimal) self-awareness. In this instance, a certain problem arises; the experiences I live through are characterized by *mineness*, but why and how can a mere object be given as *mine*? In fact, how can my awareness of an *object* constitute self-awareness? Whereas self-awareness implies some form of identity, object-consciousness is precisely characterized by an epistemic difference between the subject and the object of experience, and, as Husserl himself pointed out in the *Bernau Manuscripts*, there is always a phenomenological difference between the intentional object and the intentional experience that is conscious of the object (Hua 33/199). In this case, however, we are faced with a dilemma. To deny that we are aware of the experiences as our own is unacceptable. Yet we cannot affirm that we are aware of them as our own, as long as we maintain that we are aware of them only as objects.

Is there any alternative? The obvious way to dismantle the dilemma is to concede that we are aware of our own experiences in an immediate, prereflective, and nonobjectifying manner. If we are to avoid an infinite regress, this primitive, pre-reflective self-awareness cannot be a result of a secondary act or reflex, but must be a constitutive aspect of the experience itself. Prior to reflection, experiential states do present themselves, but not as objects. Metaphorically speaking, experiential states are characterized by a certain self-luminosity; they are self-intimating or self-presenting (see Shoemaker 1996, 51, 225). Thus, the first-personal givenness of experience should not be taken as the result of a higher-order representation, reflection, internal monitoring, or introspection, but rather should be treated as an *intrinsic feature* of experience. If genuine self-awareness is to be possible—and who would deny its existence?—this seems to be the only option. Thus, the solution is to deny that the primal givenness of the experience is an object-givenness.

Perhaps it could be objected that we need to distinguish between different types of objects. As Kortooms insists in his recent book, *Phenomenology of Time*, when saying that an experience is given as an "object," the term "object" must be placed within quotation marks, since the consciousness of the experience is not really a grasping, objectifying consciousness (Kortooms 2002, 102, 130, 192, 237). To put it another way, the experiential "object" is only a marginal, nongrasped and nonobjectified "object." In my view, however, this rescue attempt is a failure; some terminological rigor is required, and to speak of a nonobjectified object is unsatisfactory.

It is obviously necessary to distinguish thematic (focal) and marginal (peripheral) modes of consciousness. There is an obvious distinction to be made between my thematic awareness of my laptop, and my marginal awareness of the myriad objects surrounding it. We also need to dismiss any narrow conception of consciousness that equates consciousness with attention and claims that we are conscious only of that to which we pay attention. The phenomenal content of experience is not restricted to, or exhausted by, what we notice or are able to describe in any detail. There is experience that goes unnoticed, but unnoticed or unattended experience is still experience. It may even be argued that the bulk of our consciousness consists of this sort of unnoticed experience. Dainton has recently called this sphere of experience the *phenomenal background* and has argued that it has three main components: one is the diverse range of bodily experience, another is world-presenting perceptual experience, and the third component is our sense of self, an ambient inner background of what it feels like to be the conscious being we are (Dainton 2000, 31–32). All of this seems perfectly right. The crucial question is, however, whether the distinction between focal and peripheral consciousness—a distinction between two types of object-consciousness—is pertinent when it comes to an understanding of the prereflective givenness of our experiences.[7]

Husserl discussed this question extensively in his 1906–1907 lecture course *Einleitung in die Logik und Erkenntnistheorie*. He began by observing that we are aware of the perceptual object when we are engaged in a perception. But what about the sensations and the perceptual experience itself? They are also conscious, but are not given as perceptual objects; they are not perceived. What does it mean to be conscious, if not perceptually given (Hua 24/242)? Obviously, the experiential components do not form part of the objective background of the perceptual object. The perceptual object, say, a house, is always situated in a perceptual field. The house is located right in the middle of a multitude of other objects, and obviously the perceptual experience itself is not to be found among these objects, as if it were located a few centimeters to the left of the wall:

> One should not mistake the consciousness of the objective background [gegen-ständlichen Hintergrund] and consciousness understood in the sense of experiential being [Erlebtseins]. Lived-experiences [Erlebnisse] as such, do have their own being, but they are not objects of apperception (in this case we would end in an infinite regress). The background, however, is given to us objectively; it is constituted through a complex of apperceptive lived-experiences. We do not pay attention to these objects ..., but they are still given to us in a quite different manner than the mere lived-experiences themselves.... The attentional consciousness of the background and consciousness in the sense of mere experiential givenness must be completely distinguished. (Hua 24/252)

We know that we can turn our attention away from the perceptual object and toward the perceptual experience. In this sense, it is possible to reflect upon the experience. To repeat the question, how is the perceptual experience given prior to reflection; how is it pre-reflectively present (Hua 24/244)? In 1906–1907 Husserl answered the question by distinguishing between consciousness in the sense of experiential being and consciousness in the sense of intentionality. Whereas the latter involves directedness toward an object, that is, object-consciousness, the former does not. As Husserl explicitly wrote: " 'experiencing' does not mean the having of an object [Gegenständlich-Haben], nor to be 'related' to the object in this or that way and to take a position to it in this or that way and whatnot" (Hua 24/247).

The attempt to model pre-reflective self-consciousness on marginal object-consciousness by suggesting that our pre-reflective experiences remain in the background as potential themes—in precisely the same way as does, say, the hum of the refrigerator—might be tempting, but it is ultimately misleading since it remains stuck in the subject–object model. It remains committed to the idea that our experiential life must either be given as an object or not be given at all and lets the only allowed variable be whether the object is given thematically or only marginally. This line of thought is flawed, however, since it erroneously assumes that there is only one type of givenness or manifestation, that of object-givenness. Had that, in fact, been the case, self-awareness *sensu stricto* (understood as an awareness of oneself as subject) would have been impossible.

It is true, of course, that the plausibility of the claim that self-awareness and awareness of something as an object are mutually exclusive modes of awareness depends to a large extent on what we mean by "object" (see Cassam 1997, 5). From a phenomenological perspective, however, object-hood is a specific mode of givenness. For Husserl, an object is something that is constituted in a process of objectification. More specifically, he argued that something is given as an object only the moment it is experienced as being in possession of a sort of *transcendence*. It is only when we experience something as a unity within a multiplicity of adumbrations, or as an identity across differences, that is, as something that transcends its actual appearance or that can be intended as the same throughout a variety of experiential states, that we experience it as an object. Moreover, object-givenness necessarily entails an epistemic divide, a distinction between that which appears and to whom it appears, between the object and the subject of experience. For something to be given as an object of experience is for it to differ from the subjective experience that takes it as an object. In other words, an object of experience is something that, per definition, stands in opposition to or over against the subject of experience (cf. the German term *Gegen-stand*). This is one reason why object-consciousness is singularly unsuitable as a model for understanding self-awareness. Another reason, already spelled out in chapter 1, is that the attempt to construe self-awareness as a type of object-consciousness generates an infinite regress.

When we are absorbed or immersed in our daily concerns and simply live through our experiences, they are not given as objects; they are not something we observe from a distance and they do not stand opposite us. This, however, is precisely what can happen when we reflect. In reflection, we can place ourselves in contrast to a part of our own experiential life. We can distance ourselves from an experience and seize it as an object. If I reflect upon my present perception, it is given as that which remains identical across the respective differences of pre-reflective and reflective givenness, that is, it is given as the *same* as what was previously experienced unthematically. It is only in reflection, where we are confronted with a relation between two different acts, the reflecting and the reflected, that the latter can appear as transcendent vis-à-vis the first. On the pre-reflective level, where there is only one experience, it cannot appear as a temporal *object*, since it cannot appear as transcendent in relation to itself.

To sum up, I do not think the account offered by Husserl in the *Bernau Manuscripts* is systematically satisfactory.[8] However, as I have already suggested, I also believe that it is a view that Husserl himself, for the most part, rejected. This is so not only in *Logische Untersuchungen* and *Einleitung in die Logik und Erkenntnistheorie*, but also in his later writings. In the following, I propose an alternative interpretation of Husserl's investigation of inner time-consciousness that permits one to link this investigation to Husserl's account of the relation between pre-reflective and reflective self-awareness.

IV *Urbewußtsein* and Self-Affection

To speak phenomenologically of the temporality of consciousness is to speak of the temporal givenness of consciousness. To speak of the temporal givenness of consciousness is to speak of its temporal self-givenness. To suggest otherwise is to reify consciousness. Why speak of *self-givenness*? Because whereas we, in the case of the givenness of an object, have to distinguish the object that is given from the subject to whom it is given, this distinction is no longer appropriate when it comes to the givenness of our experience. The experience is given in and through and for *itself*. What this means, however, is that it would be a mistake to conceive of the relation between inner time-consciousness and the intentional experience as a relation between two separate dimensions of consciousness. When Husserl claimed that the experience is constituted in inner time-consciousness, he was not saying that the experience is brought to givenness by some other part of subjectivity, as if one part took the other as its object. Rather, to say that an experience is constituted in inner time-consciousness is to say that it is brought to awareness by its own means. It is called *inner* time-consciousness because it belongs *intrinsically* to the *innermost* structure of the experience itself. To put it differently, inner time-consciousness simply *is* the pre-reflective self-awareness of the stream of consciousness, and Husserl's account of the structure of inner time-consciousness (protention–primal presentation–retention) should consequently be appreciated as an analysis of the (micro)structure of first-personal givenness.

Husserl's position was, consequently, relatively unequivocal. An intentional experience is conscious of something different from itself, namely the object intended. At the same time, the experience also manifests itself. Thus, apart from being intentional, the experience is also characterized by inner consciousness, or by what Husserl occasionally called its *Urbewußtsein* (10/89, 118–120).

The notion of *Urbewußtsein*, which Husserl had already used in his early lecture course *Einleitung in die Logik und Erkenntnistheorie*, is not meant to denote a particular intentional experience. Rather, the term designates the pervasive dimension of pre-reflective and nonobjectifying self-consciousness that is part and parcel of any occurring experience (Hua 24/245–247). Whereas reflection is always belated and retrospective (*nachträglich*), *Urbewußtsein* is—as indicated by the prefix "Ur-"—original (*ursprünglich*) (see also Ni 1998, 80).

Subjectivity is, as such, self-temporalizing, with the intentional experiences originally given as waves in this stream of experiencing, to use Husserl's own metaphor (Hua 10/75, 29/194; Husserl Ms. C 17 63a). Originally, these experiences are moments of the self-temporalizing stream of consciousness and, therefore, precisely *not* distinct temporal objects (Hua 10/333–334, 371). Whereas Husserl claimed that our experiences—be they perceptions, recollections, anticipations, judgments, imaginations—initially reveal themselves, though not as immanently given temporal objects, he also suggested that reflection imposes a new temporal form upon our consciousness.[9] When we start to thematize our experiences through reflection, they are made into subjective or immanent temporal objects (Hua 10/285; Hua 14/29). As it is formulated in the late C manuscripts:

My *thematic* experience of I and consciousness is, by itself, the founding of a continuous validity—the founding of a lasting being, the being of the immanent. (Husserl Ms. C 12 3b; my emphasis)[10]

The pure streaming is indeed objectified only as it is [reflectively] observed, etc., and through the possibility of repetition. (Husserl Ms. C 16 59a)[11]

Prior to reflection, there is no awareness of internal objects and there is no distinction between the pre-reflective self-givenness of the experiential stream and the flow of inner time-consciousness.

To insist that the very flow of inner time-consciousness *is* the pre-reflective self-givenness of the experiences is not to deny the distinction between our singular and transitory experiences and the abiding dimension of experiencing, that is, between *die Erlebnisse* and *das Erleben* (Hua 23/326; see also 14/46). In fact, there are excellent reasons for not simply identifying the experience and the experiencing, the intentional experience and the pre-reflective givenness of the experience. It is easy to illustrate why this distinction must be kept. If we take three different experiences, say, a visual perception of a bird, an anticipation of a forthcoming holiday, and a rejection of the claim that Earth is the largest planet in our solar system, these three experiences obviously have different intentional structures. But the self-givenness of the three experiences does not have a different structure in each case. On the contrary, we are faced with the same basic structure. If that is the case, however, we do need to distinguish the experience and its self-givenness. Whereas we live through a number of different experiences, the dimension of first-personal givenness remains unchanging. It stands, to use a striking image from James, permanently, like a rainbow on a waterfall, its own quality unchanged by the events that stream through it (James 1890, I/630). In other words, it is highly appropriate to distinguish the strict singularity of the *lebendige Gegenwart* from the plurality of changing experiences. We must be sure to understand that distinguishability is not the same as separability. We are not dealing with a pure or empty field of first-personal givenness upon which the concrete experiences subsequently make their entry. The flow of inner time-consciousness has no self-manifestation of its own, but *is* the very nonobjectifying, pre-reflective self-manifestation of the experiences.

Husserl's most profound investigation of self-awareness can be found in his analysis of inner time-consciousness. Although Husserl denied that our experiences are pre-reflectively given as temporal objects, he did claim that self-awareness has a temporal infrastructure and that pre-reflective self-awareness is a type of manifestation intrinsically caught up in the structure of protention–primal presentation–retention. For these reasons, one can find an elaboration of Husserl's theory of self-awareness in his renowned analysis of the retentional process, what he specified as the double intentionality of the retention, its so-called *Quer-* and *Längsintentionalität* (transverse and longitudinal intentionality):

Our regard can be directed, in the one case, *through* the phases that "coincide" in the continuous progression of the flow and that function as intentionalities of the tone. But our regard can also be aimed *at* the flow, at a section of the flow, at the passage of the flowing consciousness from the beginning of the tone to its end. Every adumbration of consciousness of the species "retention" possesses a double intentionality: one serves for the constitution of the immanent object, of the tone; it is this intentionality that we call "primary memory" of the (just sensed) tone, or more precisely, just retention of the tone. The other intentionality is constitutive of the unity of this primary memory in the flow; namely, retention, because it is a still-being-conscious, a consciousness that holds back—because it is, precisely, retention—is also retention of the elapsed tone-retention: in its process of being continuously adumbrated in the flow, it is continuous retention of the continuously preceding phases. (Hua 10/80–81)

If P(t) is the primal presentation of a tone, then P(t) is retained in a retention, $Rp_{(t)}$, when a new primal presentation appears. As the notation makes clear, however, each retention preserves not only the preceding conscious tone, but also the preceding primal presentation. That is, the actual phase of the flow retains not only the tone, which has just been, but also the elapsing phase of the flow. In short, the retentional process not only permits us to experience an enduring temporal object—it does not merely enable the constitution of the identity of an object in a manifold of temporal phases; it also provides us with temporal self-awareness.

Whereas the flow's constitution of the duration of its object is called its *Querintentionalität*, the flow's awareness (of) its own streaming unity is called its *Längsintentionalität* (Hua 10/80–81, 379). Although the latter carries the name intentionality, it would be a decisive misunderstanding of Husserl's theory if one were to identify it with a type of object-intentionality, since Husserl's account of *Längsintentionalität* is, in fact, an analysis of the pre-reflective self-givenness of consciousness. It is precisely because consciousness is characterized by such a nonobjectifying self-awareness that it is possible to avoid an infinite regress:

The flow of the consciousness that constitutes immanent time not only *exists* but is so remarkably and yet intelligibly fashioned that a self-appearance of the flow necessarily exists in it, and therefore the flow itself must necessarily be apprehensible in the flowing. The self-appearance of the flow does not require a second flow; on the contrary, it constitutes itself as a phenomenon in itself. (Hua 10/83)

This central passage from *Zur Phänomenologie des inneren Zeitbewusstseins* has not been overlooked by Husserl's critics. It has generally been met with two distinct arguments:

1. If one claims that the stream of consciousness is characterized by self-appearance, one must ask what it is that appears when the stream appears to itself. According to Cramer, the only possible answer is that the stream appears to itself as a self-appearing stream. In his view, however, this answer

merely demonstrates that the very notion of self-appearance is both redundant and circular (Cramer 1974, 587).

The pertinence of this criticism is, however, questionable. Cramer seems to expect something of a theory of self-awareness that it, qua explication of a phenomenon *sui generis*, will forever be prevented from providing, specifically, that of a decomposition of the phenomenon into more simple elements without self-awareness. To put it another way, the impossibility of providing a noncircular account of self-awareness is hardly a problem for those who explicitly acknowledge the irreducible and fundamental status of self-awareness; it is a problem only for those who seek to explain self-awareness by means of something more basic.

2. If the self-appearance of the stream of consciousness is to be explained in terms of the notion of *Längsintentionalität*, as a kind of retentional process, are we then only self-aware of that which has just passed? Is consciousness initially nonconscious and does it only gain self-awareness the moment it is retained? This line of thought has been advocated by Derrida.

According to Derrida, it would be impossible to understand the relation between retention and primal presentation, and to comprehend the perpetual retentional modification, if the primal presentation were a simple and completely self-sufficient ground and source. The primal presentation is always already furnished with a temporal density and the retentional modification is not a subsequent addendum to, but an integral part of the primal presentation. Rather than being a simple, undivided unity, self-awareness is consequently characterized by an original complexity, by a historical heritage. The present can only appear to itself as present due to the retentional modification. Presence is differentiation; it *exists* only in its intertwining with absence (Derrida 1990, 120, 123, 127).

One then sees quickly that the presence of the perceived present can appear as such only inasmuch as it is *continuously compounded* with a nonpresence and nonperception, with primary memory and expectation (retention and protention). These nonperceptions are neither added to, nor do they *occasionally* accompany, the actually perceived now; they are essentially and indispensably involved in its possibility. (Derrida 1967a, 72 [1973, 64])

To be more precise, owing to the intimate relation between primal presentation and retention, self-presence must be conceived of as an originary *difference* or *interlacing* between now and not-now. Consciousness is never given in a full and instantaneous self-presence, but presents itself to itself across the difference between now and not-now. Experiential givenness is possible thanks to the retentional trace; it emerges on the background of a nonidentity and is haunted by the irreducible *alterity* of the past (Derrida 1990, 127–128, 168, 240). For this reason it is necessary to ascribe a transcendental or constitutive significance to a nonpresence in self-awareness (Derrida 1990, 166; 1967a, 5).

These reflections do not merely illustrate the complexity of the task of understanding the temporal articulation of self-awareness; they also have the rather disturbing implication that consciousness appears to itself, not as it is, but as it has just been. To put it differently, there appears to be a blind spot in the core of subjectivity, that is, the field of presencing is centered around a fundamental absence: initially consciousness is nonconscious, and it gains self-awareness *nachträglich* through retentional modification.

Although Husserl himself anticipated Derrida's line of thought, and even occasionally seriously considered it (Hua 10/83), he ultimately and quite explicitly rejected it:

What about the beginning-phase of an experience that is in the process of becoming constituted? Does it also come to be given only on the basis of retention, and would it be "unconscious" if no retention were to follow it? We must say in response to this question: The beginning-phase can become an object only *after* it has elapsed in the indicated way, by means of retention and reflection (or reproduction). But if it were intended *only* by retention, then what confers on it the label "now" would remain incomprehensible. At most, it could be distinguished negatively from its modifications as that one phase that does not make us retentionally conscious of any preceding phase; but the beginning-phase is by all means characterized in consciousness in quite positive fashion. It is just nonsense to talk about an "unconscious" content that would only subsequently become conscious. Consciousness is necessarily *consciousness* in each of its phases. Just as the retentional phase is conscious of the preceding phase without making it into an object, so too the primal datum is already intended—specifically, in the original form of the "now"—without its being something objective. (Hua 10/119)

Husserl's analysis is not meant to imply that consciousness becomes aware of itself only through retention. On the contrary, he explicitly insisted that the *retentional* process and modification presupposes an "impressional 'inner consciousness'" (Hua 10/110), what he also called *Urbewußtsein*, that is an original and immediate nonobjectifying self-givenness. This is so not only because consciousness is, as such, self-given, but also because a retention of a nonconscious content is impossible (Hua 10/119; 11/337).

Is it possible to specify the nature of this immediate self-givenness any further? Regrettably, Husserl was not forthcoming with details. The terminology used, and the fact that we are confronted with an occurrence by no means initiated, regulated, or controlled by the subject, suggests that we are dealing with a state of pure passivity, with a form of *self-affection*. This interpretation is confirmed by Husserl, for instance in his manuscript C 10 (1931), where he spoke of self-affection as an essential, pervasive, and necessary feature of the functioning ego. In manuscript C 16 (1931–33) he added that we are ceaselessly (*unaufhörlich*) affected by ourselves (see also Husserl Ms. C 10 3b, 5a, 7a, 9b–10a; C 16 82a; C 16 78a). Thus, along with the term *Urbewußtsein*, self-affection might be the phenomenological term of choice when it comes to designating the most fundamental level of experiential self-givenness.

Of course, it might be objected that the term "self-affection" is singularly unsuited as a designation for a pre-reflective and nonrelational type of givenness, since it seems to entail a structural difference between something that affects and something that is affected (see Derrida 1967a, 92; 1967b, 235). In reply, one might point out that Husserl was not the only phenomenologist who employed this term in his description of self-awareness. The term self-affection was used by Merleau-Ponty (1945, 469, 487), Heidegger (Heidegger GA 3: 189–190), and Michel Henry (1963, 288–292, 301) as well. Merleau-Ponty, for instance, wrote that consciousness is always affected by itself or given to itself and that the word "consciousness" has no meaning independent of this self-affection (Merleau-Ponty 1945, 488). Henry, in particular, stressed the truly immediate nature of self-affection. In his view, self-affection should not be understood in the same way as we would understand normal (outer) affection, as a process involving a difference between an organ or faculty of sensing and a sensed object. In other words, when speaking of self-affection one should simply bear in mind that we are dealing with a nonrelational type of manifestation: at this level there is no subject–object dichotomy, there is no difference between the dative and genitive of manifestation (see Zahavi 1999). The choice of the term is motivated mainly by its ability to capture the whole range of the defining features of pre-reflective self-awareness, including its immediate, implicit, nonobjectifying, and passive nature.

Pre-reflective self-awareness has an internal differentiation and articulation. Husserl insisted that only this fact can explain the possibility of temporal self-awareness, of reflection and recollection; yet to speak of self-awareness as being mediated or delayed is to remain determined by a conception that sees primal presentation and retention as two different and separate elements.[12] Consciousness is the generation of a field of lived presence. The concrete and full structure of this field of presence is protention–primal presentation–retention. There is no possible consciousness that does not entail retentional and protentional horizons (Hua 11/317, 337–338, 378). Consciousness is "immediately" given as a unity of presencing (primal presentation) and absencing (retention–protention)[13] and is not a gradual, delayed, or mediated process of self-unfolding. This seems to be what is required if one is to avoid the Scylla of an instantaneous non-temporal self-awareness and the Charybdis of a completely fractured time-consciousness that makes the consciousness of the present and the unity of the stream unintelligible.[14]

One of the decisive tasks facing a phenomenological investigation of subjectivity is to account for its givenness. How does subjectivity reveal or manifest itself? If subjectivity, rather than being an object that we encounter in the world, is the very perspective that permits any such encounter, to what extent can it then be made accessible for direct examination? Will any examination necessarily take the subject as an *object* of experience and thereby distort it beyond recognition? In other words, can subjectivity be grasped and described, or is it only approachable *ex negativo*? One of the pivotal issues in this classical debate has been the question of whether *reflection* is at all trustworthy. Does reflection genuinely give us access to the original experiential dimension, or is there, on the contrary, reason to suspect that the experiences are changed radically when reflected upon? Is reflection, in reality, a kind of falsifying mirror or telescope that transforms whatever it makes appear? Some have argued that reflection is an objectifying procedure; it turns that which it reflects upon into an object. If reflection makes us aware of an object, how then could it ever make us aware of our own subjectivity?

Let us, in the following, take a look at a dispute between Natorp and Heidegger concerning the possibility of investigating subjectivity reflectively,[1] a dispute that has had repercussions to the very definition of phenomenology.

I Natorp's Challenge

Natorp began his *Allgemeine Psychologie* from 1912 by emphasizing the radical difference between subject and object. He was not concerned with the traditional Cartesian separation between *res cogitans* and *res extensa*, but with a transcendental philosophically motivated distinction. He defined the object as that which is accessible to theoretical description and explanation. In contrast, the subject is that which stands opposed to all objects; it is that in contrast to which objects are given as objects (*Gegen-stände*). Whereas everything else can be made into an object for consciousness, the subject itself cannot be made into an object, nor can it take itself as its own object. Rather, the moment we start to think of the subject as an object, we stop thinking of it as a subject (Natorp 1912, 8, 28–29, 31).

On this background, Natorp argued that we substitute an object of consciousness for the subject of consciousness the moment we start to investigate it reflectively, that is, we transform it into its very opposite. Obviously, Natorp could not actually ban the use of reflection, but he insisted that we should at least realize that reflection is a distorting prism and that the subjectivity which we investigate reflectively is no longer our original subjectivity, but a kind of reflected image or derived representation. Reflection confronts us with an objectified subjectivity, and this should not be mistaken for the original functioning subjectivity that is performing the reflection (Natorp 1912, 30).

Allow me to slightly formalize Natorp's argument:

(1) Experience is a relation between a subject (qua experiencing) and an object (qua experienced).

(2) If the subject is to experience itself, it has to take itself as an object.

(3) If the subject experiences an object, it does not experience itself.

(4) It is impossible to experience true subjectivity.

This Kantian way of thinking also comes to the fore when Natorp wrote that the I is a principle and condition. It is not a datum, it is not something given; if it were, it would be given for somebody, that is, it would be an object, and therefore no longer an I (Natorp 1912, 40). In a similar vein, Natorp wrote that consciousness cannot be something with a temporal and spatial appearance, since only objects appear in space and time (Natorp 1912, 151, 169). For the very same reason, it is necessary to resist the attempt to describe consciousness with the help of those categories and concepts that have their legitimate use in the world of objects. To apply them to subjectivity would be a category mistake (Natorp 1912, 28).

The full title of Natorp's work is *Allgemeine Psychologie nach kritischer Methode*; from this, it is clear that Natorp's topic was not empirical psychology, but a transcendental philosophical investigation of subjectivity. Given Natorp's critical comments, how is such an investigation at all possible? Will it not inevitably be objectifying, and thus fall short of its aim? Even a simple description will make use of concepts and analyses, yet insofar as subjectivity is analyzed and subsumed under universal concepts, we are already estranging ourselves from it (Natorp 1912, 91–92, 190). In fact, if subjectivity is to be investigated it must express itself, be it in language or behavior. Every expression (*Äußerung*) is, according to Natorp, an externalization (*Entäußerung*), that is, the moment consciousness expresses itself it leaves its own domain behind and enters the realm of objects, and thereby we once again miss that which had our interest (Natorp 1912, 99). This view is clearly presented in the following passage:

> If one were oneself to try, if it were at all possible, to somehow grasp the content of immediate experience purely as it is in itself—far from every expression, every judgment, every intention—would one then not somehow be forced, nevertheless, to delimit it, to raise it above the mesh of experiencing, be it with the pointing of a finger, with a blink of an eye; would one not be forced to artificially still and interrupt the continuous stream of becoming, which surely is how inner life presents itself, to isolate the individual finding, to fixate it with the isolation in mind, to sterilize it, like the anatomist does with his specimen? But doesn't one then detach it from the experienced, from the subjective, and doesn't one then, nevertheless, make it into an object? In the end, one apparently never grasps the subjective, as such, in itself. On the contrary, in order to grasp it scientifically, one is forced to strip it of its subjective character. One kills subjectivity in order to dissect it, and believes that the life of the soul is on display in the result of the dissection! (Natorp 1912, 102–103)

This is not a very heartening conclusion. Was Natorp really claiming that a systematic investigation of subjectivity is impossible and that every description is a falsification, every conceptualization a violation? Natorp did not, in fact, give in completely to skepticism. On the contrary, he suggested the following research strategy: He took it to be established that we have no direct access to our own original subjectivity, and that we, in reflection, grasp only a paralyzed and objectified subject. We will never be able to grasp our subjectivity simply by improving and refining our forward-looking object-investigation, just as no matter how much we sharpen a knife, it will remain unable to cut itself. What other possibilities are there? According to Natorp, we have to turn around and look closely at the very condition of possibility for such an object-investigation. In order to reach subjectivity we must effectuate a process of *purification*. We have, so to speak, to neutralize the effect of reflection. That is, after having analyzed and thereby destroyed the lived unity of the experiences, we must try to reverse the process and try to unite the detached elements and thereby restore the experiences to their original state (Natorp 1912, 192). Thus, Natorp suggested that we engage in a kind of *reconstruction*. We cannot investigate our own functioning subjectivity directly; but we can start with the objectified counterpart and then proceed regressively in an attempt to recover the original subjective dimension. Ultimately, however, the dimension of pure subjectivity remains an unreachable ideal and limit case (Natorp 1912, 233).

II The Criticism of Reflective Phenomenology

In his 1919 lecture course *Die Idee der Philosophie und das Weltanschauungsproblem*, Heidegger observed that Natorp was the only one who had so far raised scientifically noteworthy objections against phenomenology (Heidegger GA 56/57: 101).[2] It is, in fact, not difficult to construe Natorp's position in *Allgemeine Psychologie* as anti-phenomenological. As we have just seen, Natorp primarily delivered two critical thrusts: 1. Phenomenology claims to describe and analyze lived subjectivity itself and, in order to do so, it employs a reflective methodology. Reflection, however, is a kind of internal perception; it is a theoretical attitude involving an objectification. As Natorp then asked, how is this objectifying procedure ever going to provide us with access to lived subjectivity itself? 2. Phenomenology aims at describing the experiential structures in their pretheoretical immediacy. Every description necessarily involves the use of language, of generalizing and subsuming concepts. For that reason, every description and expression involves a mediation and objectification that necessarily estranges us from subjectivity itself.

How did Heidegger view Natorp's criticism of what might be called "reflective phenomenology"? To some extent, he seemed to accept it. The question is whether the experiential dimension can be explored adequately by means of Husserl's reflective methodology, that is, through a method of reflective description and descriptive reflection (Heidegger GA 56/57: 100, GA 59: 194). As Heidegger pointed out, reflection is a theoretical stance, and every theoretical endeavor, every observation and demonstration involves a certain objectifying modification, a particular element of "deliving" that introduces a certain fracture between the experience and the experienced (Heidegger GA 56/57: 73–74, 98). This modification is particularly vivid in the case of reflection, since reflection turns a nonreflectively lived through experience into an observed object, that is, the moment an experience is reflectively given it is no longer lived through, but only looked at (Heidegger GA 56/57: 100). Thus, basically accepting Natorp's criticism, Heidegger wrote that reflection is a theoretical intrusion that interrupts the stream of experiencing and exercises an analytically dissective and dissolving effect upon it: "We ex-posit the experiences and so extract them from the immediacy of experience. We as it were dip into the onflowing stream of experience and scoop out one or more, which means that we 'still the stream,' as Natorp says" (Heidegger GA 56/57: 100–101). In short, to answer the question posed above, it is not possible to access the dimension of lived experiencing through reflection. Reflection is objectifying; it destroys the living life-experience, petrifies the stream, and turns experiences into isolated objects.

One should not underestimate the radical nature of this criticism. One of the standard ways of defining phenomenology is to say that its task is to describe that which is given, exactly as it is given. In consequence of his criticism, Heidegger even questioned the legitimacy of this preoccupation with *givenness*. He wrote that for something to be given is already for it to be theoretically affected, if ever so slightly (Heidegger GA 56/57: 88–89). (In his own writings from the period, however, Heidegger did not seem to respect this admonition, since he himself repeatedly spoke of something as being given.)

Despite the basic agreement, however, Heidegger was not particularly impressed with Natorp's alternative, nor did he think that Natorp had exhausted all the possibilities.

• To begin with, Heidegger pointed out that Natorp's so-called reconstruction is itself a construction; it is itself a theoretical and objectifying procedure. It is hard to understand, however, how such a mediated procedure could ever give us access to the immediacy of subjective life (Heidegger GA 56/57: 104, 107).[3]

• Since Natorp was denying that subjective life is given in any way prior to analysis, his reconstruction lacks any reliable guiding principle. He had no criteria for determining whether his reconstruction led him, in fact, to the original lived dimension (Heidegger GA 56/57: 107). To put it differently, how was Natorp at all in a position to claim that reflection transforms subjective life? Does this not presuppose the existence of a pre-reflective access to the immediacy of subjective life, and is this not exactly that of which Natorp denied existence?

• When it comes to Natorp's reservations about the adequacy of a linguistic articulation, Heidegger retorted that this objection (also found in Bergson) presupposes a much too narrow view on language. As he asked, is it true that all language is objectifying and that all concepts inevitably fragment a hitherto nonfragmented totality? (Heidegger GA 56/57: 111).

• Ultimately, however, the greatest weakness in Natorp's criticism may be its theoretical bent. Natorp simply assumed that any phenomenological intuition will be externally related to that which is to be intuited and that any description will always be foreign to that which is given. Perhaps this is simply a theoretical prejudice (Heidegger GA 56/57: 111–112). Although a phenomenology based on reflection might inevitably operate with a subject–object dichotomy and thereby be vulnerable to Natorp's criticism, the decisive question is whether phenomenology must necessarily be reflective.

What Heidegger was ultimately driving at was the possibility of basing phenomenology on a nonreflective understanding, what he called a *hermeneutical intuition* (Heidegger GA 56/57: 117). Let us take a closer look at Heidegger's own alternative.

III   A Hermeneutical Alternative

According to Heidegger, experiential life is not an object and any investigation that seeks to grasp it as an object is consequently bound to fail. For the very same reason, it would be a fundamental error to approach and investigate life using the same methods found in the positive sciences (Heidegger GA 58: 145). If we are to truly understand the fundamental structures of life, Heidegger argued, a radically new phenomenological methodology is called for (Heidegger GA 58: 237). This is also why Heidegger repeatedly spoke of phenomenology as an "originary science of life" (Heidegger GA 58: 233; cf. GA 58: 36, 79). He, however, immediately added that one should not infer from the fact that life is not an *object*, that it must then be a (traditionally conceived epistemological or psychological) *subject*. Both objectification and what he called "subjectification" are, according to Heidegger, theoretical deformations of life (Heidegger GA 58: 145–147, 236). Thus, when it comes to the study of pure life-experience, traditional categories such as inner and outer or transcendence and immanence are all misplaced (Heidegger GA 58: 253). This already indicates that when Heidegger spoke of life (*Leben*), experience (*Erlebnis*), and experiencing (*Erleben*), he was not speaking of psychological entities. To interpret the experiences as psychical processes was, in his view, already an objectification (Heidegger GA 56/57: 65–66).[4] Ultimately, the very term "experience" might be so laden with traditional connotations that it would be better to avoid it altogether, but in 1919 Heidegger still thought that it was the best term available (Heidegger GA 56/57: 66) and he did not introduce any neologism.

Heidegger's point of departure is not a psychological concept of experience, but rather, factic life-experience itself, with all its concrete articulations and tendencies. As he said, the task is to disclose the nonobjectifying and nontheoretical self-understanding of life-experience in all of its modifications (Heidegger GA 58: 155–156, 250). Thus, Heidegger resolutely rejected the idea that experiential life should be a mute, chaotic, and basically incomprehensible principle (Heidegger GA 58: 148). Rather, life-experience is imbued with meaning, is intentionally structured, has an inner articulation and rationality, and, last but not least, it has a spontaneous and immediate self-understanding. This last is why it can ultimately be interpreted from itself and in terms of itself. Life is comprehensible because it always spontaneously expresses itself, and because experiencing is, itself, a preliminary form of understanding or what might be called a pre-understanding (Heidegger GA 59: 166). Thus, Heidegger argued that there is an intimate connection between *experience, expression*, and *understanding* (Heidegger GA 59: 169). He quoted Dilthey: "Thinking is bound to life through an inner necessity; it is itself a form of life"[5] and spoke himself of philosophy as a continuation of the *reflexivity* found in life (Heidegger GA 59: 156). In other words, phenomenology must build on the familiarity that life already has with itself; it must draw on the self-referential dimension, the persistent care of self that is built into the very life stream.

In clear opposition to the view espoused by Natorp, Heidegger could consequently claim that the phenomenological articulation and conceptualization of life-experience is something that belongs to life itself. It is not something that is imposed on life arbitrarily from without, as if the conceptualization were merely driven by certain epistemological or foundational concerns. A true phenomenological description does not constitute a violation, nor is it an attempt to impose a foreign systematicity on life; rather it is something that is rooted in and motivated by factic life-experience itself (Heidegger GA 61: 87; GA 58: 59). As Heidegger wrote in the *Phänomenologische Interpretationen zu Aristoteles* lecture course from 1921–22: "The categories are nothing invented, no 'framework' or independent society of logical schemata; they are rather in an originary fashion *in life itself of life*; of life, in order to 'cultivate' it. They have their own mode of access which, however, is not such as would be foreign to life itself, imposed upon it arbitrarily from without, rather it is just the eminent way in which *life comes to itself*" (Heidegger GA 61: 88).[6]

From what has been argued so far, it should be clear that Heidegger did not subscribe to the view that experiential life becomes acquainted with itself only through reflection. On the contrary, Heidegger clearly acknowledged the existence of a more fundamental form of self-acquaintance that is part and parcel of experience. As he wrote in his 1919–20 lecture course *Grundprobleme der Phänomenologie*: "The aim is to understand this character of self-acquaintance that belongs to experience as such" (Heidegger GA 58: 157). Any worldly experiencing involves a certain component of self-acquaintance and familiarity; it is characterized by the fact that "I am always somehow acquainted with myself" (Heidegger GA 58: 251). As Heidegger repeatedly emphasized, this basic familiarity with oneself—he also spoke of a *Sich-Selbst-Haben* (Heidegger GA 58: 257)—does not take the form of a reflective self-perception or a thematic self-observation, nor does it involve any kind of self-objectification. On the contrary, we are confronted with a process of lived self-acquaintance whose distinctive feature is its nonreflective character, and which must be understood as an immediate expression of life itself (Heidegger GA 58: 159, 165, 257–258). As he also wrote, the phenomenological investigation has factic life and history as its guiding clue; history, not in the sense of the science of history, but in the sense of a going along with life as it is lived, in the sense of a certain lived self-familiarity or self-concern (Heidegger GA 58: 252, 256; GA 9: 32). Heidegger designated the self-familiarity of experiential life as the *historicity of life* (Heidegger GA 58: 159). This is why Heidegger ultimately argued that life will never be understood in its living if one excludes the problem of history from the field of phenomenology (Heidegger GA 58: 238).

When we investigate factic life-experience, we articulate it and thereby modify it. In the best of circumstances, this articulation springs from and is motivated by life itself, not imposed from without. We still, however, need to understand what exactly this modification consists of. In *Grundprobleme der Phänomenologie* from 1919–1920, Heidegger argued that prior to such a thematization, we live from one momentary phase to the next without looking back, without having a unified overview of our situation. Nevertheless, through the living a certain, relatively unarticulated, experiential context is established. When we then start to investigate factic life-experience, it is precisely this experiential context that comes to the fore. The submerged tendencies of life are brought to light and consolidated into a unified constellation. When we notice and articulate the experience, the experiential context takes on a new gestalt, it gains a new unity (Heidegger GA 58: 118).[7]

In the course of his analyses, and as early as 1919, Heidegger touched on the following central question: To what extent do the experiences contain a reference to an I? To what extent is it a conceptual and experiential truth that any episode of experiencing necessarily includes a *subject of experience*? To interpret an intentional experience, say, the experience of writing on a blackboard, as an experience where "I relate myself toward the blackboard" is, Heidegger argued, not an inadmissible objectification and reification of the experience, as such; but it nevertheless introduces something into the experience that was not there from the very start, namely an I (Heidegger GA 56/57: 66). If one really wants to describe what is there originally, one will not find any detached I, but simply an intentional life (Heidegger GA 56/57: 68). Although my experiences do not contain any explicit reference to myself, it is nevertheless the case, as Heidegger then went on to say, that the experiences are present (to me), they are rightly called *my* experiences, and are indeed part of *my* life (Heidegger GA 56/57: 69). To put it differently, there is what one might call a certain *mineness* or, to anticipate the terminology from *Sein und Zeit*, a certain *Jemeinigkeit* to the experiential dimension. Thus, whenever I experience something, my self (Heidegger preferred to speak of a self rather than of an I) is present and is, so to speak, therefore implicated. The experiences do not simply pass me by, as if they were foreign entities, but rather they are exactly *mine* (Heidegger GA 56/57: 75).

What, precisely, is this self? We are obviously confronted neither with a pure and detached ego-pole nor with some formal epistemological principle (Heidegger GA 58: 247). Rather, we should examine factic life-experience, and what we will then find is the co-givenness of self and world. Life is, as Heidegger said, world-related; it is always already living in the world and does not have to seek it out (Heidegger GA 58: 34). My self is present when I am worldly engaged; it is exactly to be found "out there." Factic life-experience is, literally speaking, "worldly tuned," it always lives in a world; it is, properly speaking, a world-life, and it always finds itself in a life-world (Heidegger GA 58: 250).

In the 1919–20 *Grundprobleme der Phänomenologie* Heidegger pursued this idea further, and described the life-world as an interpenetration of three domains: surrounding world (*Umwelt*), with-world (*Mitwelt*), and self-world (*Selbstwelt*) (Heidegger GA 58: 33, 39, 62). Of these three domains, the self-world is ascribed a certain priority—not in the sense that the other two are insignificant, but rather in the sense that the surrounding world and the with-world are structured and appropriated by the self-world (Heidegger GA 61: 95); they point, so to speak, toward the self-world.[8]

Just as the self is what it is in its worldly relations, self-acquaintance is not something that takes place or occurs in separation from our living in a world. Originally speaking, self-experience is not a question of "inner perception," introspection, or self-reflection (Heidegger GA 61: 95). In factic life-experience, I neither experience myself as a conglomerate of acts and processes nor as a detached I-object; instead I experience myself factically in what I do and suffer, in what confronts me and what I accomplish, and in my concerns and disregards. I am acquainted with myself when I am captured and captivated by the world. Self-acquaintance is indeed only to be found in our immersion in the world, that is, self-acquaintance is always the self-acquaintance of a world-immersed self. To accentuate the close connection between self and world, Heidegger also introduced the notion of self-worldly (*selbstweltliche*) experiences (Heidegger GA 61: 95). Thus, if we wish to study the self, we should look not inside consciousness in the hope of finding some elusive I, but rather at our worldly experience; therein will we find the situated self (Heidegger GA 58: 258).

Heidegger argued that we primarily encounter our self in and through our engagement in the world. There are several ways to understand this claim. According to Manfred Frank, the correct interpretation is that, at first, the self is completely lost (immersed) in the world, and it is only in a subsequent move that it turns toward itself and thereby acquires self-acquaintance. To substantiate his interpretation, Frank often refers to assertions found in the

1927 lecture course *Grundprobleme der Phänomenologie*, which, in his view, offers us "a classical formulation of the reflection model of self-awareness" (Frank 1991a, 518). In this course, Heidegger once again took up the problem of self-acquaintance and wrote that the self is somehow present and implicated in all its intentional comportments. Intentionality not only entails a being-directed toward and an understanding of that toward which one is directed, but also entails a co-disclosure of the very self which is comporting itself. Thus, the intentional directedness toward is not to be understood as an intentional act that gains a reference to the self only afterward, as if the self would have to turn its attention back upon the first act with the help of a subsequent second (reflective) act. Rather, the co-disclosure of the self belongs to intentionality as such (Heidegger GA 24: 225):

Dasein,[9] as existing, is there for itself, even when the ego does not expressly direct itself to itself in the manner of its own peculiar turning around and turning back, which in phenomenology is called inner perception as contrasted with outer. The self is there for the Dasein itself without reflection and without inner perception, *before* all reflection. Reflection, in the sense of a turning back, is only a mode of self-*apprehension*, but not the mode of primary self-disclosure. The way in which the self is unveiled to itself in the factical Dasein can nevertheless be fittingly called reflection, except that we must not take this expression to mean what is commonly meant by it—the ego bent around backward and staring at itself—but an interconnection such as is manifested in the optical meaning of the term "reflection." To reflect means, in the optical context, to break at something, to radiate back from there, to show itself in a reflection from something. (Heidegger GA 24: 226)

The last sentence is, of course, the crucial one. Heidegger seems to be saying that self-acquaintance is a *derived* and *mediated* phenomenon grounded in our world-disclosure. At first, Dasein is completely immersed in the world, and it is only in reaction that it finds itself and achieves self-understanding (Frank 1991a, 517). This is how Frank interprets Heidegger, which is why he argues that Heidegger was still operating with a version of the traditional reflection theory of self-awareness (Frank 1991a, 516–520). The question, however, is whether this is the only way to interpret Heidegger's statements. One page later in the text, Heidegger emphasized that the self (Dasein) does not need to turn back upon itself as if it were, at first, standing in front of the things and fixedly staring at them. Rather, it is exactly in the things themselves that it finds itself. It finds itself in the things primarily because by tending to them it always somehow rests in them (Heidegger GA 24: 227).

This line of thought is even more clearly articulated in the lecture course *Prolegomena zur Geschichte des Zeitbegriffs* from 1925. In this text, Heidegger asserted that Dasein itself is co-disclosed in the world. Thus, when the world is disclosed in its meaningfulness, Dasein itself is also discovered in its being-there-with (*Mitdabei-Sein*), in its intimate involvement with that which is of concern (Heidegger GA 20: 348). Heidegger could consequently write that the disclosedness (*Erschlossenheit*) of the world itself along with the fact that Dasein qua being-in-the-world is co-discovered jointly define the unified phenomena *discoveredness* (*Entdecktheit*) (Heidegger GA 20: 349). The two statements, "Dasein 'has' its world," and "Dasein finds itself" are, as Heidegger pointed out, both referring to the same basic structure of being-in-the-world (Heidegger GA 20: 352).

As Heidegger then went on to specify, in its preoccupation with the world Dasein always finds itself in this or that way, is always *affected* by this or that *mood* (Heidegger GA 20: 351–352). In fact, the co-discoveredness of being-in-the-world through being solicited and summoned by the world is possible only because Dasein originally *finds* itself, and this is why Heidegger called the primary form of the co-discoveredness of Dasein its *affected-ness* (*Befindlichkeit*). And, as he then added, the reason he chose this term was exactly to avoid construing Dasein's finding itself in its being-in-the-world as a kind of self-reflection (Heidegger GA 20: 352). At this point, Dasein is not given thematically; rather we are dealing with a modality that founds and conditions any such thematic knowledge (Heidegger GA 20: 349).

At this stage Heidegger made a clarification that elucidates his statements in *Grundprobleme der Phänomenologie,* and which ultimately questions Frank's interpretation: "The co-discoveredness of in-being itself, that I am to my Dasein itself first in a worldly way, that is, that I have myself in a self-worldly way as an accompaniment in my concerned absorption in the world: this is not a consequence of the disclosedness of the world, but is *equiprimordial* with it" (Heidegger GA 20: 350, my emphasis).[10] Disclosing a world is always already a self-finding. In fact, the discoveredness of Dasein, its finding itself, constitutes its very mode of being (Heidegger GA 20: 354).

Given all of the above, it seems reasonable to conclude that Heidegger did, in fact, operate with a form of self-acquaintance that precedes reflection. When understanding his claim that no self-acquaintance can occur independently of, or prior to, our world-disclosure, it is crucial to remember that this world-disclosure contains a dimension of self from the very start and, as well, that it cannot occur independently of or prior to a disclosure of self.[11]

Insofar as the self is present to itself precisely, and indeed only, when worldly engaged, a certain difficulty arises. Factic life-experience is not only world immersed; it also has a tendency to interpret itself in terms of worldly being. The self-understanding thereby obtained is, according to Heidegger, both inadequate and inauthentic. In the lecture course *Phänomenologische Interpretationen zu Aristoteles*, Heidegger contrasted life's tendency toward self-illumination and self-interpretation, which he called its *Reluzenz*, with its tendency toward self-forgetfulness, which he calls its *Ruinanz*, or falling (Heidegger GA 61: 119, 121). The existence of the latter tendency, which must be seen as an unavoidable existential predicament—life has an inherent tendency to objectify and cover itself up—obviously complicates the entire picture and ultimately questions Heidegger's earlier account of the hermeneutical enterprise. If factic life-experience has a tendency to cover up that which needs to be brought to light, the articulation of the fundamental structures of life will no longer be able to rely on a mere going along with the tendencies of life or be described in terms of a simple continuation of life's own inherent self-understanding. Rather, it might be more correct to describe philosophy as a counterruinant movement (Heidegger GA 61:153). To be more specific, phenomenology is the struggle against factical ruinance, it is the bringing of factic life to genuine self-givenness. This is probably why Heidegger wrote, in *Sein und Zeit*, that the existential analytic has a certain *violence* to it. The disclosure of Dasein's own primordial being can be won only in direct confrontation with Dasein's own tendency to cover things up. It must, in fact, be wrested and captured from Dasein (Heidegger 1986, 311).[12] At the same time, the existence of both tendencies permits a clarification of the conditions of philosophizing. It has been put well in the following passage by Gethmann: "Philosophizing is only possible *and* necessary, if life *on the one hand* is not transparent to itself, hazy, opaque (opacity), and *on the other* is not anonymous for itself, is not turned away from itself, but is self-related, reflected (relucence [*Reluzenz*]). Opacity and relucence are the conditions of possibility *and* necessity of philosophizing . . ." (Gethmann 1986–87, 48).

IV Pure and Impure Reflection

It is not difficult to read Heidegger's analysis of the objectifying nature of reflection as a criticism of Husserl's reflective phenomenology. In Heidegger's early writings, this criticism is rarely voiced openly, but in a recent book entitled *Hermeneutik und Reflexion* Friedrich-Wilhelm von Herrmann remedies this restraint by articulating the criticism in no uncertain manner.

As the title of the book indicates, von Herrmann operates with a distinction between hermeneutical phenomenology and reflective phenomenology. Reflective phenomenology is a theoretical enterprise, whereas hermeneutical phenomenology is atheoretical and consequently a-reflective (Herrmann 2000, 11). In contrast to reflection, which can be described as an objectifying intuition, hermeneutical understanding must be understood as an atheoretical, nonobjectifying, and merely accentuating type of intuition or understanding (von Herrmann 2000, 23). Reflection does not remain within factic life-experience; rather, it withdraws from it in order to gain the distance that is required if the intentional gaze is to bend backward and turn the experience into an object of reflection. Whereas the act of reflection interrupts and stills the living stream, and deprives the experience reflected upon from what is its own, namely its lived "*Vollzugshaftigkeit*," the hermeneutical understanding remains within and accompanies factic life and simply raises and accentuates it into a new level of transparency and expressibility. According to von Herrmann, this is precisely why the hermeneutical understanding is able to grasp the experiences in their nontheoretical immediacy; why it can interpret the structures of life in a nonviolating and nonobjectifying manner (von Herrmann 2000, 32, 58, 79). As von Herrmann writes: "Hermeneutical phenomenology does not interrupt the primal intention of life and experience in order to objectify it reflectively; rather it grasps this primal intention in order to make it phenomenologically transparent and articulate" (von Herrmann 2000, 92). The decisive difference between the reflective and the a-reflective method is consequently that the a-reflective method accentuates the experience while remaining within it; it does not stand opposed to it in an objectifying manner (von Herrmann 2000, 24). Although Husserl's reflective phenomenology claims to be true to the phenomena, this is not at all the case. As dependent on a reflective methodology as it is, it has been prevented from accessing and disclosing the atheoretical being of the experiential dimension (von Herrmann 2000, 20).

In contrast, the atheoretical, hermeneutical understanding provides us with a completely new type of access to experiences; an access that, for the first time, allows them to reveal themselves as they truly are (von Herrmann 2000, 50). In fact, the phenomenological dictum "back to the things themselves" is only fully realized the moment we avoid objectifying the experiences reflectively and instead understandingly extract their structures (von Herrmann 2000, 26). In contrast to reflection, this truly phenomenological understanding can be variously described as being immersed in life or being in sympathy with life. Ultimately, von Herrmann takes the word "*Lebenssympathie*" as the hermeneutical term of choice and alternative to the term "reflection" (von Herrmann 2000, 92).

How convincing is this line of thought? Let us take a look at some of those phenomenologists who actually do employ a reflective methodology. Like Natorp and Heidegger, Sartre also argued that the process of reflection can entail a distorting transformation of its subject matter. This is, for instance, clear from his criticism of the egological theory of consciousness. As we have already seen, Sartre took pre-reflective consciousness to lack an egological structure. As long as we are absorbed in the experience, *living* it, no ego will appear. The ego appears only when we adopt a distancing and objectifying attitude to the experience in question, that is, when we reflect upon it. When reflected upon, the original non-egological experience is submitted to an egological interpretation and thereby provided with extraneous and transcendent elements. What are the implications of this stance? Did Sartre thereby exclude the possibility of a *reflective* phenomenological description of lived consciousness? No; rather, Sartre's criticism must be seen in the context of an attempt to distinguish between two very different types of reflection, the *pure* and the *impure*. The impure reflection is the kind of reflection that we encounter daily. It operates with an epistemic duality and must be classified as a type of knowledge. It is called impure because it transcends the given and interprets the reflected in an objectifying manner, thus giving rise to the psychic unity that we know under the name *ego* (Sartre 1943, 194, 199, 201). In contrast, pure reflection presents us with a pure (unfalsifying) *thematization* of the reflected-on. It articulates the phenomena, without contaminating them with interpretive overlays, in a manner that remains true to their pre-reflective structures. Quite in keeping with this, Sartre claimed that pure reflection never learns or discovers anything new. It is not surprised by what it uncovers, since it simply discloses and thematizes that with which it was already familiar, namely, the original nonsubstantial streaming of pre-reflective consciousness (Sartre 1943, 195, 197; Sartre 1936, 48).[13] Pure reflection is the ideal form of reflection, yet it is much harder to attain since it never emerges by itself, but must be won by a sort of purifying *catharsis.*

Although one might ultimately criticize Sartre's definition and methodological use of pure reflection—he did not say much more about it and never explained how it could be attained—his distinction between the two types of reflection is useful and points to the fact that the term "reflection" is polysemical. There may, indeed, be forms of reflection and self-apprehension that are distorting, but the question is whether it might not also be appropriate to acknowledge the existence of a form of reflection that is nothing but a higher form of *wakefulness,* nothing but a simple *"schauendes Hinnehmen."* It is tempting to follow Fink when he claims that the phenomenological reflection, rather than being an explicit self-reification, is simply a more articulate and intense form of self-awareness (Fink 1992, 116–117, 128). To put it even more simply, why not understand reflection as a type of *attention?*[14] When we reflect, might we not merely be paying attention to something that was there from the very beginning?

Of course, by paying attention to something, by accentuating or articulating it, we do change its givenness. This also holds true when it comes to reflection. Reflection does not merely copy or repeat the original experience, it transforms it, or as Husserl explicitly admitted, it *alters* it (Hua 1/72). *Otherwise, there would be no need for reflection.*

The actual life and lived-experiencing is of course always conscious, but it is not therefore always thematically experienced and known. For that a new pulse of actual life is necessary, a so-called reflective or immanently directed experience. This is not merely added to the previous life, to the respective experience or experiential thinking, rather it transforms it in a specific manner. (Hua 25/89)

In a passage from *Zur Phänomenologie des inneren Zeitbewußtseins,* Husserl described this transformation in more detail. He wrote that the experience to which we turn attentively in reflection acquires a new mode of being; it becomes accentuated (*herausgehoben*). He argued that this accentuation is nothing other than its being grasped (Hua 10/129). Husserl also spoke of reflection as a process that discloses, disentangles, explicates, and articulates all those components and structures that were implicitly contained in the pre-reflective experience (Hua 24/244; 11/205, 236).

What is important is that this articulation is not necessarily imposed from without; is not necessarily foreign to the experience in question. In fact, rather than representing a distortion, it may constitute a consummation of the experience (Merleau-Ponty 1945, 207). As Husserl put it, in the beginning we are confronted with a dumb experience that through reflection must then be made to articulate its *own* sense (Hua 1/77). Rather than adding new distorting components and structures to the experience reflected upon, a reflection might, at best, simply be accentuating structures already inherent in the lived experience. In this case, the persistent fear that reflection is somehow prevented from attaining true subjectivity seems unfounded.

In Cassirer's *Philosophie der symbolischen Formen*, one can find a brief but acute criticism of Natorp that proceeds along similar lines. Cassirer argued that the linguistic and conceptual form does not stand opposed to the life-experience, but that it should rather be regarded as the latter's completion. He consequently accused Natorp of operating with too narrow an understanding of both conceptualization and language. Natorp focused exclusively on the theoretical, objectifying, and reifying side of language and thereby failed to appreciate the protean character of language. Does language not have a multiplicity of forms; does it not possess a force and mobility that enables it to seize the subjective without necessarily violating it in the process (Cassirer 1954, 62–67)? It is an irony of fate that Natorp himself spent considerable time discussing the work of Bergson and ultimately criticized him for operating with an unacceptable contrast between the concepts that were viewed as absolutely static, fixed, and immobile and the experiences that were seen as boundlessly streaming and variable (Natorp 1912, 323). Natorp failed to realize that his own position was vulnerable to the exact same criticism.

V   Reflection and Alteration

How should one appraise the reflective appropriation of lived consciousness? Can reflection make the pre-reflective accessible to us, or does it rather distort it radically? Does the reflective modification involve a necessary supplementation or an inevitable loss? As we have just seen, one way to avoid skeptical conclusions might be to understand reflection as a form of attention. In other words, the relation between pre-reflective and reflective consciousness could be structurally comparable to the relation between marginal and thematic consciousness. In both cases, the transition from one to the other can be understood in terms of an *attentional modification*. This is not to say, of course, that reflection is always trustworthy. The point is merely that reflection does not necessarily have to be untrustworthy.

The analogy to perceptual consciousness seems straightforward. To perceive an object is always to perceive an object situated in a perceptual field; whenever we pay attention to something, we single it out from its surroundings. Thus, one might describe the appearance of a thematic object as an appearance out of a field or background. It seems absurd to suggest that our attentive examination of something should change it beyond recognition.

Although much might be won by understanding reflection in terms of attention, there are also limits to this endeavor. First, the concepts of attention and attentional modification are taken from the domain of object-consciousness and are related to the distinction between thematic and marginal objects. The attentional modification is what is at stake when we shift our focus between different objects, bringing those at the margin into the center of attention. To straightforwardly identify the process of reflection with an attentional modification, however, would be to remain committed to the view that our pre-reflectively lived through experiences linger in the background as marginal objects, and, as we have already seen in chapters 1 and 3, this will not do. Second, reflection is ultimately in possession of its own unique traits and cannot be simply identified with some kind of inner attention. As Husserl argued in both *Logische Untersuchungen* and *Ideen I*, attention is a particular feature or mode of our primary act; it is not a new act (Hua 19/425; Hua 3/75–76). To pay attention to something is not to engage in two processes or activities, but to change or modify one's first-level experience or activity. Reflection, by contrast, is precisely a new (founded) act; it never occurs in isolation, but only together with the act reflected upon. Thus, reflective self-awareness must be appreciated as involving a *relation* between two different experiences (Hua 3/78). It entails the coexistence of a double(d) subject: a reflected and a reflecting. As Husserl also frequently put it, it entails a kind of doubling or fracture or *self-fission* (Hua 8/89–90, 92–93, 111, 114, 306). Following Husserl, Fink even speaks of reflection as a *self-multiplication*, wherein I exist together or in communion with myself (Fink 1987, 62). Of course, this should not be taken too literally. Reflection does not split me into two different egos; it does not turn me into a true other to myself. When I reflect, I am not confronted with the experiential life of a stranger. If I was, I would not say, "I perceive an emerald," but "Somebody perceives an emerald." By saying "I," I am affirming the identity between the reflecting and the reflected subject. Thus, reflection is not a kind of empathy, nor is it a kind of multiple personality disorder; it is a kind of *self*-awareness. It is, however, a kind of self-awareness that is essentially characterized by an internal division, difference, and *alterity*. As Asemissen put it:

> It is a distinctive feature of reflection that in it the I qua first-person singular effectuates and suffers a kind of inner pluralization. It is only in reflection that the I can become thematic, but it can only become thematic by paying the price of a dividing self-alienation, in which it distances itself from itself. (Asemissen 1958–59, 262)

To some extent, reflective self-awareness is distinguished by a certain detachment and withdrawal, since reflection deprives the original experience of its naïveté and spontaneity. To put it another way, reflective self-awareness does not differ from pre-reflective self-awareness merely by its intensity, articulation, and differentiation, but also by its quality of *othering*. Becoming a theme to oneself is a matter of becoming divided from oneself. Reflective self-awareness involves a form of alienation. It is characterized by a type of *self-fragmentation* that we do not encounter on the level of pre-reflective self-awareness.

This observation has at least three significant implications:

• Reflection is a precondition for self-critical deliberation. If we are to subject our different beliefs and desires to a critical, normative evaluation, it is not sufficient simply to have first-personal access to the states in question. It is not enough to be immediately and implicitly aware of them. Rather, when we reflect, we step back from our ongoing mental activities and, as Moran has recently pointed out, this stepping back is a metaphor of distancing and separation, but also one of observation and confrontation. The reflective distancing is what allows us to relate critically to our mental states and put them into question; it ultimately forces us to act for reasons (Moran 2001, 142–143).

• If reflection involves a kind of self-fission, it remains necessary to explain how such a fractured self-awareness can arise out of a supposedly unified pre-reflective self-awareness. As Sartre poignantly reminds us: The problem is not to find examples of pre-reflective self-awareness—they are everywhere—but to understand how one can pass from this self-awareness that constitutes the being of consciousness to the reflective knowledge of self, which is founded upon it (Sartre 1948, 63). Thus, it will not do to conceive of pre-reflective self-consciousness in such a manner that the transition to reflective self-consciousness becomes incomprehensible. Sartre was, by no means, trying to deny the difference between a reflective and a pre-reflective self-awareness, yet he insisted that the two modes of self-awareness must share a certain affinity, a certain structural similarity. Otherwise, it would be impossible to explain how the pre-reflective cogito could ever give rise to reflection. It is a significant feature of the lived experience that it allows for reflective appropriation; a theory of self-consciousness that can *only* account for pre-reflective self-consciousness is not much better than a theory that only accounts for reflective self-consciousness. To phrase it differently, it is no coincidence that we speak of a pre-*reflective* self-consciousness; the very choice of words indicates that there remains a connection. The reason reflection remains a permanent possibility is precisely that pre-reflective self-consciousness already entails a temporal articulation and differentiated infrastructure (Sartre 1943, 113, 194). In fact, reflection draws on the unity of unification and differentiation inherent in the pre-reflective lived presence: its ecstatic-centered structure of protending, presencing, retaining. Thus, most phenomenologists (Michel Henry is a notable exception) would argue that pre-reflective self-consciousness must be conceived not as a static self-identity, but as a dynamic and temporal self-differentiation.

▪ If reflection is characterized by a kind of self-fragmentation, there will always remain an unthematic and anonymous spot in the life of the subject. Even a universal reflection will contain a moment of naiveté since it is necessarily prevented from grasping itself (Hua 9/478). Reflection will forever miss something important, namely itself qua anonymously functioning subject-pole (Hua 14/29). As Husserl wrote, I cannot grasp my own functioning subjectivity because I am it; that which I am cannot be my *Gegenstand*, cannot stand opposed to me (Hua 8/412). Experiential life can thematize and disclose itself, but it can never do so exhaustively and completely. This insight was repeated by Merleau-Ponty, when he wrote that our temporal existence is both a condition for and an obstacle to our self-comprehension. Temporality contains an internal fracture that permits us to return to our past experiences in order to investigate them reflectively, yet this very fracture also prevents us from fully coinciding with ourselves. There will always remain a difference between the lived and the understood (Merleau-Ponty 1945, 76, 397, 399, 460). Thus, both Husserl and Merleau-Ponty questioned the absolute power of reflection.[15]

That there is a connection between reflection and *alterity* or *otherness*— that reflection involves a moment of self-alteration (or even self-alienation)— will be even more obvious if we turn from the merely accentuating type of reflection to the more interpretative form. To recapitulate, according to Sartre, the impure reflection is called impure because it transcends the given and interprets the reflected in an objectifying manner (Sartre 1943, 194, 199, 201). One of the examples given by Sartre touches on our experience of *pain*. Assume that you are sitting late at night trying to finish a book. You have been reading most of the day and your eyes are hurting. How does this pain originally manifest itself? According to Sartre, not immediately as a thematic object of reflection, but by influencing the way in which you perceive the world. You might become restless, irritated, or have difficulties in focusing and concentrating; the words on the page may tremble or quiver. Even though the pain is not yet apprehended as a psychical object, it is not absent or unconscious. It is not yet thematized, but given as a vision-in-pain, as a pervasive affective atmosphere that influences and colors your intentional interaction with the world (Sartre 1943, 380–381). As Sartre wrote:

I exist the pain in such a way that it disappears in the ground of corporeality as a structure subordinated to the corporal totality. The pain is neither absent nor unconscious; it simply forms a part of that distance-less existence of positional consciousness for itself. (Sartre 1943, 383 [1956, 334])

So far, the pain is only given pre-reflectively, but this of course can change. You can start to reflect (impurely) upon it. If you do this, you adopt, in keeping with Sartre, a distancing and objectifying attitude to the experience in question, and, as a result, the experience is transformed. You transcend the lived pain and posit the pain as an object, that is, as a transcendent unity: Different isolated twinges of *pain* are apprehended as manifestations of one and the same *suffering* (Sartre 1943, 385–386). Apart from turning the pain into a psychical object, however, the reflection also situates it within an ego-logical context. That is, the pain is henceforward given as being owned by, or belonging to, an ego. More generally, when experiences are reflected upon, they are interpreted as manifesting states, traits, and qualities that belong to somebody. Sartre actually took this distancing transformation to be so radical that he described impure reflection as an attempt to capture the experience reflected-on as if it were the experience of somebody else. This description might gain some credibility if we follow Sartre yet another step in his analysis of pain. After all, you might not only apprehend a concrete pain as the manifestation of a suffering. You can also describe and classify it through acquired medical concepts: It is a case of glaucoma. At this stage, the pain is taken as the manifestation of a *disease*, and it is now accessible to others who can describe and diagnose it even better than yourself. When you conceive of your pain in a similar manner, you have adopted an alienating third-person perspective on it (Sartre 1943, 405–407).

Strictly speaking, we are now confronted with a type of reflection that is intersubjectively mediated. Thus, for both Husserl and Sartre there are forms of reflection that entail a self-apprehension from the perspective of the other, and which therefore have the encounter with the other and the other's intervention as their condition of possibility. There are, in other words, types of self-apprehension that do not have their origin in the self but depend on *radical alterity*.

Husserl frequently distinguishes between two types of alienating self-apprehensions. Through an other subject, I can learn to apprehend myself as a person among persons, that is, I can learn to adopt a *personalistic* attitude on myself. I can also learn to conceive of myself as a causally determined object among objects or, in other words, to adopt a *naturalistic* attitude on myself. By assuming the objectifying perspective of the other on myself, I learn to apprehend myself both as a person or human being, a socialized subject of the kind studied by the humanities and social sciences, and as a psyche or psychophysical entity, a naturalized subject of the kind studied by the natural sciences (Hua 8/71; 5/146; 4/142–143; 4/174–175). Neither of these attitudes is immediately accessible; both entail a fundamental change of attitude toward oneself that is occasioned by the other. It is the other that teaches me to apprehend myself from a third-person perspective as the bearer of cultural and natural properties. As Husserl said, I cannot experience my own intersubjective "*Realitätsform*" directly, but only mediated through empathy which, as he then added, leads to self-alienation (Hua 4/200; 13/342, 462; 4/90, 111; 15/19, 589, 634; 14/418).

Sartre also spoke of the *existential alienation* occasioned by my encounter with the other. This alienation is, for instance, manifest in my attempt to grasp my own being by way of what can be revealed in language, that is, through something that throws me outside of myself. Thus, for Sartre language is not just something added on to my intersubjective being; if anything, it expresses my being-for-others in a preeminent way, since it confers significance upon me that others have already found words for (Sartre 1943, 404, 422–423). To apprehend myself from the perspective of the other is to apprehend myself as seen in the midst of the world, as a thing among things with properties and determinations that I am without having chosen them. The gaze of the other thrusts me into worldly space and time. I am no longer given to myself as the temporal and spatial center of the world. I am no longer simply "here," but next to the door, or on the couch; I am no longer simply "now," but too late for the appointment (Sartre 1943, 309, 313, 317, 481, 581). Sartre also characterized my being-for-others as an *ecstatic* and *external* dimension of being (Sartre 1943, 287, 314, 334, 582).

One rather marked difference between Husserl and Sartre is that Husserl viewed the process of alienation more positively than Sartre. In Husserl's view, it can lead to a maturation and enrichment of subjectivity. I am not only the subject of occurrent experience but also of diverse developing personality structures (Hua 4/345), and, according to Husserl, my *personhood* is intersubjectively constituted (Hua 14/175; 6/315; 4/204–205; 15/177, 603). It is only when I apprehend the other as apprehending me and take myself as other to the other that I apprehend myself in the same way that I apprehend them and become aware of the same entity that they are aware of, namely, myself as a person (Hua 6/256; 14/78, 418). It is no wonder that Husserl often asserts that the personal reflection, in contrast to the pure reflection, is characterized by a complex and indirect intentional structure (Hua 4/242, 250).

To summarize the results: Although Husserl, Sartre, and Merleau-Ponty all rejected the view that reflection necessarily implies a distortion of lived experience, they also insisted that reflection presents us with a kind of self-alteration or even self-alienation. One might see their position as situated between two extremes. On the one hand, we have the view that reflection merely copies or mirrors pre-reflective experience faithfully, and on the other, we have the view that reflection distorts lived experience. The middle course is to recognize that reflection involves a gain and a loss. For Husserl, Sartre, and Merleau-Ponty, reflection is constrained by what is pre-reflectively lived through. It is answerable to experiential facts and is not constitutively self-fulfilling. At the same time, however, they recognized that reflection qua thematic self-experiences does not simply reproduce the lived experiences unaltered and that this is precisely what makes reflection cognitively valuable. The experiences reflected upon are transformed in the process, to various degrees and manners depending on the type of reflection at work. Subjectivity consequently seems to be constituted in such a fashion that it can and, at times, must relate to itself in an othering manner. This self-alteration is something inherent to reflection; it is not something that reflection can overcome.[16]

VI Reflective versus Hermeneutical Phenomenology

Let us, after this long detour, return to Heidegger. According to von Herr-mann, Heidegger rejected Husserl's reflective phenomenology and offered his own nonreflective alternative. But is this really true? Although Heidegger largely seems to have accepted Natorp's criticism of reflective phenom-enology, this does not prove that his own hermeneutical alternative is nonreflective. On the contrary, there are good reasons to insist that Heideg-ger's hermeneutical intuition is in fact nothing but a special type of reflection.

As we have seen, Heidegger distinguished between an objectifying reflec-tion and a nonobjectifying hermeneutical thematization and articulation. As we have also just seen, however, a number of other phenomenologists would make the same distinction but use different terms. They would insist that one should distinguish different types of reflection and that whereas some are merely accentuating, others are distorting and reifying.[17] In my view, it is reasonable to argue that what Heidegger has really done is to describe the former type of reflection in some detail. Thus, contrary to what von Herr-mann is claiming, Heidegger's real contribution might be taken to consist in an analysis of a phenomenological type of reflection that can precisely provide us with an access to lived subjectivity that is not vulnerable to the objections posed by Natorp.

Perhaps it could be objected that it is misleading and confusing to operate with different notions of reflection, but then again, this is exactly what Heidegger himself was also doing in the passage from *Grundprobleme der Phänomenologie* quoted earlier (Heidegger GA 24: 226; see also GA 61: 95).

When all is said and done, hermeneutical phenomenology seeks to thematize and articulate experiential structures. It seeks to make us pay heed to something that we normally live through but fail to notice owing to our absorption in the surrounding world. Insofar as this is what hermeneutical phenomenology does, it remains a reflective enterprise.

Recently, Crowell has made the same point and has argued that Heidegger's formal indicative concepts "repeat" the self-interpretation of life, but that this repetition is more than a mere going-along with life, more than a mere reliving of life; rather, it is an "explicitly cognitive-illuminative self-recollection (reflection)" that is oriented toward intuitive self-having (Crowell 2001, 125–127). To put it another way, the reflective methodology is not abandoned; rather, it reappears in Heidegger's conception of philosophy as a distinctive sort of *questioning* comportment (Crowell 2001, 131). Philosophizing is a self-referential movement; if I am to philosophize on the basis of authentic evidence, I must attend to my own mode of being, I must concern myself with my own questioning being, and this involves reflection. Thus, Heidegger's notion of hermeneutical understanding or hermeneutical intuition must ultimately be seen as "a reappropriation, rather than a rejection, of the genuinely phenomenological concept of reflection" (Crowell 2001, 137; cf. 140, 144).[18]

The fact that Heidegger himself did not describe the hermeneutical intuition *expressis verbis* as a kind of reflection should not be cause for undue concern. To some extent, Heidegger's silence is only to be expected. Had he, in fact, described his own method in reflective terms, he would have had a harder time making the case that his hermeneutical phenomenology really was a new form of phenomenology, and Heidegger was always concerned to emphasize his own originality vis-à-vis his old mentor. In other words, it would not be the first time that Heidegger had employed a Husserlian methodology without acknowledging it.

If one accepts this conclusion, one pertinent question is, of course, whether *reflective phenomenology* and *hermeneutical phenomenology* are really to count as two radically different types of phenomenology. Alternately, should the distinction between a *reflective phenomenology* and a *hermeneutical phenomenology* be preserved or rather be abandoned? Given how they have been defined above and given that the distinction is taken to rest solely upon the methodological use of reflection, I would argue that it is utterly artificial. But, of course, the distinction is frequently taken to touch on quite different issues as well, including the status of subjectivity, the role of the epoché, and the more general stance toward transcendental philosophy. Often, it is actually taken to be a distinction between a pure and transcendental type of phenomenology on the one hand, and an existential and hermeneutical kind on the other. Whether this distinction is artificial as well, and whether it is largely based on something approaching a serious misunderstanding of Husserl's transcendental turn is something I have discussed elsewhere.[19,20]

What is the relation between (phenomenal) consciousness and the self? Must we evoke a subject of experience in order to account for the unity and continuity of experience, or rather, are experiences anonymous mental events that simply occur without being anybody's states? When we speak of self-awareness, do we then necessarily also speak of a self? Is there always a self involved in self-awareness, or is it also possible to speak of self-awareness without assuming the existence of anybody being self-aware? Answers to these questions are of obvious importance when it comes to a proper understanding both of the structure of consciousness and of what it means to be a self.

I The Non-egological Challenge

Let me illustrate two alternatives by means of Gurwitsch's classical distinction between an egological and a non-egological theory of consciousness (Gurwitsch 1941). An *egological* theory would claim that when I watch a movie by Bergman, I am not only intentionally directed at the *movie*, nor merely aware of the movie being *watched*, I am also aware that it is being watched by *me*, that is, that *I* am *watching* the *movie*. In short, there is an object of experience (the movie), there is an experience (the watching), and there is a subject of experience, myself. Thus, an egological theory would typically claim that it is a conceptual and experiential truth that any episode of experiencing necessarily includes a subject of experience (see Shoemaker 1968, 563–564). In contrast, a *non-egological* theory, also known as the *no-ownership* view (see Strawson 1959, 95), would deny that every experience is for a subject. It would, in other words, omit any reference to a subject of experience and simply say that there is an awareness of the watching of the movie. Experiences are egoless; they are anonymous mental events that simply occur, and minimal self-awareness should, consequently, be understood as the acquaintance that consciousness has with *itself* and *not* as an awareness of an experiencing *self*.

It is not difficult to find arguments against an egological theory of self-awareness and in favor of a non-egological position in twentieth-century philosophy. According to Henrich and Pothast, for instance, to speak of a self or an ego is to speak of an *agent*, that is, some principle of activity and volition. Pre-reflective self-awareness, however, is not something that we initiate or control; it is something that precedes all performances and should, consequently, not be attributed to an ego, but rather be understood as an egoless occurrence. Moreover, if one conceives of the ego qua subject of experience as something that *has* the experience, one obviously makes a distinction between the ego and the experience; they are not identical. In this case, however, it is difficult to understand why the ego's awareness of the experience should count as a case of *self*-awareness. Thus, Henrich and Pothast conclude that it is better to avoid introducing any ego into the structure of basic self-awareness (Henrich 1970, 276, 279; Pothast 1971, 76, 81; cf. Frank 1991b, 252; Cramer 1974, 573).

This view has affinities with the position advocated by Sartre, though he frequently phrased his discussion in terms of the relation between consciousness and self, rather than in terms of the relation between self-awareness and self. In chapter 2, I presented Sartre's position in some detail, so let me just quickly recapitulate a few of his main points. It has often been argued that mental life would dissipate into a chaos of unstructured and separate sensations were it not supported by the unifying, synthesizing, and individuating function of a central and atemporal ego. However, as Sartre pointed out, this reasoning misjudges the nature of the stream of consciousness. The stream of consciousness does not need an exterior principle of individuation, since it is, per se, individuated. Nor is it in need of any transcendent principle of unification, since the stream of experiences is self-unifying (Sartre 1936, 21–23). Sartre then went on to point out that an unprejudiced phenomenological description of lived consciousness will simply not include an ego, understood as an inhabitant in or possessor of consciousness. Lived pre-reflective consciousness has no egological structure. As long as we are absorbed in the experience, *living* it through, no ego appears. It is only when we adopt a distancing and objectifying attitude toward the experience in question, that is, when we reflect upon it, that an ego appears. Even then, however, we are dealing not with an I-consciousness, since the reflecting pole remains non-egological, but merely with a consciousness *of* an ego. The ego is not the subject, but the object of consciousness. It is not something that exists in or behind consciousness, but in front of it (Sartre 1936, 34, 43–44). Thus, Sartre accepted Lichtenberg's famous critique of Descartes: the traditional rendering of the cogito affirms too much. What is certain is not that "I am aware of this chair," but only that "there is awareness of this chair" (Sartre 1936, 31–32, 37).

Sartre's position was not original. Not only was it anticipated—as we have already seen—by Husserl in *Logische Untersuchungen*, but similar views were also advocated by Hume and Nietzsche, who both insisted that the positing of a conscious self or subject is descriptively unwarranted. If we describe the content of our consciousness accurately and pay attention to that which is given, we will not find any self. As Hume famously wrote in *A Treatise of Human Nature*:

For my part, when I enter most intimately into what I call *myself*, I always stumble on some particular perception or other, of heat or cold, light or shade, love or hatred, pain or pleasure. I never can catch *myself* at any time without a perception, and never can observe any thing but the perception. (Hume 1888, 252)

One finds the following statement in one of Nietzsche's manuscripts from the 1880s:

The "subject" is not something given, it is something added and invented and projected behind what there is. (Nietzsche 1960, 903 [1968, 267])

Thus, rather than having experiential reality, the self must be classified as a linguistic construct or as a product of reflection.

Recently, a rather different type of skepticism regarding the self has gained popularity. According to this approach, it is not at all crucial whether or not the self is a given. Whether something is real is not a question of its appearance or of whether it is experienced as real; rather it is a question of whether it can be naturalized and explained by means of the principles and methods employed by natural science. According to this criteria, the self has been weighed and has been found wanting.

One exponent of this view is Metzinger, who in his recent book *Being No One* offers a representationalist and functionalist analysis of what a consciously experienced first-person perspective is. The conclusion he reaches is quite unequivocal: "no such things as selves exist in the world: Nobody ever *was* or *had* a self" (Metzinger 2003a, 1). Thus, for all scientific and philosophical purposes, the notion of a self can safely be eliminated. It is neither necessary nor rational to assume the existence of a self, since it is a theoretical entity that fulfills no indispensable explanatory function. In reality, the self is not an actually existing object or an unchangeable substance, but a representational construct. All that has been explained previously by reference to a phenomenological notion of "self" can consequently be better explained with the notion of a phenomenally transparent self-model whose representational, or more important, *mis*representational (hallucinatory) nature cannot be recognized by the system using it (Metzinger 2003a, 337, 563, 626). The way in which we are given to ourselves on the level of conscious experience must consequently count as a deficit. Biological organisms exist, but an organism is not a self. Some organisms possess self-models, but such self-models are not selves, but merely complex brain states (Metzinger 2003a, 563). Whenever we speak of a "self," we consequently commit what Metzinger alternately calls the phenomenological fallacy, or the error of phenomenological reification. We confuse the content of an ongoing subpersonal self-representational process with a real existing entity (Metzinger 2003a, 268). All that really exist are certain types of information-processing systems engaged in operations of self-modeling, and we should not commit the mistake of confusing a model with reality (Metzinger 2003b, 370, 385, 390). To be more precise (since there is no I, you, or we), owing to an autoepistemic closure or lack of information, owing to a special form of epistemic darkness, the self-representing system is caught up in a naive-realistic self-misunderstanding (Metzinger 2003a, 332, 436–437, 564). Properly speaking, there is no one who confuses herself with anything, since there is no one who could be taken in by the illusion of a conscious self (Metzinger 2003a, 634). The self is a mere appearance, and on several occasions Metzinger compares the recognition of the illusionary or fictitious character of one's own self with the kind of insight that is one of the main goals of Buddhist enlightenment (Metzinger 2003a, 550, 566).

We will have occasion to return to Metzinger later on, but it is already appropriate now to present a few critical remarks. Metzinger argues that there are no such things as selves or subjects of experience in the world. All that exist are phenomenal selves, that is, selves that are nothing but properties of complex representational processes (Metzinger 2003a, 577).

Granted that this is true, however, why does Metzinger adopt a no-self doctrine? Why does he take the self to be an illusion? Why does he not, rather, argue like Churchland, who writes "The brain makes us think that we have a self. Does that mean that the self I think I am is not real? No, it is as real as any activity of the brain. It does mean, however, that one's self is not an ethereal bit of 'soul stuff'" (Churchland 2002, 124)? Part of the reason for this seems to be that Metzinger, himself, remains committed to the rather classical definition of the self, according to which the self is a mysteriously unchanging essence, a process-independent ontological substance that could exist all by itself, that is, in isolation from the rest of the world (Metzinger 2003a, 577, 626). Metzinger denies the existence of such an entity and then concludes that no such things as selves exist. The only reason to accept his conclusion would be if this notion of self were the only one available. And as we will shortly see, this is by no means the case. It is obviously possible to speak of the self or ego the way Henrich, Pothast, Sartre, Hume, Nietzsche, and Metzinger do. One problem with their skeptical reservations, however, is that they all presuppose rather specific concepts of self, which they then proceed to criticize. Yet is it at all clear what, precisely, a self is?

II Different Notions of Self

On closer examination, it should be obvious that it is an exaggeration to claim that the notion of "self" is unequivocal and that there is widespread consensus about what, exactly, it means to be a self. Quite to the contrary, if one looks at contemporary discussions one will find them to be literally bursting with completing and competing definitions of the self. In a well-known article from 1988, Neisser distinguished five types of self: the ecological, interpersonal, extended, private, and conceptual self (Neisser 1988, 35). Eleven years later, Strawson summed up a recent discussion on the self in the *Journal of Consciousness Studies* by enumerating no fewer than twenty-one concepts of self (Strawson 1999, 484). Given this escalating abundance, it is quite easy to talk at cross-purposes, particularly in an interdisciplinary context. It is a simple fact that the concept of self connotes different things in different disciplines—sometimes radically different things. What is urgently needed is, consequently, a clarification of the relationships between these various conflicting and/or complementary notions of self. Moreover, such a taxonomic clarification is indispensable if one is to evaluate the merits of the no-self doctrine. What I intend to do in the following is to contrast a rather classical understanding of the self that, to a large extent, is targeted by the non-egological criticism with two alternate and more contemporary ways of conceiving of the self.

A Kantian Perspective: The Self as a Pure Identity-Pole
This traditional view insists on distinguishing between the identical self on the one hand and the manifold of changing experiences on the other. In turn, I can taste an ice cream, smell a bunch of roses, admire a statue by Michelangelo, and recollect a hike in the Alps. We are here faced with a number of different experiences, but they also have something in common; they all have the same subject, they are all lived through by one and the same self, namely myself. Whereas the experiences arise and perish in the stream of consciousness, the self remains as one and the same through time. More specifically, the self is taken to be a distinct *principle of identity* that stands apart from and above the stream of changing experiences and which, for that very reason, is able to structure it and give it unity and coherence (cf. Kant 1956: B 132–133).

The notion of self at work here is obviously a formal and abstract one. Every experience is always lived through *by* a certain subject; it is always an experience *for* a certain subject. The self is, consequently, understood as the pure subject, or ego-pole, that any episode of experiencing necessarily refers back to. It is the subject of experience rather than the object of experience. Instead of being something that can itself be given as an object for experience, it is a necessary condition of the possibility for (coherent) experience. We can infer that it must exist, but it is not itself something that can be experienced. It is an elusive principle, a presupposition, rather than a datum or something that is itself given. Were it given, it would be given for someone, that is, it would be an object, and therefore no longer a self (see Natorp 1912, 8, 40). As Kant wrote in *Kritik der reinen Vernunft*: "It is . . . evident that I cannot know as an object that which I must presuppose to know any object" (Kant 1956, A 402).

A Hermeneutical Perspective: The Self as a Narrative Construction
A quite different way of conceiving the self takes its point of departure in the fact that self-comprehension and self-knowledge, rather than being something that is given once and for all, is something that has to be appropriated and can be attained with varying degrees of success. As long as life goes on,

there is no final self-understanding. The same, however, can also be said for what it means to be a self. The self is not a thing; it is not something fixed and unchangeable, but rather something evolving. It is something that is realized through one's projects, and it therefore cannot be understood independently of one's own self-interpretation. As Jopling puts it: "Selfhood is best viewed as a kind of ongoing project that serves as a response to the question of how to be" (Jopling 2000, 83). In short, one is not a self in the same way as one is a living organism. One does not have a self in the same way that one has a heart or a nose (Taylor 1989, 34). To have a self, or better, to be a self, is something in which one is existentially involved.

According to this view, which has become increasingly popular lately, the self is assumed to be a construction. It is the product of conceiving and organizing one's life in a certain way. When confronted with the question "Who am I?" we will tell a certain story and emphasize aspects that we deem to be of special significance, to be that which constitutes the *leitmotif* in our life, that which defines who we are, that which we present to others for recognition and approval (Ricoeur 1985, 442–443). This narrative, however, is not merely a way of gaining insight into the nature of an already existing self. On the contrary, the self is first constructed in and through the narration. Who we are depends on the story we (and others) tell about ourselves. The story can be more or less coherent, and the same holds true for our self-identity. The narrative self is, consequently, an open-ended construction that is under constant revision. It is pinned on culturally relative narrative hooks and organized around a set of aims, ideals, and aspirations (Flanagan 1992, 206). It is a construction of identity starting in early childhood and continuing for the rest of our life, which involves a complex social interaction. Who one is depends on the values, ideals, and goals one has; it is a question of what has significance and meaning for one, and this, of course, is conditioned by the community of which one is part. Thus, as has often been claimed, one cannot be a self on one's own, but only together with others, as part of a *linguistic* community. As Taylor puts it, "There is no way we could be inducted into personhood except by being initiated into a language" (Taylor 1989, 35).

A Phenomenological Perspective: The Self as an Experiential Dimension

The phenomenological alternative I now consider can be seen as a replacement of the first notion of self and as a necessary founding supplement for the second notion of self. The crucial idea is that an understanding of what it means to be a self calls for an examination of the structure of experience, and vice versa. In other words, the investigations of self and experience have to be integrated if both are to be understood. More precisely, the self is claimed to possess experiential reality, is taken to be closely linked to the first-person perspective, and is, in fact, identified with the very first-personal *givenness* of the experiential phenomena. As Michel Henry would have put it, the most basic form of selfhood is the one constituted by the very self-manifestation of experience (Henry 1963, 581; 1965, 53). To be conscious of one*self*, consequently, is not to capture a pure self that exists in separation from the stream of consciousness, but rather entails just being conscious of an experience in its first-personal mode of givenness; it is a question of having first-personal access to one's own experiential life. Thus, the self referred to is not something standing beyond or opposed to the stream of experiences but is rather a feature or function of its givenness. In short, the self is conceived neither as an ineffable transcendental precondition, nor as a mere social construct that evolves through time; it is taken to be an integral part of our conscious life with an immediate experiential reality.

This third notion of self, just like the Kantian notion, is a very formal and minimalist notion, and it is obvious that far more complex forms of selves exist. With this said, however, the phenomenological notion nevertheless strikes me as being of pivotal significance. It is fundamental in the sense that nothing that lacks this dimension deserves to be called a self. Thus, in my view, this experiential sense of self deserves to be called the *minimal self* or the *core self*. In order to substantiate this suggestion, we must look closer at the last two concepts of self, the hermeneutical and the phenomenological. Let us start with the former.

III The Narrative Concept of Self

It has recently been argued that it is impossible to discuss the issues of self-hood and personal identity in abstraction from the temporal dimension of human existence (Ricoeur 1990, 138). Human time, however, is neither the subjective time of consciousness nor the objective time of the cosmos. Rather, human time bridges the gap between phenomenological and cosmological time. Human time is the time of our life stories; a narrated time structured and articulated by the symbolic mediations of narratives (Ricoeur 1985, 439). What contributions do such narratives make to the constitution of the self? It has been suggested that they make up the essential form and central constitutive feature of self-understanding and self-knowledge.

In order to know who you are, in order to gain a robust self-understanding, it is not enough to simply be aware of oneself from the first-person perspective. It is not sufficient to think of oneself as an I; a narrative is required. To answer the question "Who am I?" is to tell the story of a life (Ricoeur 1985, 442). I attain insight into who I am by situating my character traits, the values I endorse, the goals I pursue within a life story that traces their origin and development; a life story that tells where I am coming from and where I am heading. This narrative, however, is not merely a way of gaining insight into the nature of an already existing self. On the contrary, the self is the product of a narratively structured life. As MacIntyre puts it, the unity of the self "resides in the unity of a narrative which links birth to life to death as narrative beginning to middle to end" (MacIntyre 1985, 205). Thus, for MacIntyre, personal identity is the identity presupposed by the unity of the character that the unity of the narrative requires, or, to put it differently, the notion of a character in a story is more fundamental than the concept of a person. The latter concept is simply the concept of a character abstracted from its history (MacIntyre 1985, 217–218).

Why is it natural for us to think of the self in terms of narrative structures? This is because human activities are enacted narratives; our actions gain intelligibility by having a place in a narrative sequence. We live out narratives in our lives and we understand our own lives in terms of such narratives: "Stories are lived before they are told—except in the case of fiction" (MacIntyre 1985, 212). Stories involve agents and patients, people who act and suffer. It is within the framework of such narratives that we can ask the central who-questions: "Who is this?"; "Who did this?"; "Who is responsible?" The answers to these questions are provided by the narrative itself. The self is the "who" of the story, the one upon whom the story confers an identity (Villela-Petit 2003, 3). To ask for the identity of the one who is responsible is, consequently, to ask for his narrative identity. This is why, according to MacIntyre, any attempt to elucidate the notions of selfhood or personal identity independently of and in isolation from the notions of narrativity, intelligibility, and accountability is bound to fail (MacIntyre 1985, 218).

Ricoeur has sought to clarify the concept of narrative identity by means of two further concepts of identity: identity as sameness (*mêmeté*) and identity as selfhood (*ipséité*). The first concept of identity, the identity of the same (Latin: *idem*), conceives of the identical as that which can be reidentified again and again, as that which resists change. The identity in question is that of an unchangeable substance, or substrate, that remains the same over time. As Ricoeur points out, not all problems of personal identity can be conceived as problems concerning the possibility of reidentification and tackled by means of the concept of sameness. Thus, the second concept of identity, the identity of the self (Latin: *ipse*), has very little to do with the persistence of some unchanging personality core. It is, primarily, not a question concerning the kinds of causal links that are required if we are to identify P_2 at t_2 as the same as P_1 at t_1. Rather, its identity condition is linked to the question of self-understanding, to the question "who am I" (Ricoeur 1990, 12–13, 140). When confronted with this question, I am forced to reflect on and evaluate my way of living, the values I honor, and the goals I pursue. I am forced to confront the life I am living. Thus, the answer to the question is not immediately accessible; rather it is the fruit of an examined life.

Whereas questions such as "What is x" or "Is x at t_1 identical to y at t_2"— questions regarding *idem*-identity—can be answered from a third-person perspective and be given definite and informative answers, questions regarding *ipse*-identity, such as "Who am I," must include an approach from the first-person perspective and will never find an exhaustive answer.

Ricoeur has occasionally presented his own notion of narrative identity as a solution to the traditional dilemma of having to choose between the Cartesian notion of the self as a principle of identity that remains the same throughout the diversity of its various states and the positions of Hume and Nietzsche, who held an identical subject to be nothing but a substantialist illusion (Ricoeur 1985, 443). Ricoeur suggests that we can avoid this dilemma if we replace the notion of identity that they respectively defend and reject with the concept of narrative identity. The identity of the narrative self rests on narrative configurations. Unlike the abstract identity of the same, the narrative identity can include changes and mutations within the cohesion of a lifetime. The story of a life continues to be reconfigured by all the truthful or fictive stories a subject tells about him- or herself. It is this constant reconfiguration that makes "life itself a cloth woven of stories told" (Ricoeur 1985, 443 [1988, 246]).

Any consideration of narrative identity obviously entails a reference to others, since there is a clear social dimension to the achievement of narrative self-understanding. Narrative self-understanding requires maturation and socialization and the ability to access and issue reports about the states, traits, and dispositions that make one the person one is. I come to know who I am and what I want to do with my life by participating in a community. To come to know oneself as a person with a particular life history and particular character traits is, consequently, both more complicated than knowing one's immediate beliefs and desires and less private than it might initially seem (Jopling 2000, 137). When I interpret myself in terms of a life story, I might be both the narrator and the main character, but I am not the sole author. Whereas I, as the author of a literary text, am free to determine the beginning, middle, and end of the story, the beginning of my own story has always already been made for me by others, and the way the story unfolds is determined only in part by my own choices and decisions. As MacIntyre points out:

> [W]e are never more (and sometimes less) than the co-authors of our own narratives. Only in fantasy do we live what story we please. In life, as both Aristotle and Engels noted, we are always under certain constraints. We enter upon a stage which we did not design and we find ourselves part of an action that was not of our making. (MacIntyre 1985, 213)

Who we are depends on the stories told about us, both by ourselves and by others. Our narrative self is multiple-authored and under constant revision. The story of any individual life is not only interwoven with the stories of others (parents, siblings, friends, etc.), it is also embedded in a larger historical and communal meaning-giving structure (MacIntyre 1985, 221). The concepts I use to express the salient features of the person I take myself to be are concepts derived from tradition and theory that will vary widely from one historical period to the next and across social class and culture. To think of oneself as a citizen, an academic, a European, as hot tempered, handsome, clever, weak willed, amblyopic, anorectic, or anemic is to think of oneself by means of concepts that are embedded within diverse theoretical frameworks, be they of a sociological, biological, psychological, or religious provenience (see Neisser 1988, 53–54).

Ricoeur has frequently been regarded as one of the main proponents of a narrative approach to the self. Although it is undeniable that he has made decisive contributions to the discussion, Ricoeur himself has also pointed to some of the limitations of this approach. As he states in *Temps et recit*, narrative identity is the name of a problem at least as much as it is that of a solution (Ricoeur 1985, 446). Let us, then, take a closer look at this problem, or, to be more precise, at some of these problems.

Fiction and Confabulation

It is possible to tell different, even incompatible, stories about one and the same life, but not all of them can be true. The fact that our narration can, and does, include fictional components gives rise to at least two questions. First, how do we distinguish true narratives from false narratives? It is obvious that a person's sincere propagation of a specific life story does not guarantee its truth. In fact, in some cases the stability of our self-identity might be inversely proportional to the fixed stories we tell about ourselves. Elaborate storytelling might serve a compensatory function as an attempt to make up for the lack of a coherent self-identity.

Since the internal coherency of a story is no guarantee of its accuracy, it must be complemented by other constraints. Jopling has recently suggested some additional constraints. A self-narrative should not only be (1) internally coherent, it should also be (2) externally coherent, that is, it should fit with the narratives told about me by other people, and it should be (3) applicable to my current life situation, since a self-narrative is not meant to be relevant only for the understanding of the past, but is also meant to entail a forward-looking commitment to a broadly unified set of possible actions. Finally, it should (4) fit with narrative-transcendent facts (Jopling 2000, 50).

This reference to narrative-transcendent facts, however, calls attention to the second, more worrying issue: What is a narrative self-understanding an understanding of? What is the question "Who am I?" a question about? Is the self an independently existing entity that makes the questions we ask about it true or false? Is it something whose nature we gradually unearth, or rather, is it wholly constituted and constructed by our descriptions? Some defenders of a narrative approach to selfhood have argued that the self is nothing but a linguistic and social invention. As Dennett puts it, biological organisms with brains like ours cannot prevent themselves from inventing selves. We are hardwired to become language users, and the moment we make use of language, we begin spinning our stories. The self is produced in this spinning, but it has no reality; it is merely a fictional center of narrative gravity (Dennett 1991, 418; see also 1992). It is the abstract point where various stories about us intersect. Thus, on this reading, the narrative account turns out to be a variant of the no-self doctrine.

Dennett has compared the notion of self to the notion of a center of gravity. The latter is an abstractum, and although it has a well-defined role to play within physics, it remains a theorist's fiction; it is not a real thing in the universe. The situation is quite similar when it comes to selves, Dennett claims. They are theoretical fictions that we find it perspicuous to employ when we engage in the interpretation and prediction of behavior. It facilitates our predictions to organize our interpretations around such a central abstraction, but this does not change the fact that the self is, and remains, a fiction.

According to Dennett, selves are theoretical fictions that differ from theoretically inferred entities, such as subatomic particles, by having only the properties endowed by the theory that constitutes them. There are no theory-transcendent constraints; there is nothing to be discovered. To ask *what* a self really is, or to ask—as some neuroscientists do—*where* the self is, is quite simply a category mistake (Dennett 1992).

Some might argue that fictional selves depend on real selves for their creation. Dennett, however, considers this suggestion mistaken. He asks us to consider the following scenario: Let us imagine a highly sophisticated computer that has been designed to write novels. The first novel it writes is the apparent autobiography of some fictional person called Gilbert. Gilbert is a fictional self, yet its creator—the computer—is not a real self. There may have been human designers who built the computer, but the narrative construction of Gilbert did not involve any selves. Dennett then asks us to expand upon the story. Let us turn the novel-writing computer into a robot and assume that it is outfitted with wheels and cameras and that it can move around in the world. It still writes a novel about Gilbert, but strangely enough, the adventures of Gilbert bear a striking relationship to the adventures of the robot. If you hit the robot with a baseball bat, the story about Gilbert will, shortly thereafter, include a section that describes how he was hit with a baseball bat by somebody looking like you. If you instead help the robot, it will send you a note saying "Thank you. Love, Gilbert." Thus, Gilbert seems to be real, seems to be the robot. In truth, however, there is no Gilbert, there is no self. All that exists are patterns of behavior that can be interpreted by means of a narrative that includes a reference to a self. Needless to say, on Dennett's view, this holds true not only in the case of the robot and Gilbert, but in the case of each of us as well (Dennett 1992).

Let us grant that the narrative self is a construction. It is not something innate, and the material used for its construction consists not only of real-life materials, but also ideals and fictive ideas. Let us grant that our narrative identity is subject to constant revisions and that it is organized around numerous narrative hooks that differ from culture to culture. Does this, then, justify the claim that the self is nothing but a fiction? Let us not forget that there are constraints; some self-narratives are more true than others. As Flanagan points out, it is undeniable that the self plays a crucial role in our psychological and social life by giving it organization, meaning, and structure. Thus, in his view, the narrative self might be a construction, but that does not make it unreal (Flanagan 1992, 205–210). Ricoeur and MacIntyre would, obviously, agree. Although both reject the idea of a substantial self, they would insist that human life has a natural narrative structure. To declare everything peculiar to human life fictitious simply because it cannot be naturalized, because it cannot be grasped by a certain mode of scientific comprehension, merely reveals one's prior commitment to a naive scientism, according to which (natural) science is the sole arbiter of what there is.

I fully share this view with Flanagan, Ricoeur, and MacIntyre; yet a lingering doubt remains. Is it possible to resist Dennett's conclusion as long as the self is taken to be nothing but a narrative construction? Does the narrative self not require some kind of experiential support?

Finitude
We are finite creatures. No finite, fallible creature can explicate the full story of its life. Self-narratives may capture something important about who we are, but are they capable of capturing the full complexity of the self? Is it legitimate to reduce our selfhood to that which can be narrated? Could it not be argued that we actually learn more about ourselves when confronted with situations that make us step out of smooth, unifying narratives, that make us act "out of character"? Furthermore, it might not only be objected that stories are told rather than lived and that narratives differ from life, it might also be argued that the very attempt to present human life in the form of a narrative will necessarily transform it. The storyteller will inevitably impose an order on the life events that they did not possess while they were lived. To form a self-narrative more must be done than simply recall and

recount certain life events. One must also consider these events reflectively and deliberate on their meaning to decide how they fit together. All of this involves a certain element of confabulation that goes beyond the lived life itself (see Gallagher 2003a).

MacIntyre's reply to the latter kind of objection is that the only picture we can envisage of a human life, prior to its alleged misinterpretation by a narrative, is in the form of a sequence of disjointed fragments or snapshots, which, in his view, simply proves his point. To talk of the sequence as being fragmented is to measure it against the narrative that continues to remain the framework of intelligibility (MacIntyre 1985, 212–215). This rejoinder, however, is too easy. Although it might be true that many of our actions easily lend themselves to narrative articulation, human life is made up of more than just actions. Moreover, it is one thing to claim that actions can be narrated, and something quite different to claim that they can all be fitted into one unifying narration without thereby imposing more unity upon them than they had to start with. As Drummond has recently put it:

> Narratives are reflective selections and organizations of a life. In this sense the narrative captures less than an individual's life, for not all of a life as pre-reflectively lived can be fitted into a narrative, which best suits goal-directed action. From the opposite perspective, narratives, by virtue of their selectivity, impose more unity than life itself has manifested. . . . [W]e should not confuse the reflective, narrative grasp of a life with an account of the pre-reflective experience that makes up that life prior to that experience being organized into a narrative. (Drummond 2004, 119)

Ethics and Beyond

Despite his being heralded as one of the leading protagonists of the narrative approach to selfhood, one of Ricoeur's conclusions, reached in *Temps et recit* but only fully developed in *Soi-meme comme un autre*, is that the discussion of narrative identity does not exhaust the question concerning the identity of the self. Selfhood cannot be reduced to narrative identity since the identity of the self is only fully revealed the moment we include the *ethical dimension*.

As Ricoeur argues, personal identity has two poles, and narrative identity is what links the two (Ricoeur 1990, 195). The first pole is constituted by *character*, which is, as he puts it, the *what* in the *who* (Ricoeur 1990, 147). The character is the totality of our enduring dispositions and habits, those distinctive traits that enable others to recognize and reidentify us. Our character, consequently, has a temporal dimension; it expresses permanence in time. As a second, acquired nature my character is I, myself, but it is also a dimension of self that announces itself as *idem*. To speak of character is to speak of the self in the manner of the same. It is the limit point where a discussion of *ipse* is indiscernible from a discussion of *idem* (Ricoeur 1990, 143). The second pole is constituted by what Ricoeur calls *faithfulness of self*, that is, by the ethical dimension of the self. This is the dimension of pure *ipseity* where *ipse* and *idem* are completely dissociated and where the question of self-identity is a question of *accountability* and *responsibility* (Ricoeur 1990, 143, 179, 195). As Ricoeur already pointed out in 1950, in *Philosophie de la volonté*:

I form the consciousness of being the author of my acts in the world and, more generally, the author of my acts of thought, principally on the occasion of my contacts with an other, in a social context. Someone asks, who did that? I rise and reply, I did. Response-responsibility. To be responsible means to be ready to respond to such a question. (Ricoeur 1950, 55 [1966, 56–57])

Thus, to be a self is not simply a question of storytelling. It is also a question of adopting certain norms as binding; to be bound by obligation or loyalty. It is to remain true to oneself in promise keeping. It is to be somebody others can count on. It is to assume responsibility for one's past actions and for the future consequences of one's present actions, regardless of how much one's self-narrative might change (Ricoeur 1990, 341–342). Thus, Ricoeur ends up arguing that the narrative take on selfhood must be complemented by a different perspective that includes the issue of *ethical responsibility*.[1]

Although I fully agree with Ricoeur's concession that a discussion of narrative identity is insufficient if we want to understand the full complexity of the self, I will not follow Ricoeur on his excursion into ethics. Rather, I want to suggest that the narrative or hermeneutical take on self must be complemented by an experiential or phenomenological take on the self. To put it very simply, it takes a self to experience one's life as a story. In order to begin a self-narrative, the narrator must be able to differentiate between self and nonself, must be able to self-attribute actions and experience agency, and must be able to refer to him- or herself by means of the first-person pronoun. All of this presupposes that the narrator is in possession of a first-person perspective.

IV The Self as an Experiential Dimension

The term "*ipseity*" (selfhood, from the Latin, *ipse*) has gained a recent popularity as a result of Ricoeur's writings on narrative and what he calls his "herméneutique de l'ipséité" (Ricoeur 1990, 357). However, Ricoeur is by no means the first French thinker to employ the term, and if we look briefly at the way the term has been used by some of his phenomenological predecessors (Merleau-Ponty, Sartre, and Henry) we will begin to gain a better understanding of what the phenomenological concept of self amounts to.

Merleau-Ponty occasionally spoke of the subject as realizing its *ipseity* in its embodied being-in-the-world (Merleau-Ponty 1945, 467). He also, however, referred to Husserl's investigations of inner time-consciousness and wrote that the original temporal flow involves a self-manifestation. Consciousness constitutes itself in terms of itself and, as Merleau-Ponty then stated, the temporal explosion of the present toward the future counts as the archetypical relationship of self to self and traces out an interiority or *ipseity* (Merleau-Ponty 1945, 487–488).

We have already come across Sartre's dismissal of an egological account of consciousness in *La transcendance de l'ego*. Whereas Sartre, in that early work, had characterized non-egological consciousness as *impersonal*, he described this view as mistaken in both *L'être et le néant* and in his important 1948 article "Conscience de soi et connaissance de soi." Although no ego exists on the pre-reflective level, consciousness remains personal because consciousness is, at bottom, characterized by a fundamental self-givenness or self-referentiality that Sartre called *ipseity*:

> Thus, the ego appears to consciousness as a transcendent in-itself, as an existent in the human world, not as *of* the nature of consciousness. Yet we need not conclude that the for-itself is a pure and simple "impersonal" contemplation. The ego is far from being the personalizing pole of a consciousness which, without it, would remain in the impersonal stage; on the contrary, it is consciousness in its fundamental ipseity which, under certain conditions, allows the appearance of the ego as the transcendent phenomenon of that ipseity. (Sartre 1943, 142 [1956, 103; translation modified]. see also 1943, 162, 284; 1948, 63)

Sartre's crucial move was, consequently, to distinguish between ego and self. From the context, it is obvious that Sartre had nothing like narrative identity in mind when he spoke of *ipseity*. He was referring to something much more basic, something characterizing consciousness as such. It is something that distinguishes my very mode of existence, and, although I can fail to articulate it, it is not something I can fail to be. As he also wrote, "prereflective consciousness is self-consciousness. It is this same notion of *self* which must be studied, for it defines the very being of consciousness" (Sartre 1943, 114 [1956, 76]).

The most focused discussion of *ipseity*, however, is to be found in the work of Michel Henry. Henry repeatedly characterized selfhood in terms of an interior self-affection (Henry 1963, 581, 584, 585). Insofar as subjectivity reveals itself to itself, it is an *ipseity* (Henry 2003, 52). As he put in his early work, *Philosophie et phénoménologie du corps*: "The interiority of the immediate presence to itself constitutes the essence of ipseity" (Henry 1965, 53 [1975, 38]). For Henry, there was a clear connection between being a self and being self-aware. It is because consciousness is characterized, as such, by self-awareness that we can ascribe it a fundamental type of *ipseity*.

What we find in all three thinkers is, consequently, an attempt to link a basic sense of self to the first-personal givenness of experiential life. Let us take a closer look at the structure of first-personal givenness in order to better understand this line of thought.

What It Is Like

Whereas we cannot ask what it feels like to be a piece of soap or a radiator, we can ask what it is like to be a cat, a wolf, or another human being, because we take them to be conscious and to have experiences. Experiences are not something that one simply has, like coins in the pocket. On the contrary, experiences have a subjective "feel" to them, that is, a certain (phenomenal) quality of "what it is like" or what it "feels" like to have them. This is obviously true of bodily sensations like pain or nausea. It is also the case for perceptual experiences, as well as desires, feelings, and moods. There is something it is like to taste an omelet, touch an ice cube, crave chocolate, have stage fright, or to feel envious, nervous, depressed, or happy. Should one limit the phenomenal dimension of experience to *sensory* or *emotional* states alone? Is there nothing it is like to simply think of, rather than perceive, a green apple? What about abstract beliefs; is there nothing it is like to believe that the square root of nine equals three?

In *Logische Untersuchungen* (1900–1901), Husserl argued that conscious thoughts have experiential qualities and that episodes of conscious thoughts are experiential episodes. In arguing for this claim, Husserl drew some distinctions that remain relevant. According to Husserl, every intentional experience possesses two different but inseparable moments. Every intentional experience is an experience of a specific type, be it an experience of judging, hoping, desiring, regretting, remembering, affirming, doubting, wondering, fearing, and so on. Husserl called this aspect of the experience the *intentional quality* of the experience. Every intentional experience is directed at something, is also about something, be it an experience of a deer, a cat, or a mathematic state of affairs. Husserl called the component that specifies what the experience is about the *intentional matter* of the experience (Hua 19/425–426). The same quality can be combined with different matters, and the same matter can be combined with different qualities. It is possible to doubt that "the inflation will continue," that "the election was fair," or that "one's next book will be an international bestseller," just as it is possible to deny that "the lily is white," to judge that "the lily is white," or to question whether "the lily is white." Husserl's distinction between the intentional matter and the intentional quality, therefore, bears a certain resemblance to the contemporary distinction between propositional content and propositional attitudes, though it is important to emphasize that Husserl, by no means, took all intentional experiences to be propositional in nature.

Furthermore, and this is of course the central point, Husserl considered these cognitive differences to be *experiential* differences. Each of the different intentional qualities has its own phenomenal character. There is an *experiential* difference between affirming and denying that Hegel was the greatest of the German idealists, just as there is an *experiential* difference between expecting and doubting that Denmark will win the 2006 FIFA World Cup. What it is like to be in one of these occurent intentional states differs from what it is like to be in another of these occurrent intentional states.[2] Similarly, the various intentional matters each have their own phenomenal character. There is an *experiential* difference between entertaining the occurrent belief that "thoughts without content are empty" and the belief that "intuitions without concepts are blind," just as there is an *experiential* difference between denying that "the Eiffel Tower is higher than the Empire State Building" and denying that "North Korea has a viable economy." To put it differently, a change in the intentional matter entails a change in what it is like to undergo the experience in question.[3] These experiential differences, these differences in what it is like to think different thoughts, are not simply sensory differences.[4]

In the same work, Husserl also called attention to the fact that one and the same object can be given in a variety of modes. This is not only the case for spatiotemporal objects—the same tree can be given from this or that perspective, as perceived or recollected, and so on—but also for ideal or categorial objects. There is an experiential difference between thinking of the theorem of Pythagoras in an empty and signitive manner, without really understanding it, and doing so in an intuitive and fulfilled manner by actually thinking it through with comprehension (Hua 19/73, 667–676). In fact, as Husserl pointed out, our understanding of signs and verbal expressions can illustrate these differences most clearly:

Let us imagine that certain arabesques or figures have at first affected us merely aesthetically, and that we then suddenly realize that we are dealing with symbols or verbal signs. In what does this difference consist? Or let us take the case of a man attentively hearing some totally strange word as a sound-complex without even dreaming it is a word, and compare this with the case of the same man afterwards hearing the word, in the course of conversation, and now acquainted with its meaning, but not illustrating it intuitively. What in general is the surplus element distinguishing the understanding of a symbolically functioning expression from the uncomprehended verbal sound? What is the difference between simply looking at a concrete object A, and treating it as a representative of "any A whatsoever"? In this and countless similar cases it is the act-characters that differ. (Hua 19/398 [2001, II/105])

Strawson has argued more recently in a similar fashion. He asks us to consider a situation wherein Jacques, a monoglot Frenchman, and Jack, a monoglot Englishman, are both listening to the same French news program. The experiences of Jacques and Jack are certainly not the same, for only Jacques is able to understand what is being said. Only Jacques is in possession of what might be called an experience of understanding. To put it another way, there is normally something it is like, experientially, to understand a sentence. There is an experiential difference between hearing something that one does not understand, and hearing and understanding the very same sentence. This experiential difference is not a sensory difference, but a cognitive one (Strawson 1994, 5–6). This is why Strawson can write that

the apprehension and understanding of cognitive content, considered just as such and independently of any accompaniments in any of the sensory-modality-based modes of imagination or mental representation, is part of experience, part of the flesh or content of experience, and hence, trivially, part of the qualitative character of experience. (Strawson 1994, 12)

Every conscious state, be it a perception, an emotion, a recollection, or an abstract belief, has a certain subjective character, a certain phenomenal quality of "what it is like" to live through or undergo that state. This is what makes the mental state in question *conscious*. In fact, the reason we can distinguish occurrent conscious mental states from each other is exactly because there is something it is like to be in those states. The widespread view that only sensory and emotional states have phenomenal qualities must, therefore, be rejected. Such a view is not only simply wrong, phenomenologically speaking, but its attempt to reduce phenomenality to the "raw feel" of sensation marginalizes and trivializes phenomenal consciousness and is detrimental to a correct understanding of its cognitive significance.[5]

First-personal Givenness

When asked to exemplify the "what it is like" quality of experience, one will often find references to what have traditionally been called secondary sense qualities, such as the smell of coffee, the color of red silk, or the taste of a lemon. These answers reveal an ambiguity in the notion of "what it is like." Normally, the "what it is like" aspect is taken to designate experiential properties. If, however, our experiences are to have qualities of their own, they must be qualities over and above whatever qualities the intentional object has. It is exactly the silk that is red, and not my perception of it. Likewise, it is the lemon that is bitter, and not my experience of it. The *taste* of the lemon is a qualitative feature of the lemon and must be distinguished from whatever qualities my *tasting* of the lemon has. Even if there is no other way to gain access to the gustatory quality of the lemon than by tasting it, this will not turn the quality of the object into a quality of the experience. In this situation, however, a certain problem arises. There is definitely something it is like to taste coffee, just as there is an experiential difference between tasting wine and water. When one asks for this quality and for this qualitative difference, it seems hard to point to anything beside the taste of coffee, wine, or water, though this is not what we are looking for. Should we consequently conclude that there is, in fact, nothing in the tasting of the lemon apart from the taste of the lemon itself?

Recently a number of philosophers have defended what might be called an *intentionalistic* interpretation of phenomenal qualities. The point of departure has been the observation that it can often be quite difficult to distinguish a description of certain objects from a description of an experience of these very same objects. Back in 1903, G. E. Moore called attention to this fact and dubbed it the peculiar *diaphanous* quality of experience: When you try to focus your attention on the intrinsic features of experience, you always seem to end up attending to that *of* which it is an experience. As Tye argues, the lesson of this transparency is that *"phenomenology ain't in the head"* (Tye 1995, 151). To discover what it is like, you must look at what is being intentionally represented. Thus, as the argument goes, experiences do not have intrinsic and nonintentional qualities of their own; rather, the qualitative character of experience consists entirely, as Dretske writes, in the qualitative properties objects are experienced as having (Dretske 1995, 1). In other words, the phenomenal qualities are qualities of that which is represented. Differences in what it is like are, in fact, intentional differences. An experience of a red apple is subjectively distinct from an experience of a yellow sunflower in virtue of the fact that different kinds of objects are represented. Experiences acquire their phenomenal character simply by representing the outside world. Consequently, all phenomenal qualities are intentional.

Dretske's and Tye's intentionalistic interpretation of phenomenal qualities bears a certain resemblance to views found in phenomenology. Phenomenologists would not interpret phenomenal experience as some kind of internal movie screen that confronts us with mental representations. Rather, we are *"zunächst und zumeist"* directed at real, existing objects. The so-called qualitative character of experience, the taste of a lemon, the smell of coffee, the coldness of an ice cube—these are not at all qualities belonging to some spurious mental objects, but qualities of the presented objects. Instead of saying that we experience *representations*, it would be better to say that our experiences are *presentational*, that they *present* the world as having certain features (see also Sartre 1943, 26–28, 363).[6]

Both Tye and Dretske explicitly criticize the attempt to draw a sharp distinction between the intentional or (re)presentational aspects of our mental lives and their phenomenal, subjective, or felt aspects. They deny the existence of epiphenomenal qualia and relocate the phenomenal from the "inside" to the "outside." To repeat the earlier question, does this justify the claim that there is nothing in the tasting of the lemon apart from the taste of the lemon itself?

I think such a conclusion would be overhasty, since it fails to realize that there are two sides to the question of "what it is like." In *Ideen I*, Husserl distinguished between the intentional object in "the how of its determinations" (*im Wie seiner Bestimmtheiten*) and in "the how of its givenness" (*im Wie seiner Gegebenheitsweisen*) (Hua 3/303–304). Although this distinction is introduced as one that falls within the noematic domain, rather than a distinction between the noetic and the noematic domain, it nevertheless points us in the right direction. There is a difference between asking about the property the object is experienced as having (what does the object seem like to the perceiver) and asking about the property of the experience of the object (what does the perceiving feel like to the perceiver). Both questions pertain to the phenomenal dimension, but whereas the first question concerns a worldly property, the second concerns an experiential property.[7] Contrary to what both Dretske and Tye are claiming, we consequently need to distinguish between (1) what the object is like for the subject and (2) what the experience of the object is like for the subject (see also Carruthers 1998; McIntyre 1999). Insisting on this distinction, however, is not enough; the tricky part is then to respect the lesson of transparency and avoid misconstruing the experiential properties as if they belong to some kind of mental objects. It is not the case that worldly properties, such as blue or sweet, are matched one to one by experiential doublets of an ineffable nature, let us call them *blue or *sweet, or that both kinds of properties are present in ordinary perception. How, then, is the distinction to be phenomenologically redeemed?

We are never conscious of an object *simpliciter*, but always of the object as appearing in a certain way; as judged, seen, described, feared, remembered, smelled, anticipated, tasted, and so on. We cannot be conscious of an object (a tasted lemon, a smelt rose, a seen table, a touched piece of silk) unless we are aware of the experience through which this object is made to appear (the tasting, smelling, seeing, touching). This is not to say that our access to, say, the lemon is *indirect,* or that it is mediated, contaminated, or blocked by our awareness of the experience; the given experience is not itself an object on a par with the lemon, but instead constitutes the access to the appearing lemon. The object is given through the experience; if there is no awareness of the experience, the object does not appear at all. If we lose consciousness, we, or more precisely our bodies, will remain causally connected to a number of different objects, but none of these objects will appear to us. In short, the red cherry is present for me, through my seeing it. Experiences are not objects, but rather, they provide us with access to objects; I attend to the objects through the experiences. Experiential properties are not properties like red or bitter; they are properties pertaining to these various types of access. These accesses can take different forms; the same object, with the exact same worldly properties, can present itself in a variety of manners. It can be given as perceived, imagined, or recollected, and so on.

The moment we are dealing with manifestation or appearance we are faced with the phenomenal dimension. In fact, "what it is like" is exactly a question of how something appears to me, that is, it is a question of how it is given to and experienced by me. When I imagine a unicorn, desire an ice cream, anticipate a holiday, or reflect upon an economic crisis, all of these experiences bring me into the presence of different intentional objects. What this means is that not only am I phenomenally acquainted with a series of worldly properties such as blue, sweet, or heavy, but also the object is there *for me* in different modes of givenness (as imagined, perceived, recollected, anticipated, etc).

Whereas the object of John's perception, along with all its properties, is intersubjectively accessible in the sense that, in principle, it can be given to others in the same way that it is given to John, it is different with John's perceptual experience. Whereas John and Mary can both perceive the exact same cherry, each of them have his or her own distinct perception of it and can share these just as little as Mary can share John's bodily pain. Mary might certainly realize that John is in pain, she may even sympathize with John; but she cannot actually feel John's pain in the same way John does. It is here customary to speak of an epistemic asymmetry and say that Mary has no access to the *first-personal givenness* of John's experience.

This first-personal givenness of experiential phenomena is not something incidental to their being, a mere varnish that the experiences could lack without ceasing to be experiences. On the contrary, this first-personal givenness makes the experiences *subjective*. To put it another way, their first-personal givenness entails a built-in self-reference, a primitive experiential self-referentiality.

In contrast to the redness of the tomato or the bitterness of the tea, both of which are worldly properties, the first-personal givenness of the perception of the redness or bitterness is not a worldly property, but an experiential property. When asked to specify "what the experience of the object is like for the subject," this first-personal givenness is precisely one of the features to mention. In short, the experiential dimension does not have to do with the existence of ineffable qualia; it has to do with the dimension of first-personal experiencing.

To reiterate: the "what it is like" question has two sides to it: "what is the object like for the subject" and "what is the experience of the object like for the subject." Although these two sides can be distinguished conceptually, they cannot be separated. It is not as if the two sides or aspects of phenomenal experience can be detached and encountered in isolation from one another. When I touch the cold surface of a refrigerator, is the sensation of coldness that I then feel a property of the experienced object or a property of the experience of the object? The correct answer is that the sensory experience contains two dimensions, namely one of the *sensing* and one of the *sensed*, and that we can focus on either. Phenomenology pays attention to the givenness of the object, but it does not simply focus on the object exactly as it is given; it also focuses on the subjective side of consciousness, thereby illuminating our subjective accomplishments and the intentionality that is at play in order for the object to appear as it does. When we investigate appearing objects, we also disclose ourselves as datives of manifestation, as those to whom objects appear.

To put it differently, when speaking of a first-person perspective, or of a dimension of first-personal experiencing, it would be a mistake to argue that this is something that exclusively concerns the type of access a given subject has to his or her own experiences. Access to objects in the common world is independent of a first-person perspective, precisely in that it involves a third-person perspective. This line of thought will not do; obviously, I can be directed at intersubjectively accessible objects, and although my access to these objects is of the very same kind available to other persons, this does not imply that there is no first-person perspective involved. Rather, intersubjectively accessible objects are intersubjectively accessible precisely insofar as they can be accessed directly from each first-person perspective. They thereby differ from experiences, which are accessible in a unique way from the very same first-person perspective they, themselves, help constitute. Phrased another way, every givenness, be it the givenness of mental states or the givenness of physical objects, involves a first-person perspective. There is no pure third-person perspective, just as there is no view from nowhere. To believe in the existence of such a pure third-person perspective is to succumb to an objectivist illusion. This is, of course, not to say that there is no third-person perspective, but merely that such a perspective is exactly a perspective from somewhere. It is a view that *we* can adopt on the world. It is a perspective founded upon a first-person perspective, or to be more precise, it emerges out of the encounter between at least two first-person perspectives; that is, it involves intersubjectivity.[8]

Let me summarize the line of argumentation. The phenomenal dimension covers both the domains of (1) what the object is like for the subject, and (2) what the experience of the object is like for the subject. Both the worldly properties of the appearing object and the experiential properties of the modes of givenness are part of the phenomenal dimension. They are not to be separated, but neither are they to be confused.

Mineness and Selfhood

Although the various modes of givenness (perceptual, imaginative, recollective, etc.) differ in their experiential properties, they also share certain features. One common feature is the quality of *mineness*, that is, the fact that the experiences are characterized by a first-personal givenness that immediately reveals them as one's own. When I (in nonpathological standard cases) am aware of an occurrent pain, perception, or thought from the first-person perspective, the experience in question is given immediately, noninferentially and noncriterially as *mine*. If I feel hunger or see a sunrise, I cannot be in doubt or be mistaken about who the subject of that experience is, and it is nonsensical to ask whether I am sure that I am the one who feels the hunger. Whether a certain experience is experienced as mine or not, however, depends not on something apart from the experience, but precisely on the givenness of the experience. If the experience is given in a first-personal mode of presentation, it is experienced as *my* experience, otherwise not (see James 1890, I/226–227). Obviously, this form of egocentricity must be distinguished from any explicit I-consciousness. I am not (yet) confronted with a thematic or explicit awareness of the experience as being owned by or belonging to myself. The mineness is not something attended to; it simply figures as a subtle background presence. Nevertheless, the particular first-personal givenness of the experience makes it mine and distinguishes it for me from whatever experiences others might have (Klawonn 1991, 5, 141–142; Hua 8/175; Hua 13/28, 56, 307). As Husserl put it in a manuscript now published in *Zur Phänomenologie der Intersubjektivität II*:

What is most originally mine is my life, my "consciousness," my "I do and suffer," whose being consist in being originally pre-given to me qua functioning I, i.e., in the mode of originality, in being experientially and intuitively accessible as itself. (Hua 14/429)

It could be argued that it is misleading to suggest that experiences can be given in more than one way. Either an experience is given from a first-person perspective, or it is not given at all. However, I think this objection is mistaken. It is correct that experiences must always be given from a first-person perspective, for otherwise they would not be experiences; this does not, however, prevent them from being given from a second-person perspective as well. Let us assume that I get into a car accident, and that I am being scolded by the driver whose car I have just damaged. That the driver is angry is not something I establish by way of a hypothesis; it is something I experience. That I experience the anger of the driver does not imply that the experience is infallible (perhaps the driver is actually happy about the accident, since he can now finally get a new car, but he does not show his real feelings), nor does it imply that the driver's anger is given to me in the same way that it is given to the driver himself. The anger is exactly given from a second-person perspective for me. To deny the possibility of this is to face the threat of solipsism. (I will return to these issues in detail in chapters 6 and 7.)

Contrary to what some of the self-skeptics are claiming, one does not need to conceive of the self as something standing apart from or above experiences, nor does one need to conceive of the relation between self and experience as an external relation of ownership. It is also possible to identify this pre-reflective sense of *mineness* with a minimal, or core, sense of self. To again quote Henry, the most basic sense of self is the one constituted by the very self-givenness of experience (Henry 1963, 581; 1965, 53). In other words, the idea is to link an experiential sense of self to the particular first-personal givenness that characterizes our experiential life; it is this first-personal givenness that constitutes the *mineness* or *ipseity* of experience. Thus, the self is not something that stands opposed to the stream of consciousness, but is, rather, immersed in conscious life; it is an integral part of its structure.

One advantage of this view is that, incidentally, it makes it clear that self-awareness is not to be understood as an awareness of an isolated, worldless self, nor is the self located and hidden in the head. To be self-aware is not to interrupt the experiential interaction with the world in order to turn the gaze inward; on the contrary, self-awareness is always the self-awareness of a world-immersed self. The self is present to itself precisely and indeed only when worldly engaged. It would consequently be a decisive mistake to interpret the present notion of a core, or minimal, self as a Cartesian-style mental residuum, that is, as some kind of self-enclosed and self-sufficient interiority.[9] The phenomenological notion of an experiential self is fully compatible with a strong emphasis on the fundamental intentionality, or being-in-the-world, of subjectivity.[10] It is no coincidence that even Heidegger employed such a minimal notion of self (see chapter 4 above).

An effective way to capture this basic point is to replace the traditional phrase "subject of experience" with the phrase "subjectivity of experience." Whereas the first phrasing might suggest that the self is something that exists apart from, or above, the experience and, for that reason, is something that might be encountered in separation from the experience or even something the experience may occasionally lack, the second phrasing excludes these types of misunderstanding. It makes no sense to say that the subjectivity of the experience is something that can be detached or isolated from the experience, or to say that it is something the experience can lack. To stress the subjectivity of experience is not an empty gesture; it is to insist on the basic *ipseity* of the experiential phenomena.

In order to have a self-experience, it is, consequently, not necessary to apprehend a special self-object, it is not necessary to have a special experience of self alongside yet different from other experiences; rather what is required is simply an episode of pre-reflective self-awareness. What is needed is an acquaintance with the experience in its first-personal mode of presentation.[11] Thus, from Hume's famous passage in *A Treatise on Human Nature*, wherein he declared that he could not find a self when he investigated his own mental life, but only particular perceptions or feelings, it would be natural to conclude that he had overlooked something in his analysis, namely the specific givenness of his own experiences. He was looking for the self in the wrong place, so to speak. As Evans states, "from the fact that the self is not an object of experience it does not follow that it is non-experiential" (Evans 1970, 145).

One possible countermove would be to insist that first-personal access to individual mental states is not sufficient for self-experience. Self-experience involves some reference to self, but one can be aware of a mental happening from the first-person perspective and fail to realize that the happening occurs to oneself. As already mentioned, the non-egological theory would claim that our experiences are normally impersonal, in the sense that they do not include any reference, not even an implicit reference, to oneself as the subject of the experience. Thus, even if one has to concede that two persons who have two simultaneous and qualitatively identical experiences would still have two distinct experiences, the fact that they are distinct is not due to each of the experiences having a different *subject*. To quote Parfit, "one of these experiences is *this* experience, occurring in *this* particular mental life, and the other is *that* experience, occurring in *that* other particular mental life" (Parfit 1987, 517).

However, is it true that the primary difference between my perception and my friend's perception is that my perception is *this* one and his *that* one? Is this not, as Klawonn has argued, a parasitic and derived characterization? Is it not, rather, the case that an experience is *this* one exactly because it is *mine*, that is, given in a *first-personal mode of presentation*, whereas the other's experience is not given in a first-personal mode for *me*, and precisely therefore, is no part of *my* mental life (Klawonn 1991, 28–29)?

For the same reason, the validity of Sartre's revision of the cogito in *La transcendance de l'ego* must also be questioned. It does not seem adequate to render the cogito as "there is a perception of a chair," nor for that matter as "somebody perceives a chair" (Merleau-Ponty 1945, 249, 277), since both formulations overlook one significant detail. If the reader and I look at the same chair, these two perceptions of the chair might very well be impersonal or anonymous in the sense of lacking any *thematic* self-reference. In fact, on the pre-reflective level there is no explicit awareness of the experience being mine. The two perceptions, however, are definitely *not* anonymous in the sense of being undifferentiated and indistinguishable, regardless of whether this is taken to imply strict numerical identity or mere qualitative identity. On the contrary, the moment we take the first-person perspective seriously, it is obvious that there is a vital difference between the two perceptions; only one of them is given in a first-personal mode of presentation for me.

It might be objected that the current proposal makes the thesis concerning the experiential reality of the self acceptable but also quite trivial. However, as long as the thesis is routinely denied by advocates of the different impersonality theses, that is, by adherents to the no-ownership view or the non-egological account, it does not seem superfluous to make the point. Moreover, as both Wittgenstein and Heidegger remarked, one of the tasks of philosophy is exactly to call attention to and elucidate those fundamental aspects that are so familiar to us, so taken for granted, that we often fail to realize their true significance and even deny their existence.

Another countermove would be to follow Metzinger and argue that it is a phenomenological fallacy to conclude to the literal properties of the self from the content and structure of phenomenal self-experience. In his view, a phenomenological account of selfhood has no metaphysical impact. Our self-experience, our primitive, pre-reflective feeling of conscious selfhood, is never truthful in that it does not correspond to any single entity inside or outside of the self-representing system (Metzinger 2003a, 565). Why, however, should the reality of the self depend on whether it faithfully mirrors either subpersonal mechanisms or external (mind-independent) entities? If we were to wholeheartedly endorse such a restrictive metaphysical principle, we would declare illusory most of the world we live in and know and care about. Why not rather insist that the self is real if it has experiential reality and that the validity of our account of the self is to be measured by its ability to be faithful to experience, by its ability to capture and articulate (invariant) experiential structures?

As Strawson has recently argued, if we wish to answer the metaphysical question concerning whether or not the self is real, we will first need to know what a self is supposed to be. In order to establish this, our best chance will be to look at self-experience, since self-experience is what gives rise to the question in the first place by giving us a vivid sense that there is something like a self. Thus, as Strawson readily concedes, the metaphysical investigation of the self is subordinate to the phenomenological investigation. The latter places constrains on the former. Nothing can count as a self unless it possesses those properties attributed to the self by some genuine form of self-experience (Strawson 2000, 40).[12]

Although the minimal notion of self might seem overly inclusive, it does, in fact, exclude several nonexperiential candidates. Some have argued that no organism can survive or act without being able to distinguish between self and nonself (see Dennett 1991, 174, 414). According to this proposal, however, whether to ascribe selfhood to, say, bacteria would depend on whether bacteria can be said to possess phenomenal experiences. It would not be sufficient that the bacterium was able to nonconsciously differentiate itself from the environment.

Let me return to the three notions of self that I distinguished in the beginning of the chapter. How does the self as experiential dimension stand to the self as a pure identity-pole, and to the self as a narrative construction? As already mentioned, it can replace the first and supplement the second. If we start with the latter, that is, with the relation between the self as experiential dimension and the self as narrative construction, the case is relatively straightforward. The two notions of self are so different that they can easily complement each other. In fact, on closer consideration it should be clear that the notion of self introduced by the narrative model is not only far more complex than, but also phenomenologically and ontologically dependent, on the experiential self. Only a being with a first-person perspective could make sense of the ancient dictum "know thyself"; only a being with a first-person perspective could consider her own aims, ideals, and aspirations *as* her own and tell a story about them. To avoid unnecessary confusion, one might opt for a terminological differentiation. When dealing with the experiential self, one might retain the term "self," since we are dealing precisely with a primitive form of self-givenness or self-referentiality. By contrast, it may have been better to speak not of the self, but of the *person* as a narrative construction. After all, what is being addressed by this model is the nature of my personal character or personality, a personality that evolves through time and is shaped by the values I endorse and by my moral and intellectual convictions and decisions.

The fact that narrative personhood presupposes experiential selfhood (but not vice versa) does not diminish the significance of the former. Owing to the first-personal givenness of experience, our experiential life is inherently individuated. It is, however, a purely formal kind of individuation. In contrast, a more concrete kind of individuality manifests itself in my personal history, in my moral and intellectual convictions and decisions. It is through such acts that I define myself; they have a character-shaping effect. I remain the same as long as I adhere to my convictions; when they change, *I* change (Hart 1992, 52–54). Ideals can be identity defining; acting against one's ideals can mean the disintegration (in the sense of a dis-integrity) of one's wholeness as a person (see Moland 2004). These convictions and endorsed values are all intrinsically social; it is no coincidence that Husserl distinguished the subject taken in its bare formality from the personalized subject and claimed that the origin of personality must be located in the social dimension (see p. 95 above). I am not simply a pure and formal subject of experience, but also a person with abilities, dispositions, habits, interests, character traits, and convictions, and to focus exclusively on the first is to engage in an abstraction (Hua 9/210). Given the right conditions and circumstances, the self acquires a personalizing self-apprehension, that is, it develops both into a person and as a person. This development depends heavily on social interaction. To exist as a person is to exist socialized into a communal horizon, where one's bearing to oneself is appropriated from the others. To put it differently, the self is fully developed only when personalized intersubjectively; I become a person exclusively through my life with others in our communal world (Hua 4/265; 14/170–171).[13]

Usually, the self under consideration is already personalized or at least in the process of developing into a full-blown person. Although a narrow focus on the experiential core self might, therefore, be said to involve an abstraction, there is no reason to question its reality; it is not a *mere* abstraction. Not only does it play a foundational role, but, as we will shortly see, the notion of an experiential core self has also found resonance in empirical science. There are limit situations where this minimal self might, arguably, be encountered in its purity.

Whereas the relation between the self as experiential dimension and the person as narrative construction is relatively straightforward, the situation is slightly more complicated when it comes to the relation between the self as an experiential phenomenon and a pure identity-pole. One advantage of the view just outlined is that it may be capable of accounting for some of the features normally associated with the pure identity-pole model, particularly its ability to account for the identity of the self through time without actually having to posit the self as a separate entity over and above the stream of consciousness. Although the phenomenological account sketched above is intended mainly as an account of the conditions of selfhood (what properties must x have in order to count as a self), it could, ultimately, also have something to say concerning the conditions of persistency (the conditions required for x to remain the same from t_1 to t_2).

To show why this is so, let us briefly return to Husserl. As already mentioned, Husserl operated with a whole range of various notions of self. He not only spoke of it in terms of the first-personal givenness of an experience, he also introduced the notion of an act-transcendent ego. This was explained as the self considered as an identity-pole, a principle of focus, shared by all experiences belonging to the same stream of consciousness (Hua 13/248; 9/207; 4/277). What is new in this characterization is obviously the attempt to *differentiate* between the self and the experiences. Such a differentiation seems warranted the moment we pass beyond a narrow investigation of the self-givenness of a single experience and consider the case of a plurality of experiences. After all, not only is it possible to be aware of one's own toothache, it is also possible to be aware of oneself as the common subject of a manifold of simultaneous experiences. The same holds true wherein one can be self-aware across temporal distance and recall a past experience as one's own. In these latter cases, it is necessary to distinguish the self from any single experience, as the self can preserve its identity whereas experiences arise and perish in the stream of consciousness, replacing one another in a permanent flux (Hua 4/98; 17/363). Husserl then went on to emphasize, however, that although the ego must be distinguished from the experiences in which it lives and functions, it cannot exist in any way independently of them. It is a transcendence, but in Husserl's now famous phrase, it is *a transcendence in the immanence* (Hua 3/123–124, 179; 4/99–100; 13/246; 14/43).

If we relate the question concerning the act-transcendent self to the discussion of self-awareness, the obvious question to ask is: When does my self-awareness contain a reference to such an overarching identity? I think a plausible answer would be that the self-givenness of a single experience is a necessary, but not a sufficient, condition for this type of self-awareness to occur. The latter entails more than a simple and immediate self-awareness; it also entails a difference or distance that is bridged, that is, it involves a *synthesis*. This is so because the self cannot be given as an act-transcendent identity in a *single* experience (Kern 1989, 60–62; 1975, 66; Marbach 1974, 110, 112). It is only by comparing several experiences that we can encounter something that retains its identity through changing experiences (Hua 13/318; 4/208; 11/309–310).

What has all of this to do with the earlier discussion of the self as an experiential dimension? At first glance, the answer might be "nothing." After all, whereas the current point seems to be that one should distinguish self and experience, the earlier discussion attempted to abolish this difference. Such a response would be premature, however; as it was already pointed out in the discussion of Husserl's theory of inner time-consciousness from chapter 3, it is quite legitimate to insist on the *difference* between our singular and transitory experiences and the abiding dimension of first-personal experiencing (see Hua 23/326; 14/46). In other words, the moment we expand the focus to include more than a single experience, it becomes not only legitimate but also highly appropriate to distinguish the strict singularity of the field of first-personal givenness from the plurality of changing experiences. Although the act-transcendent identity of the self is revealed only in acts of synthesis, it does not arise out of the blue, but is grounded in the pervasive dimension of first-personal experiencing. Whereas we live through a number of different experiences, the dimension of first-personal experiencing remains the same. In short, although the self, as an experiential dimension, does not exist in separation from the experiences, and is identified by the very first-personal givenness of the experiences, it may still be described as the *invariant* dimension of first-personal givenness throughout the multitude of changing experiences.

The pertinence of this account for the problem concerning the diachronic persistency of the self should be obvious. To determine whether a past experience is mine, I do not first need to assure myself of the uninterrupted, temporal continuity between my present recollection and the past experience. If I have first-personal access to the past experience, it is automatically given as *my* past experience. There is more to episodic memory than the simple retrieval of information about the past. The subjective experience of remembering involves the conviction that the remembered episode was once experienced by me. Obviously, this is not to say that episodic memory is infallible (I might have false beliefs about myself), but only that it is not subject to the error of misidentification (see Campbell 1994, 98–99). To question the unity of mind by pointing to alleged interruptions in the stream of consciousness (dreamless sleep, coma, etc.) is consequently pointless, since one thereby makes the erroneous assumption that it is the *continuity* and *contiguity* between two experiences that makes them belong to the same self, rather than their shared mineness, or their shared manner of givenness.[14]

V Empirical Implications

The narrative concept of self has found resonance not only in different philosophical traditions (Ricoeur, MacIntyre, Dennett), but also in a variety of empirical disciplines, such as developmental psychology, neuroscience, and psychiatry (see Gallagher 2000a). The same holds true for the phenomenological concept of an experiential core self. In the following, I will briefly discuss some relevant psycho- and neuropathological findings.

The study of pathological phenomena might not only serve as a demonstration of the empirical relevance of the phenomenological analysis of self; on its own it might enrich our understanding of the nature of selfhood. Pathological cases can function as a heuristic device that shocks one into an awareness of what is normally taken for granted. They may be employed as a means of gaining distance from the familiar, in order better to explicate it. To put it another way, core features of subjectivity, including fundamental aspects of self-experience, can be sharply illuminated through a study of their pathological distortions. These distortions may reveal, through their very absence, aspects of normal existence that frequently remain unnoticed. In using pathology as a contrast, it will also become clear that normality cannot be taken for granted; it is, itself, an achievement.

The Case of Schizophrenia

In his *Allgemeine Psychopathology*, Jaspers famously wrote that schizophrenia is characterized by its un-understandability or incomprehensibility. What he meant by this was that schizophrenic symptoms are so strange and bizarre that they remain inaccessible to empathy and meaningful reconstruction. More specifically, Jaspers distinguished between *static un-understandability*, which refers to their inaccessibility to empathy, and *genetic un-understandability*, which refers to the impossibility of understanding the development or emergence of psychotic symptoms (Jaspers 1959, 24, 251, 483–486). By implication, there is not much to be won by paying close attention to the first-person accounts of schizophrenic patients. Their disturbed self-descriptions do not present us with a key to an understanding of schizophrenia; rather they must be seen as senseless ravings or morbid eruptions of a malfunctioning brain.

Jaspers's claims were based on a study of the chronic stages of schizophrenia. In recent years, however, Parnas and Sass have argued that a study of the advanced stages of the illness is of limited value if one wishes to understand the core features of the illness. This is so not only because of the apparent incomprehensibility of the symptoms, but also because the advanced stages confront one with the results of a long-standing interaction between multiple factors, such as the effects of medication, social isolation, and stress. This complexity inevitably makes it much harder to isolate the primary pathogenetic factors.

Parnas and Sass have suggested that it would make more sense to examine the highly informative antecedent stages of schizophrenia. One should study the early symptoms detectable in the first (initial) prodromal stage, that is, the stage immediately preceding and leading to the onset of a schizophrenic psychosis, as well as the abnormalities present in the even earlier so-called premorbid phase, since these symptoms might, in a much sharper manner, express the essential core of the illness. This change of focus may, incidentally, also be of direct benefit to the patient, since it allows for earlier detection and therapeutic intervention.

What will one find if one investigates these prepsychotic stages? According to Parnas and Sass, one will find a diverse assortment of self-disorders involving a variety of alterations and transformations to the very basic sense of self, including disturbances of the first-person perspective, the first-personal givenness of experience, and the dimension of mineness. Parnas and Sass argue that these self-disorders may even be ascribed a generating, pathogenic role. They antecede, underlie, and shape the emergence of later and psychotic pathology and may thus unify what, from a purely descriptive psychiatric standpoint, may seem to be unrelated or even antithetical syndromes and symptoms (Sass and Parnas 2003, 428). To put it differently, a focus on the psychopathology of chronic schizophrenia might present one with such a diversity of apparently unconnected symptoms that it thereby raises doubts about the unity of the diagnostic category. A focus on the earlier stages of the illness will reveal the sought-after unity. The heterogeneity of the symptoms, both negative and positive, encountered in advanced stages is merely ostensible; at its root, schizophrenia is a disorder of the self (Sass and Parnas 2003, 427–428). The concept of self in use, however, is not the narrative concept, but the phenomenological concept of *ipseity*, the concept of an experiential core self. This commitment to a phenomenological understanding of selfhood is articulated by Parnas and Sass themselves (see Sass 2000, 152; Parnas 2003, 219).

Although the most recent versions of the psychiatric diagnostic systems (DSM-IV and ICD-10) do not include a reference to the self, varieties of self-disorders have always figured, at least implicitly, as an important component in the clinical picture of schizophrenia. As early as 1913, the concept of *"Ichstörungen"* (self-disturbances) was introduced by Jaspers. One year later, Berze proposed that a basic transformation of self-consciousness was at the root of schizophrenia. As Parnas and Sass point out, however, the most detailed analysis of schizophrenic self-disorders is to be found in phenomenologically oriented psychiatry (Minkowski 1927; Conrad 1958; Laing 1960; Blankenburg 1971; Tatossian 1979). As Minkowski wrote:

The madness . . . does not originate in the disorders of judgment, perception or will, but in a disturbance of the innermost structure of the self. (Minkowski 1997, 114)

Patients will frequently complain about having lost something fundamental. The phrasing may range from "I don't feel myself," "I am not myself," "I have lost contact with myself," to "My I is disappearing for me" or "I am turning inhuman." The patients may sense an inner void, a lack of an undefinable "inner nucleus," a diminished sense of presence, or an increased distance from the world, and an incipient fragmentation of meaning. As described by an eighteen-year old patient:

I am more and more losing contact with my environment and with myself. Instead of taking an interest in what goes on and caring about what happens with my illness, I am all the time losing my emotional contact with everything including myself. What remains is only an abstract knowledge of what goes on around me and of the internal happenings in myself. (Quoted in Frith and Johnstone 2003, 2)

Parnas has argued that all these complaints point to a diminished *ipseity*, where the sense of self no longer automatically saturates the experience (Parnas 2003; Parnas, Bovet, and Zahavi 2002). We are faced with an experiential disturbance on a pre-reflective level that is far more basic than the kind of feelings of inferiority, insecurity, and unstable identity that we find in personality disorders outside the schizophrenic spectrum.

Some patients are able to articulate these subtle disturbances better than others. One of Parnas's patients reported that the feeling that his experiences were his own always came with a split-second delay; another that it was as if his self was somehow displaced a few centimeters back. A third explained that he felt an indescribable inner change that prevented him from leading a normal life. He was troubled by a very distressing feeling of not being really present or even fully alive. This experience of distance or detachment was accompanied by a tendency to observe or monitor his inner life. He summarized his affliction by saying that his first-personal life was lost and replaced by a third-person perspective (Parnas 2003, 223).

Contrary to a traditional view according to which phenomenology is a descriptive rather than an explanatory enterprise—its task is to describe and define experiential structures rather than to account for the causal mechanisms that bring them about—Sass and Parnas have also argued for the explanatory relevance of phenomenological psychiatry (Sass and Parnas 2006). Some grounds for this claim are as follows:

• First, phenomenological descriptions must act as constraining conditions for any neuroscientific explanation. That is, the neuroscientific explanation must be compatible with the facts about the subjective dimension. After all, the subjective dimension is precisely the explicandum that a satisfactory causal explanation is supposed to account for. The phenomenological investigation can be seen as an unfolding of the various facets of conscious life in order to gain a richer insight into its lived texture and internal structure. In this sense, a descriptive account remains indispensable for any causal account.

• Second, a phenomenological understanding of the fundamental structures of self-experience and self-disturbance may allow one to make sense of seemingly incomprehensible actions and beliefs. "One may, e.g., come to see how the person's actions or beliefs are in some respect *inspired* or *justified* by the kinds of experiences the person is having, or one may see these actions or beliefs in the light of general features of the person's experience of time, space, causality, or selfhood" (Sass and Parnas 2006, 65). To put it differently, and contrary to Jaspers's claim, many so-called bizarre delusions pathognomonic of schizophrenia, are, in fact, psychologically comprehensible. A phenomenological approach might allow one to understand these bizarre experiences as arising from, and in a sense, expressing aspects of the profoundly altered form of consciousness characterizing schizophrenia (Sass and Parnas 2006). Following is Sass and Parnas's attempt to account for the symptom of schizophrenic perplexity:

normal ipseity . . . provides a point of orientation: it is what grounds human motivation and organizes our experiential world in accordance with needs and wishes, thereby giving objects their "affordances," their significance for us as obstacles, tools, objects of desire, and the like. In the absence of this vital yet implicit self-affection, and the lines of orientation it establishes, the structured nature of the worlds of both thought and perception will be altered or even dissolved. For then there can no longer be any clear differentiation of means from goal; any reason for certain objects to show up in the focus of awareness while others recede; or any reason for attention to be directed outward toward the world rather than inward toward one's own body or processes of thinking. Without normal self-affection, the world will be stripped of all the affordances and vectors of concern by which the fabric of normal, common-sense reality is knitted together into an organized and meaningful whole. This, we believe, is the basis of the distinctively schizophrenic "perplexity" (Ratlosigkeit) described in classic German psychopathology. (Sass and Parnas 2006, 78–79)

• Finally, and related to the previous point, experiential disturbances should not be regarded as mere epiphenomena or something that can be discounted in the scientific search for the core of schizophrenia. Rather, the experiential disturbances found at the prodromal stage can even partially explain the subsequent progression of the disease. Once the field of experience is disturbed, quite possibly as a result of neurobiological abnormalities, new types of experience arise in reaction to the changes in question. In this sense, subjective experience can play an important causal role in the progressive experiential transformation that we encounter in the development of schizophrenia (Sass and Parnas 2006). As a case in point, one might mention the fact that many schizophrenic patients engage in compulsive self-monitoring. This is what Conrad called a convulsive reflection or a reflective spasm (*Reflexionskrampf*) and is an aspect of what Sass has more recently dubbed *hyperreflexivity*. According to Sass, this hyperreflexivity manifests itself in a variety of ways, depending on whether it occurs (1) as a facet of the basic defect itself, (2) as a consequence of the more basic disturbance, or (3) as defensive compensation for the more basic disturbance (Sass 2000, 153). At first, hyperreflexivity is not a volitional kind of self-consciousness; it occurs in a more or less automatic manner and has the effect of disrupting experiences and actions that would normally remain in the background of awareness. Thus, the normal stream of consciousness is interrupted by sensations, feelings, or thoughts that suddenly become the focus of attention with an objectlike quality (*basal hyperreflexivity*). These primary disruptions and disturbances then attract further attention and thereby elicit a process of self-scrutiny and self-objectification, or reflective turning-inward of the mind (*consequential hyperreflexivity*). Finally, such patients might voluntarily engage in reflective self-monitoring in an attempt to compensate for their diminished self-presence (*compensatory hyperreflexivity*):

I forgot myself at the Ice Carnival the other night. I was so absorbed in looking at it that I forgot what time it was and who and where I was. When I suddenly realized I hadn't been thinking about myself I was frightened to death. The unreality feeling came. I must never forget myself for a single minute. (Patient quoted in Laing 1960, 109)

Needless to say, rather than restoring what has been lost, such excessive self-monitoring may only exacerbate the problem by further objectifying, alienating, and dividing the experiential life (Sass 1994, 12, 38, 91, 95). A patient, studied and described in detail by Sass, offered the following insights:

> "My downfall was insight," he explained, ". . . too much insight can be very dangerous, because you can tear your mind apart." "Well, look at the word 'analysis,' " he said on another occasion. "That means to break apart. When it turns in upon itself, the mind would rip itself apart." Lawrence spoke of "doing six self-analyses simultaneously" and of how he needed to change his living environment often, because he knew that, once everything around him had been scrutinized, his mind would then turn inward and begin undoing itself, leading him eventually to the feeling of having no real mind at all: "Once I started destroying [my mind], I couldn't stop." (Sass 1992, 337–338)

Neurological Findings

Damasio argues in his recent book, *The Feeling of What Happens*, that a sense of self is an indispensable part of the conscious mind. As he writes: "If 'self-consciousness' is taken to mean 'consciousness with a sense of self,' then all human consciousness is necessarily covered by the term—there is just no other kind of consciousness as far as I can see" (Damasio 1999, 19). When I think thoughts, read a text, perceive a windowsill, a red book, or a steaming teacup, my mind is configured in such a manner that I automatically and relentlessly sense that I, rather than anyone else, am doing it. I sense that the objects I now perceive are being apprehended from my perspective and that the thoughts formed in my mind are mine and not anyone else's. Thus, as Damasio puts it, there is a constant but quiet and subtle presence of self in my conscious life, a presence that never falters as long as *I* am conscious. Were it absent, there would no longer be a self (Damasio 1999, 7, 10, 127).

Consciousness is not a monolith, however, and Damasio finds it reasonable to distinguish a simple, foundational kind, which he calls *core consciousness*, from a more complex kind, which he calls *extended consciousness*. Core consciousness has a single level of organization and remains stable across the lifetime of the organism. It is not exclusively human and does not depend on conventional memory, working memory, reasoning, or language. In contrast, extended consciousness has several levels of organization. It evolves across the lifetime of the organism and depends on both conventional and working memory. It can be found in a basic form in some nonhumans, but attains its highest peak only in language-using humans.

According to Damasio, these two kinds of consciousness correspond to two kinds of self. He calls the sense of self that emerges in core consciousness *core self* and refers to the more elaborate sense of self provided by extended consciousness as *autobiographical self* (Damasio 1999, 16–17, 127).[15]

The relation between core consciousness and extended consciousness and thus, between core and autobiographical self, is foundational. Extended consciousness is built on the foundation of core consciousness. It presupposes a core, which it then extends by linking it to both the lived past and the anticipated future. From a developmental perspective, there are little more than simple states of core self in the beginning, but as experience accrues, memory grows and the autobiographical self can be deployed (Damasio 1999, 175).

When we speak of a persisting personal identity, we are referring to the autobiographical self. This self is based on a repository of memories that can be reactivated and, thereby, provide continuity to our lives (Damasio 1999, 217). By contrast, Damasio takes the core self to be a transient and ephemeral entity. It is generated anew, in a pulsative fashion, for every set of contents of which we are to be conscious. It also possesses a remarkable degree of structural invariance, as it is remade time and again in essentially the same form across a lifetime. It is this invariance that allows it to provide stability to the mind (Damasio 1999, 17, 126, 135, 173–176).

As Damasio points out, neuroscience, particularly neuropathology, provides empirical evidence in support of his distinction. The investigation of neurological diseases permits us to tease apart the layers and functions of consciousness:

The results of neurological disease validate the distinction between core consciousness and extended consciousness. The foundational kind of consciousness, core consciousness, is disrupted in akinetic mutisms, absence seizures, and epileptic automatisms, persistent vegetative state, coma, deep sleep (dreamless), and deep anesthesia. In keeping with the foundational nature of core consciousness, when core consciousness fails, extended consciousness fails as well. On the other hand, when extended consciousness is disrupted, as exemplified by patients with profound disturbances of autobiographical memory, core consciousness remains intact. (Damasio 1999, 121–122).

This shows that neuropathology can reveal that impairments of extended consciousness allow core consciousness to remain intact, whereas impairments that begin at the level of core consciousness cause extended consciousness to collapse as well (Damasio 1999, 17). In illustration, Damasio presents data from a patient whose temporal lobes had both sustained major damage from a case of encephalitis. This patient's memory was limited to a window of less than one minute; he was unable to learn any new facts and unable to recall many old facts. In fact, the recall of virtually any unique thing, individual, or event from his entire life was denied to him. Whereas his autobiographical memory had been reduced to a skeleton, and the autobiographical self that could be constructed at any moment was severely impoverished, he retained a core consciousness for the events and objects in the here and now and, thereby, also a core self (Damasio 1999, 115–119).

The Use and Misuse of Pathology

One of the customary methods of testing the validity of philosophical analyses has been to look for invalidating counterexamples. If none can be found, so much the better for the proposed thesis. This search has often been carried out by means of imagination. We don't necessarily have to come across (f)actual counterexamples; it is sufficient if we can imagine them. Thus, *imaginability* has often been taken as a mark of *possibility*: If something is imaginable, then it is, if not practically or physically possible, at least possible in principle, that is, conceptually or metaphysically possible. If this is the case, then the exceptions are relevant and should be taken into account when assessing the validity of the philosophical claims.

Much contemporary philosophy, particularly analytical philosophy of mind, abounds with thought experiments meant to test and challenge our habitual assumptions about the nature of consciousness, the mind–body relation, personal identity, and so on. Thus, one often comes across references to zombies, brain transplants, Twin Earths, and teletransporters. This way of doing philosophy has, to put it mildly, not been met with universal approval.[16] One understandable reaction has been to ask whether it is legitimate to draw substantial philosophical conclusions from the mere fact that certain scenarios are imaginable. Is our imagination always trustworthy; does it always attest to metaphysical possibility, or might it occasionally reflect nothing but our own ignorance?

As Wilkes has pointed out, if thought experiments are to be of value, they must be performed with as much attention to detail and as many stringent constraints as real experiments conducted in the laboratory. One important requirement is that we are clear about the background conditions against which the experiment is set. In other words, we need to know exactly what is being altered and what remains the same when the imagined scenario is compared to the actual world. If there are too many variables, if too many parameters are changed, we would not know which of them were responsible for the outcome, and it would, consequently, be impossible to draw any clear conclusion from the experiment (Wilkes 1988, 2, 6). Another obvious prerequisite is that we actually know something about the topic under discussion. Otherwise, we might easily end up in a situation where we believe that we have succeeded in imagining a possible state of affairs, yet, in reality, we have done nothing of the sort, as we will realize when we acquire more information and are able to think the scenario through more carefully.

To illustrate the importance of these requirements: If we ask somebody whether he can imagine a candle burning in a vacuum, or a gold bar floating on water, and the answer is yes, should we then conclude that there must be some possible world where gold bars have a different molecular weight while remaining gold bars, and where candles can burn despite a lack of oxygen, or should we rather conclude that the person has succeeded only in imagining something that superficially resembles gold bars and burning candles? It certainly seems necessary to distinguish between imagining something in the sense of having a loose set of fantasies and imagining it in the sense of thinking it through carefully. Surely only the latter is of any value if we wish to establish whether a certain scenario is possible or not. The lesson to learn is, undoubtedly, that the more ignorant we are, the easier it will seem to imagine something since "the obstructive facts are not there to obtrude" (Wilkes 1988, 31). What seems to be an imaginable possibility might, on closer examination, turn out to be an impossibility in disguise. If we wish to derive any interesting conclusions from our thought experiments, we must assure ourselves that we are not faced with such impossibilities. As Dennett puts it, "When philosophical fantasies become too outlandish—involving time machines, say, or duplicate universes or infinitely powerful deceiving demons—we may wisely decline to conclude *anything* from them. Our conviction that we understand the issues involved may be unreliable, an illusion produced by the vividness of the fantasy" (Dennett 1981, 230).

This criticism should not be misunderstood. Thinking about exceptional cases "is indispensable if we wish to avoid mistaking accidental regularities for regularities which reflect a deeper truth about the world" (Gendler 1999, 463). Yet since so many details must be attended to if a thought experiment is to be truly conclusive, it might, occasionally, be better to abandon fiction altogether and instead pay more attention to the startling facts found in the actual world. Real-life deviations can serve the same function as thought experiments. If we are looking for phenomena that can shake our ingrained assumptions and force us to refine, revise, or even abandon our habitual way of thinking, all we have to do is to turn to psychopathology, along with neurology, developmental psychology, and ethnology; all of these disciplines present us with rich sources of challenging material. In other words, if we wish to test our assumptions about the unity of mind, the privacy of mental states, the nature of agency, or the role of emotions, far more may be learned from a close examination of pathological phenomena such as depersonalization, thought insertion, multiple personality disorder, cases of apraxia, or states of anhedonia than from thought experiments involving swapped brains or teletransporters. The former phenomena can also probe and test our concepts and intuitions and in a far more reliable way, since the background conditions are known to us. As they are real phenomena, they do not harbor any concealed impossibilities.

This said, a word of caution is appropriate. Pathological phenomena and other empirical findings are, of course, open to interpretation. Their interpretation usually depends on the framework within which one is operating. Thus, the theoretical impact of an empirical case is not necessarily something that is easily determined. One might agree with Metzinger that it is important not to underestimate the richness, complexity, and variety of conscious phenomena and that nonstandard cases of conscious self-experience can test the validity of a theory of self. He may, however, be overstating his point when he writes that "many classical theories of mind, from Descartes to Kant, will have to count as having been refuted, even after consideration of the very first example" of such pathological cases (Metzinger 2003a, 429). Contrary to what Metzinger suggests, it is rather doubtful that one will find many classical philosophers who subscribed to the thesis that unnoticed errors about the content of one's own mind are logically impossible (Metzinger 2003a, 429, 431). Even if they had, it is by no means clear what type of conclusions one should draw from pathological cases. Are these cases mere anomalies? Are they the exceptions that prove the rule? Should they, rather, force us to abandon our habitual classification of behavior and experience with the realization that the normality that has been our point of departure has no priority, but is merely one variation among many? Does pathology reveal some hidden fundamental feature of normal experience, or does it rather reflect or manifest an abnormal mode or a compensatory attempt to deal with dysfunction (see Marcel 2003, 56)? Whatever the precise answer to these questions turns out to be, it does seem problematic to simply draw unqualified conclusions about normal cases on the basis of pathology.

Metzinger spends considerable time discussing pathological cases, and although he repeatedly emphasizes how important it is to listen closely to the patients and take their phenomenology seriously (Metzinger 2003a, 446, 455), I also think he underestimates the difficulty of actually doing the latter. He frequently, and mistakenly, equates it with taking the patients' first-person assertions at face value. The danger of doing this comes to the fore in his analysis of both thought insertion and Cotard's syndrome.

According to Metzinger, the phenomenology of schizophrenia is so well known that it is superfluous to offer any explicit case study of it (Metzinger 2003a, 445). One prominent feature of schizophrenia is that it typically involves forms of alienated self-consciousness. In what is known as thought insertion, for example, the patient may have direct access to his or her own mental states but still experience them not only as being controlled or influenced by others, but as alien, as belonging to another. As one patient complained:

Thoughts are put into my mind like "Kill God." It is just like my mind working, but it isn't. They come from this chap, Chris. They are his thoughts. (Quoted in Frith 1992, 66)

Thus, as Metzinger puts it, schizophrenia confronts us with situations wherein patients experience introspectively alienated conscious thoughts for which they have no sense of agency or ownership. He takes this to demonstrate that the phenomenal quality of mineness is not a necessary precondition for conscious experience (Metzinger 2003a, 334, 382, 445–446).

As Metzinger himself observes, however, "phenomenal mineness is not an all-or-nothing phenomenon" (Metzinger 2003a, 443). It comes in degrees, and perhaps the situation is slightly less clear-cut than Metzinger seems to think. Gallagher has recently argued for a distinction between a *sense of ownership* and a *sense of agency*. Whereas the sense of agency refers to the sense of being the initiator or source of an action or thought, the sense of ownership refers to the sense that it is *my* body that is moving, that the experiences I am living through are given as mine. In normal voluntary action, the sense of agency and ownership coincide. When I reach for a cup, the movement is felt as mine, and I have a sense of initiating or generating the movement. In cases of involuntary action, the two can come apart. If I am pushed or if I am undergoing spasms, I will experience ownership of the movement(s)—I, rather than somebody else, am the one moving—but I will lack a sense of agency; I will lack an experience of being the agent or initiator of the movement (Gallagher 2000b, 204). The fact that ownership can persist without agency, but not vice versa, might suggest that the former is more fundamental than the latter.[17]

It may not be difficult to find first-person statements about thought insertions that, if taken in isolation and at face value, seem to offer ample evidence in support of the claim that some experiential states completely lack a quality of *mineness*. One should, however, not overlook that the subjects of thought insertions clearly recognize that they are the subjects in whom the alien episodes occur. They are not confused about where the alien thoughts occur; they occur in the patients' own minds. That is why they suffer from and complain about it (see Stephens and Graham 2000, 8, 126). To put it another way, there is nothing obviously wrong in thinking that foreign thoughts occur in other minds; it is only the belief that alien thoughts occur in one's *own* mind that is pathological and dreadful. Even if the inserted thoughts are felt as intrusive and strange, they cannot completely lack the quality of mineness and first-personal mode of givenness, since the afflicted subject is quite aware that it is he, himself, rather than somebody else, who is experiencing the alien thoughts. When schizophrenics assert that their thoughts are not their own, they do not mean that they themselves are not having the thoughts, but, rather, that someone else has inserted them and that they, themselves, are not responsible for generating them. Thus, rather than involving a lack of a sense of ownership, passivity phenomena like thought insertions involve a lack of a sense of authorship, or self-agency, and a misattribution of agency to someone or something else.[18]

Cotard's syndrome, an extreme kind of nihilistic delusion named for the French neurologist and psychiatrist Jules Cotard, comprises any one of a series of delusions ranging from the fixed and unshakable belief that one has lost money, organs, blood, or body parts to believing that one has died and is a walking corpse. In its most profound form, the delusion takes the form of a professed belief that one does not exist. Thus, patients suffering from Cotard's syndrome might deny their own existence, may explicitly state, not only that they are dead, but also that they do not exist.

According to Metzinger, patients suffering from Cotard's syndrome are *truthfully* denying their own existence (Metzinger 2003a, 455). This choice of term might be slightly surprising, since one may have thought that the appropriate term would have been "sincerely." Given Metzinger's own adherence to a no-self doctrine, perhaps he believes such patients are actually closer to the truth than nonpathological subjects. In any case, according to Metzinger, such delusional statements must be understood literally, and he, therefore, argues that they can function as knock-down arguments against any form of Cartesianism. But does nihilistic delusion really testify to the complete absence of pre-reflective self-intimacy (Metzinger 2003a, 459)? The patients might cease using the first-person pronoun, but does this imply that they lack first-personal access to their own experiences?

In his own description of the syndrome, Metzinger provides a further piece of information that should make us hesitate before accepting any literal interpretation. This is the fact that Cotard patients frequently express a coexisting belief in their own *immortality* (Metzinger 2003a, 456)! These patients will, moreover, typically engage in activities that are quite incongruent with the professed belief. In other words, they frequently demonstrate what is known in the psychiatric literature as "double bookkeeping." This feature is rather typical of schizophrenia, where patients with paranoid delusions or delusions of grandeur might express the belief that the nursing staff is poisoning their food or that they are the German emperor while unhesitatingly eating their lunch or cleaning the floors, respectively. The fact that the patients frequently fail to act on their delusions in the appropriate way questions any straightforward literal interpretation of the delusions and suggests that it might be wrong to interpret the delusions as if they were simply strongly held ordinary beliefs that happen to be false.

To reject a literal interpretation of delusional statements and argue that such a type of interpretation is unsatisfactory is not intended as an endorsement of the Jaspersian principle of un-understandability. Delusional statements are not meaningless, not simply empty speech acts, or, for that matter, merely extravagant metaphors used to describe otherwise normal situations. Rather, they are attempts to express highly unusual and frequently dreadful experiential situations that inevitably stretch ordinary language to its limit.

I do not, however, intend to offer an alternative positive account or interpretation of delusions since they are a highly complex topic in need of careful analysis.[19] The only point I wish to make is that pathological phenomena, like any other empirical phenomena, are open to interpretation and that their proper elucidation frequently requires long clinical experience with patients. To identify a phenomenological approach to psychopathology with a literal interpretation of first-person statements is much too facile and belittles the major contributions provided by phenomenological psychiatrists such as Minkowski, Binswanger, Tatossian, Tellenbach, and Blankenburg, among others.

VI   A Sense of Self

At the start of this chapter, I posed the question of whether there is an intimate link between self and self-awareness. Does self-awareness involve a reference to a self, or is it possible to speak of self-awareness without assuming the existence of anybody being self-aware? In short, is *self*-awareness to be understood as an awareness of *a self*, or, rather, as the awareness that a specific experience has of *itself*? This phrasing of the question has turned out to be misleading. First, it presents us with a false alternative. Self-awareness is not *either* an awareness of a self *or* the awareness that an experience has of itself. On the contrary, it must be realized that there are different kinds of self-awareness. I can be pre-reflectively aware of my current psychological states, be they perceptions, memories, desires, or bodily sensations, and I can reflect on and, thereby, thematize these individual states. However, I can also reflect on myself as the subject of experience, that is, I can reflect on myself as the one who thinks, deliberates, resolves, acts, and suffers. If I compare that which is given in two different acts of reflection, say, a perception of birds and a recollection of a walk, I can focus on that which has changed, namely the intentional acts, but also on that which remains identical, the subject(ivity) of experience. Second, the formulation suggests that if self-awareness were merely a matter of the awareness that an experience had of itself, we would be dealing with a non-egological or subjectless type of self-awareness. As I hope to have made clear this suggestion is mistaken since it overlooks the *ipseity* of the experiential dimension. Ultimately, this is why Gurwitsch's distinction between an egological and a non-egological theory turns out to be too crude a distinction.

Thus, my conclusion is that there is a minimal sense of self present whenever there is self-awareness. Self-awareness is there not only when I realize that *I* am perceiving a candle, but whenever I am acquainted with an experience in its first-personal mode of givenness, that is, whenever there is something it is like for me to have the experience. In other words, pre-reflective self-awareness and a minimal sense of self are integral parts of our experiential life.[20]

One of the standard objections to phenomenology has been its alleged failure to tackle the problem of intersubjectivity. This failure could be by way of omission, by simply failing to recognize the philosophical significance of intersubjectivity, or by way of an inborn shortcoming, by being fundamentally incapable of addressing this issue in a satisfactory manner. A classical argument has been that the task of phenomenology is to investigate the conditions of possibility for manifestation; if this proceeds by means of a narrow focus on the relation between the constituting subject and that which is given for it, that is, the constituted phenomenon, then: phenomenology will always be prevented from giving an adequate analysis of the other. To speak of a foreign subject, of an other, is to speak of something that, for essential reasons, will always transcend its givenness for me. Qua foreign subject, it will be in possession of a self-givenness that, in principle, is inaccessible to me. For this reason, phenomenology will be unable to account for it and must, therefore, remain solipsistic, in its foundation as well as in its results.

This criticism is related to what has often been regarded as one of the decisive paradigm shifts in twentieth-century philosophy: the turn from a philosophy of subjectivity to a philosophy of language. It has been argued that language is at the root of intersubjectivity and that only a philosophy of language can accommodate intersubjectivity in an adequate way. This stance is exemplified in the work of Habermas, who takes phenomenology to be burdened with a number of insurmountable aporias, precisely because it remains blind to *linguistic intersubjectivity*. Habermas even argues that a look at the phenomenological theory of intersubjectivity will illustrate why we need to take language, rather than subjectivity, as our starting point. In contrast to a theory of communication, which assumes an intersubjectivity already provided by language, the difficulty with phenomenology is that it attempts to derive intersubjective relationships from a monological point of departure. Insofar as a phenomenological account will always proceed from the I, there will always remain a persisting asymmetry between the subject and the other. As long as this is the case, that is, as long as the account cannot ensure full reciprocity between the subjects involved, it is doomed to failure (Habermas 1981, 197; 1984, 58; 1988, 16, 88).

In retrospect, a good part of this criticism seems somewhat off the mark. Not only has the linguistic turn, in more recent years, been replaced by a return to consciousness, but more important, no one truly familiar with the phenomenological tradition can endorse the claim that phenomenology should have failed to recognize the philosophical significance of inter-subjectivity. Intersubjectivity, be it in the form of a concrete self–other relation, a socially structured life-world, or a transcendental principle of justification, is ascribed an absolutely central role by phenomenologists. It is, in fact, difficult to point to a philosophical tradition that has been more concerned with doing justice to the different aspects of intersubjectivity than phenomenology.

In the following, I will present some facets of this rich discussion that, at the same time, will allow for a more nuanced perspective of the relation between selfhood and otherness. I will also introduce some new issues related to the question of embodiment, which will be crucial for the discussion in the final chapter of the book.

I Expression and Empathy

In some traditions, the problem of intersubjectivity has been identified with the problem of other minds. The only mind I have direct access to is my own. My access to the mind of another is always mediated by his bodily behavior. How, though, can the perception of another person's body provide me with information about his mind? One of the classical attempts to come to grips with this problem is known as the *argument from analogy*. In my own case, I can observe that I have experiences when my body is causally influenced and that these experiences frequently bring about certain actions. I observe that other bodies are influenced and act in similar manners, and I, therefore, infer by analogy that the behavior of foreign bodies are associated with experiences similar to those I have myself. In my own case, being scalded by hot water is associated with the feeling of intense pain, and this experience then gives rise to the quite distinct behavior of screaming. When I observe other bodies being scalded by hot water and screaming, I can assume that it is likely that they are also feeling pain. Thus, the argument from analogy can be interpreted as an inference to best explanation bringing us from observed public behavior to a hidden mental cause. Although this inference does not provide me with indubitable knowledge about others and does not allow me to actually experience other minds, at least it gives me more reason to believe in their existence than to deny it.

This way of accounting for our experience of others has not exactly been met with much enthusiasm by phenomenologists. They have all criticized it. The criticism has been massive and multifaceted, and in Max Scheler's work *Wesen und Formen der Sympathie* (originally published in 1912) we find a whole list of objections (Scheler 1973, 232–234):

- To assume that our belief in the existence of other minds is inferential in nature is to opt for a far too intellectualistic account. After all, both animals and infants seem to share this belief, but in their case, it can hardly be the result of a process of conscious inference.
- For the argument to work, there has to be a similarity between the way in which my own body is given to me, and the way in which the body of the other is given to me. However, my own body as it is proprioceptively felt by me does not resemble the other's body as it is perceived visually by me. If I am to see the similarity between, say, my laughing or screaming and the laughing or screaming of somebody else, I need to understand the bodily gestures as expressive phenomena, as manifestations of joy or pain, and not simply as physical movements. If such an understanding is required for the argument from analogy to proceed, however, the argument presupposes that which it is supposed to establish. In other words, we employ analogical lines of reasoning only when we are already convinced that we are facing minded creatures but are simply unsure about precisely how we are to interpret the expressive phenomena in question (see also Gurwitsch 1979, 14, 18).
- How can the argument from analogy explain that we can empathize with creatures whose bodies in no way resemble our own, for example, a suffering bird or fish?
- Even if these problems could be overcome, the argument from analogy would still be formally invalid. In noticing the connection between my own mind and my bodily behavior, and in observing the analogy between my own bodily behavior and the behavior of a foreign body, all that I am entitled to

infer is that the foreign body is probably also linked with *my own* mind (see also Wittgenstein 1953, §302).[1]

Scheler also questioned two crucial presuppositions in the argument from analogy. First, the argument assumes that my starting point is my own consciousness. This is what is given to me in a quite direct and unmediated fashion, and it is this purely mental self-experience that is then taken to proceed and make possible the recognition of others. One is at home in oneself and one must then project onto the other, whom one does not know, what one already finds in oneself. Incidentally, this implies that one is able to understand only those psychological states in others that one has already experienced in oneself. Second, the argument assumes that we never have direct access to another person's mind. We can never *experience* her thoughts or feelings; we can only infer that they must exist based on what is actually presented to us, namely her bodily behavior. Although these two assumptions may seem perfectly obvious, Scheler rejected them both. As he put it, the argument from analogy underestimates the difficulties involved in self-experience and overestimates the difficulties involved in the experience of others (Scheler 1973, 244–246). We should not ignore what can be directly perceived about others, nor should we fail to acknowledge the embodied and embedded character of self-experience. Scheler consequently denied that our initial self-acquaintance is of a purely mental nature that takes place in isolation from others. He also denied that our basic acquaintance with others is inferential in nature. As he argued, there is something highly problematic about claiming that intersubjective understanding is a two-stage process of which the first stage is the perception of meaningless behavior and the second an intellectually based attribution of psychological meaning. On the contrary, in a face-to-face encounter, we are not confronted with a mere body, or with a hidden psyche, but with a unified whole. It is in this context that Scheler used the term "expressive unity" (*Ausdruckseinheit*). It is only subsequently, through a process of abstraction, that this unity can be divided and our interest then proceed "inward" or "outward" (Scheler 1973, 255).

Scheler opposed the view in which our encounter with others is, first and foremost, an encounter with bodily and behavioral exteriorities devoid of any psychological properties. According to such a view, defended by behaviorists and Cartesians alike, behavior, considered in itself, is neither expressive nor significant. All that is *given* are physical qualities and their changes. Seeing a radiant expression means seeing certain characteristic distortions of the facial muscles. Naturally, such a setup gives rise to the following skeptical question: How can we pass from a perception of the other as a "bag of skin moving over ground" (Gopnik and Meltzoff 1994, 166) to a full-blown experience of the other as a minded creature?

For Scheler, this view of behavior presents us with a distorted picture not only of behavior, but also of the mind. Affective and emotional states are not simply qualities of subjective experience; rather, they are given *in* expressive phenomena, that is, they are expressed in bodily gestures and actions, and they thereby become visible to others. This idea is also to be found in the works of other authors. To quote Merleau-Ponty and Wittgenstein:

We must reject the prejudice which makes "inner realities" out of love, hate or anger, leaving them accessible to one single witness: the person who feels them. Anger, shame, hate and love are not psychic facts hidden at the bottom of another's consciousness: they are types of behavior or styles of conduct which are visible from the outside. They exist *on* this face or *in* those gestures, not hidden behind them. (Merleau-Ponty 1996, 67 [1964, 52–53])

We do not see facial contortions and *make the inference* that he is feeling joy, grief, boredom. We describe a face immediately as sad, radiant, bored, even when we are unable to give any other description of the features. (Wittgenstein 1980, §570)

In general I do not surmise fear in him—I *see* it. I do not feel that I am deducing the probable existence of something inside from something outside; rather it is as if the human face were in a way translucent and that I were seeing it not in reflected light but rather in its own. (Wittgenstein 1980, §170)

Wittgenstein's response to the skeptic did not consist of postulating a noncontingent relation between what the skeptic takes to be given in our experience of others and our psychological judgments about it. He was not out to argue that the inferential move from overt behavior to covert inner states is, in fact, justified; rather, Wittgenstein was out to reject the skeptic's conception of what is given and make us recognize the proper nature of our experience of others. In Wittgenstein's view, the skeptics have replaced the human being with a philosophically generated concept of a human body, understood as a merely material object. Rather than attempting to solve the skeptical problem by somehow adding psychological meaning onto this impoverished object, we should simply restore the concept of a human being to its proper place as a seamless whole, of whose unity we should not have originally lost sight (McDowell 1998, 384). The phenomenologists would concur with this approach. Instead of attempting to secure an access to the minded life of others through technical detours, they argue what is required is a new understanding of the given (Gurwitsch 1979, 29–30). If the realm of expressive phenomena is accepted as the primary datum or primitive stratum of perception, access to the minds of others will no longer present the same kind of problem. As Scheler wrote,

> For we certainly believe ourselves to be directly acquainted with another person's joy in his laughter, with his sorrow and pain in his tears, with his shame in his blushing, with his entreaty in his outstretched hands, with his love in his look of affection, with his rage in the gnashing of his teeth, with his threats in the clenching of his fist, and with the tenor of his thoughts in the sound of his words. If anyone tells me that this is not "perception," for it cannot be so, in view of the fact that a perception is simply a "complex of physical sensations," and that there is certainly no sensation of another person's mind nor any stimulus from such a source, I would beg him to turn aside from such questionable theories and address himself to the phenomenological facts. (Scheler 1973, 254 [1954, 260]; cf. Gurwitsch 1979, 56)

In short, the basic idea is that we should avoid construing the mind as something visible to only one person and invisible to everyone else. The mind is not something exclusively inner, something cut off from the body and the surrounding world, as if psychological phenomena would remain precisely the same even without bodily and linguistic expressions. As Overgaard has recently formulated it, psychological phenomena stretch their arms in many directions, that is, they play many publicly observable roles, and to cut off all of these public arms would leave us with a severely distorted picture of the mind (Overgaard 2005).

It should be clear that the view proposed here is not behaviorism. The view does not identify or reduce mental states to behavior, nor does it rule out that some experiential states are covert. However, not all experiences can lack a natural expression if intersubjectivity is to get off the ground. There is more to the mind than its behavioral manifestation, but we should recognize that behavior is already soaked with the meaning of the mind and that the expressive relation holding between "inner" mental states and "external" bodily behavior is stronger than that of a mere contingent causal connection (see Rudd 2003). One can occur without the other, which is why playacting or stoic suppression is possible, but this is not the norm. Our understanding of affective and emotional states, such as sorrow, shame, love, hate, disgust, and fear, is deeply informed and influenced by their behavioral manifestations. Moreover, expressions are not merely exterior manifestations of something that was already internally present. Rather, what is expressed is fully realized only in the expression. As Cassirer formulated it in his *Philosophie der symbolischen Formen*, "Life cannot apprehend itself by *remaining* absolutely within itself. It must give itself form; for it is precisely by this 'otherness' of form that it gains its 'visibility,' if not its reality" (Cassirer 1954, 46 [1957, 39]; see also Cassirer 1954, 43–47). When consciousness expresses itself in behavior or language, when it externalizes itself in words and deeds, we are faced with an articulation, with a "*sich-selbst-finden*," or "*sich-selbst-bestimmen*."

Pathology might provide some empirical support of this idea. Reporting on persons born with Möbius syndrome, a lifetime facial paralysis that prevents those afflicted from making any facial expressions, Cole has recently suggested that the loss of facial animation might lead to a reduced intensity of feeling within oneself, as if the displaying of the emotion on the face enables its full feeling within. This could be the result of a lack of internal feedback from skin and muscle movements in the face that might make the emotion more clearly defined. Another option is that it is a result of lack of feedback from others, a social feedback that can be highly significant for what we feel: as Merleau-Ponty wrote, "I live in the facial expressions of the other, as I feel him living in mine" (Merleau-Ponty 1960b, 69 [1964, 146]). The specific cause can be difficult to resolve, but it is likely that both types of feedback contribute to the formation of our moods and emotions (Cole 1998).

Expressive and meaningful behavior is a visible manifestation of the life of the mind. It differs, however, from the direct manifestation available from the first-person perspective. We should respect and maintain the asymmetry between first-person and second- (and third-) person access to psychological states, but this is not a difference between an immediate certainty on one side, and an insecure inference on the other. As Wittgenstein wrote, "My thoughts are not hidden from [the other], but are just open to him in a different *way* than they are to me" (Wittgenstein 1992, 34–35). Nor should we make the mistake of confusing different kinds of access with different degrees of certainty; as Wittgenstein also pointed out, even if I had no uncertainty with regard to the mental state of an other (say, in the case where I observe the victim of a car accident writhing in pain), that would not make it *my* state (Wittgenstein 1982, §963). We should recognize that each type of access has its own strengths and weaknesses. The second- (or third-) person access "falls short" of the first-person access only if it is assumed that the latter is privileged and that it is the internal aspiration of the former to approximate the latter as closely as possible (Moran 2001, 157).

Phenomenologists would argue that we should reject the view according to which behavior, considered as such, is neither expressive nor significant. Such a view does not merely fail to recognize the true nature of behavior, it also presents us with a misleading perspective on the mind, suggesting as it does that the mind is a purely internal happening located and hidden in the head and thereby giving rise to the skeptical conundrum (see McDowell 1998, 393).

One reason the problem of other minds seems so persistent is that we have conflicting intuitions about the accessibility of the mental life of others. On the one hand, there is something right about the claim that the feelings and thoughts of others are manifest in their expressions and actions. In many situations, we do have a direct, pragmatic understanding of the minds of others. We see the anger of the other, we empathize with his sorrow, we comprehend his linguistically articulated beliefs; we do not have to *infer* their existence. On the other hand, there also seems to be something right in the Cartesian idea that the mental life of another is, in some respect, inaccessible. There are situations wherein we have no reason to doubt that the other is angry, in pain, or just plain bored. But there are also situations where we have no clue as to their precise state of mind. It seems wrong to claim that the mental life of others is essentially inaccessible, but it also seems wrong to claim that everything is open to view. The challenge is to reconcile both intuitions, rather than letting one of them go (Overgaard 2005, 250).

Most phenomenologists have argued that it makes no sense to speak of an other unless the other is in some way given and accessible. That I have an actual experience of the other and do not have to do with a mere inference does not imply, however, that I can experience the other in the same way as she herself does; nor does it imply that the other's consciousness is accessible to me in the same way as is my own. Second- (and third-) person access to psychological states differs from first-person access, but this difference is not an imperfection or a shortcoming; rather, it is constitutional. It makes the experience in question an experience of an other, rather than a self-experience. As Husserl wrote: Had I had the same access to the consciousness of the other as I have to my own, the other would cease being an other and instead become a part of myself (Hua 1/139). To put it differently, the first-personal givenness of the mind of the other is inaccessible to me, but it is exactly this inaccessibility, this limit, which I can experience, and which makes the experience in question, an experience of an other (Hua 1/144). We experience the behavior of others as expressive of mental states that transcend the behavior that expresses them. Thus, the givenness of the other is of a most peculiar kind. The otherness of the other is exactly *manifest* in his elusiveness and inaccessibility. As Lévinas observed, the absence of the other is exactly his presence as other (Lévinas 1979, 89). To demand more, to claim that I would have a real experience of the other only if I experienced her feelings or thoughts in the same way as she herself does, is nonsensical. It would imply that I would experience an other only if I experienced her in the same way that I experience myself, that is, it would lead to an abolition of the difference between self and other, a negation of the *alterity* of the other, of that which makes the other other.

What must be realized is that bodies of others differ radically from inanimate objects, and that our perception of these minded bodies is unlike our ordinary perception of objects. As Sartre pointed out, it would be a decisive mistake to think that my ordinary encounter with the body of another is an encounter with the kind of body described by physiology. The body of another is always given to me in a situation or meaningful context that is supported by that very body (Sartre 1943, 395). The relation between self and other is not established by way of an inference to best explanation; on the contrary, we should recognize the existence of a distinctive mode of consciousness, often called *empathy* or "*Fremderfahrung*," that allows us to experience behavior as expressive of mind. This is what allows us to access the feelings, desires, and beliefs of others in their expressive behavior.

Our experience and understanding of others is fallible. This should not cause us to conclude that we cannot understand others and that empathy is to be distrusted. Other people can fake or conceal their experiences. There is, however, a genuine difference between our everyday uncertainty about exactly what others might be thinking about and the nightmare vision of the solipsist. Although we may be uncertain about the specific beliefs or intentions of others, this uncertainty does not make us question their very existence. In fact, as Merleau-Ponty pointed out, our relation to others is deeper than any specific uncertainty we might have regarding them (Merleau-Ponty 1945, 415).

The description and analysis of empathy has often been taken to be a distinctive feature of phenomenology. To be more specific, empathy has typically been taken to constitute a unique and irreducible form of intentionality, and one of the classical tasks of phenomenological analysis has been to clarify its precise structure and spell out the difference between it and other forms of intentionality, such as perception, imagination, and recollection. In fact, the *empathic approach* has occasionally been assumed to constitute *the* phenomenological approach to intersubjectivity. In the following, however, I will contest this claim. Some of the most interesting and far-reaching phenomenological analyses of intersubjectivity are characterized precisely by going *beyond empathy*—not in the sense that they deny the existence of empathy or the validity of the criticism of the argument from analogy, but because empathy understood as a *thematic encounter with a concrete other* is taken to be a derived rather than a fundamental form of intersubjectivity. Empathy is taken to disclose rather than to establish intersubjectivity. I will also argue that there are aspects of intersubjectivity that simply cannot be addressed as long as one remains narrowly focused on empathy.

II Embodied Subjectivity and Internal Otherness

Although the investigation of empathy is a step forward compared to the argument from analogy, the investigation of intersubjectivity cannot end there. We cannot take our ability to experience others as simply a primitive and unanalyzable fact, as Husserl accused Scheler of doing (Hua 14/335). On the contrary, the emergence and specific presuppositions of an encounter with an other require clarification. We must investigate such an encounter's conditions of possibility, particularly those that concern the nature of the experiencing subject. One argument developed by both Husserl and Merleau-Ponty is that my encounter with the other, my ability to interact with and recognize another embodied subject as a foreign subjectivity, is preempted by and made possible through the very structure of my own *embodied* subjectivity.

How and why should our subjective embodiment prepare the way for an encounter with the other? If we begin with Husserl, one of the issues explicitly emphasized in his phenomenological analysis of the body is its peculiar two-sidedness. My body is given to me as an interiority, a volitional structure, and as a dimension of sensing, but it is also given as a visually and tactually appearing exteriority. What is the relation between that which Husserl called the "*Innen-*" and the "*Aussenleiblichkeit*," that is, what is the relation between the lived bodily inwardness on the one side, and the externality of the body on the other (Hua 14/337)? In both cases, I am confronted with my own body, but why is the visually and tactually appearing body at all experienced as the exteriority of *my* body? When I touch my own hand, the touched hand is not given as a mere object, since it feels the touch itself. Had the touched hand lacked this experience, it would no longer be felt as *my* hand. Anybody who has fallen asleep with his arm as a pillow will know how strange it is to wake up with an insensible arm. When it is touched, it does not respond in the appropriate way and feels, most of all, like the arm of another. The decisive difference between touching one's own body and anything else, be it an inanimate object or the body of another, is precisely that it implies a *double-sensation*. It presents us with an ambiguous setting in which the hand alternates between two roles, that of touching and that of being touched. It provides us with an experience of the dual nature of the body, since it is the very same hand that can appear in two different fashions, as touched and touching. The relation is reversible, since the touching is touched, and the touched is touching, and according to Husserl, this reversibility shows the interiority and the exteriority of the body to be different manifestations of the same (Hua 13/263; 14/75). To put it differently, my bodily self-exploration permits me to confront *my own* exteriority and, according to Husserl, this experience is crucial for empathy (Hua 15/652). One reason I am able to recognize other embodied subjects is that my own bodily self-experience is characterized by this remarkable interplay between *ipseity* and *alterity* (Hua 8/62; 14/457; 13/263). When my left hand touches my right, or when I perceive another part of my body, I am experiencing myself in a manner that anticipates both the way in which an other would experience me and the way in which I would experience an other. This might be what Husserl was referring to when he wrote that the possibility of sociality presupposes a certain intersubjectivity of the body (Hua 4/297).

The contrast to Sartre is striking. Sartre explicitly denied that my body-awareness from the very start contains a dimension of exteriority. In his view, it is the other who teaches me to adopt an alienating attitude toward my own body. Thus, Sartre claimed that the appearance of one's own body as an object is a relatively late occurrence. It presupposes a pre-reflective acquaintance with one's lived body (for more on this notion, see pp. 205–206 below), a consciousness of the world, and most significantly a perception of the body of the other. The infant has used her body to explore the world and examine others before she starts looking at her own body and discovers its exteriority (Sartre 1943, 385–386, 408–409).

For the same reason, Sartre attempted to belittle the significance of the touching–touched reversibility. As he wrote, it is a matter of empirical contingency that I can perceive and touch myself and thereby adopt the other's point of view on my own body, that is, make my own body appear to me as the body of an other. It is an anatomical peculiarity, and neither something that can be deduced from the fact that consciousness is necessarily embodied nor something that can serve as the basis for a general theory of the body (Sartre 1943, 351, 408). The body's being-for-itself and the body's being-for-others are two radically distinct ontological dimensions of the body:

> To touch and to be touched, to feel that one is touching and to feel that one is touched—these are two species of phenomena which it is useless to try to reunite by the term "double sensation." In fact they are radically distinct, and they exist on two incommunicable levels. (Sartre 1943, 351 [1956, 304])

This claim must be questioned, however, since it replaces an unbridgeable dualism between mind and body with an equally unbridgeable dualism between the lived body and the perceived body. Rather than dealing with different dimensions or manifestations of the *same* body, we seem to be left with distinct bodies. This conclusion is unacceptable, not the least because Sartre's position also makes it incomprehensible how we should ever be able to recognize other embodied subjects.

Merleau-Ponty, whose own position can be seen as a continuation and radicalization of Husserl's view, voiced the same criticism of Sartre. As he asks at one point in *Phénoménologie de la perception*:

> How can the word "I" be put into plural, how can a general idea of the *I* be formed, how can I speak of an *I* other than my own, how can I know that there are other *I*'s, how can consciousness which, by its nature, and as self-knowledge, is in the mode of the *I*, be grasped in the mode of Thou, and through this, in the world of the "One"? (Merleau-Ponty 1945, 400–401 [1962, 348])

Merleau-Ponty's answer to this question was unequivocal. He claimed that the self-experience of subjectivity *must* contain a dimension of otherness, if it did not, intersubjectivity would be impossible. Thus, Merleau-Ponty took self-coincidence and the relation with an other to be mutually incompatible determinations. Had subjectivity and selfhood been an exclusive first-person phenomenon, present only in the form of an immediate and unique inwardness, I would know of only one case—my own—and would never get to know any other. Not only would I lack the means of ever recognizing other bodies as embodied subjects, I would also lack the ability to recognize myself in the mirror, and more generally, I would be unable to grasp a certain inter-subjectively describable body as myself:

If the sole experience of the subject is the one which I gain by coinciding with it, if the mind, by definition, eludes "the outside spectator" and can be recognized only from within, my *cogito* is necessarily unique, and cannot be "shared in" by another. Perhaps we can say that it is "transferable" to others. But then how could such a transfer ever be brought about? What spectacle can ever validly induce me to posit outside myself that mode of existence the whole significance of which demands that it be grasped from within? Unless I learn within myself to recognize the junction of the *for itself* and the *in itself*, none of those mechanisms called other bodies will ever be able to come to life; unless I have an exterior others have no interior. The plural-ity of consciousness is impossible if I have an absolute consciousness of myself. (Merleau-Ponty 1945, 427–428 [1962, 373])

As Merleau-Ponty pointed out, however, subjectivity is not a "motionless identity with itself"; rather, it is essential for subjectivity to "to go forth from itself" and to open itself to the other (Merleau-Ponty 1945, 487). Subjec-tivity is not hermetically sealed up within itself, remote from the world and inaccessible to the other. It is, above all, a relation to the world, and Merleau-Ponty accordingly wrote that access to others is secured the moment that I define both others and myself as coexisting relations to the world (Merleau-Ponty 1964, 114).

To rephrase Merleau-Ponty's point in a more familiar terminology: Unless self-experience is embodied and embedded, intersubjectivity will be neither possible nor comprehensible. If we adopt what McCulloch has recently called a behavior-rejecting mentalism (McCulloch 2003, 94), that is, if we deny that embodiment and bodily behavior have an essential role to play in experience and cognition, if we deny that embodiment and environmental embedding are essential to having a mind, we will have a hard time escap-ing solipsism.[2] We will be faced with what is known as the *conceptual problem of other minds*. What does the argument consist in? If my self-experience is, in the primary instance, of a purely mental nature, that is, if my body does not figure essentially in my self-ascriptions of (some) psycho-logical states, while my ascriptions of mental states to others are based solely on their bodily behavior, what, then, should guarantee that we are, in fact, ascribing the same type of states to self and to others? How would we ever come to be in possession of a truly general concept of mind that is equally applicable to different subjects (see Davidson 2001, 207; Avramides 2001, 135, 224)?

As we have just seen, the notion of expressive behavior is crucial if one is to avoid this problem. We normally learn of our mental states through the situations in which we express them and, as Rudd points out, the language we learn for these states "is initially acquired from others in contexts where they are aware of us expressing those states, and it is a language that we learn to apply to others even as we learn to apply it to ourselves" (Rudd 2003, 114). More generally speaking, the proper way to respond to this skeptical challenge is by abandoning any radical division between mind and body. This was also Merleau-Ponty's view. He considered subjectivity to be essentially embodied. To exist embodied is, however, to exist as neither pure subject nor as pure object, but to exist in a way that transcends both possibilities. It does not entail losing self-awareness—on the contrary, self-awareness is intrinsically embodied self-awareness—yet it does entail a loss or, perhaps rather, a release from transparency and purity, thereby permitting intersubjectivity.

The other can be evident to me because I am not transparent for myself, and because my subjectivity draws its body in its wake. (Merleau-Ponty 1945, 405 [1962, 352])

Since intersubjectivity is, in fact, possible, there must exist a bridge between my self-acquaintance and my acquaintance with others; my experience of my own subjectivity must contain an anticipation of the other, must contain the seeds of *alterity* (Merleau-Ponty 1945, 400–401, 405, 511). If I am to recognize other bodies as embodied foreign subjects, I have to be in possession of something that will allow me to do so. When I experience myself and when I experience others, there is, in fact, a common denominator. In both cases, I am dealing with *embodiment*, and one of the features of my embodied subjectivity is that it, per definition, entails an acting and living in the world. When I go for a walk, write a letter, or play ball, to use P. F. Strawson's classic examples (Strawson 1959, 111), I am experiencing myself, but in a way that anticipates the manner in which I would experience an other and an other would experience me.

It could be argued, of course, that any account of the mind must take subjectivity and the first-person perspective seriously, and that a focus on behavior and action will consequently lose sight of what is essential to the mind.

This worry is, however, misguided. There is nothing reductive in the reference to action, since subjectivity figures centrally in the concept. Action, according to at least one venerable philosophical tradition, joins mind and body, or more precisely, it deconstructs the artificial divide between inner and outer. Action is the action of subjects; it is the action of minded individuals. Normally, we do not have to infer the existence of hidden mental happenings if we are to interpret someone else's bodily movements as intentional, such as the buying of a newspaper or the kicking of a ball. Rather, there is much to suggest that such intentions are manifested directly in goal-directed movements. Just as we are aware of what we are doing, we can directly and noninferentially observe other people acting with intent. Being presented with the behavior of others is more like being confronted with a language than with mere physical movements; even a foreign and incomprehensible language is perceived as meaningful and not simply as noise (see Waldenfels 2000, 219). When you see somebody use a hammer, feed a child, or clean a table, you might not necessarily understand every aspect of the action, but it is immediately given as a meaningful action. In fact, it seems as if we have the ability to recognize immediately whether our action shares or does not share crucial properties with the action of an other. When I am playing football, I do not need to draw any inferences to see that you and I are fighting for the same ball. Without the benefit of such an immediate recognition, action-coordination—and survival—would be much more cumbersome than it actually is (Dokic 2003, 332).

According to Merleau-Ponty, I can experience others because I am never so close to myself that the other is completely and radically foreign and inaccessible. I am always already a stranger to myself and, therefore, open to others. In other words, it is because I am not a pure disembodied interiority, but an incarnated being in the world, that I am capable of encountering and understanding others who exist in the same way (Merleau-Ponty 1960a, 215; 1964, 74). Thus, the standard question, "How do I find an access to the other?" is mistaken. It signals that I am enclosed in my own interiority, and that I must then employ specific methods to reach the other who is outside. Such a way of framing the problem fails to recognize the nature of embodiment. To exist embodied is to exist in such a way that one exists under the gaze of the other, accessible to the other; my bodily behavior always has a public side to it. This is not to say that a focus on embodiment will eradicate the difference between self-ascription and other-ascription, between a first-person perspective and a second-person perspective. We should respect this difference, but we should also conceive of it in a manner that avoids giving rise to the mistaken view that only my own experiences are given to me and that the behavior of the other shields his experiences from me and makes their very existence hypothetical (Avramides 2001, 187).

Some phenomenologists have interpreted the endeavor to locate a form of internal *alterity* in the structure of embodied subjectivity as a step toward downplaying the radical difference between self and other. Some have gone even further and claimed that intersubjectivity will remain a puzzle as long as self and other are seen as absolutely different and distinct, and that the only way to avoid the threat of solipsism is by conceiving of the difference between the two as a founded and derived difference arising out of a common, shared, undifferentiated, and anonymous life. *In concreto*, it has been argued that our personal subjectivity is founded upon an obscure, impersonal, and anonymous existence. That is, lived, pre-reflective subjectivity has been taken to lack a personal or egological structure. It is not truly *I* who perceive; rather, perception "happens" and something "is perceived." Insofar as the subject is permeated by a fundamental anonymity, the experience of others presents no difficulty. There is no problem of an *alter ego* because it is neither I nor the other who perceives but, as Merleau-Ponty wrote, an "anonymous visibility" that inhabits us both (Merleau-Ponty 1964, 187 [1968, 142]). It is only the moment I forget that I belong to a common perceptual field, and reduce myself to what reflection makes of me, that the experience of others becomes problematic.

In a similar vein, it has been maintained that intersubjectivity does not present a problem for infants, that is, that the experience of others is only a problem for the adult. The reason given is that we, at the beginning of life, will find neither self-experience nor empathy, but simply a shared anonymous existence without differentiation:

The solitude from which we emerge to intersubjective life is not that of the monad. It is only the haze of an anonymous life that separates us from being; and the barrier between us and others is impalpable. If there is a break, it is not between me and the other person; it is between a primordial generality we are intermingled in and the precise system, myself–the others. What "precedes" intersubjective life cannot be numerically distinguished from it, precisely because at this level there is neither individuation nor numerical distinction. (Merleau-Ponty 1960a, 220 [1964, 174]; see also Merleau-Ponty 1960b, 33)[3]

This view is not without its own difficulties and I will return to some of these presently. It should be emphasized, however, that there is a distinction between a theory that seeks to deny the individuality of subjectivity and a theory that seeks to introduce something impersonal into the heart of subjectivity. Ultimately, individuality and anonymity do not have to be two possible conceptions of the subject between which we must choose; rather, both notions can belong to the structure of concrete selfhood.

III Beyond Empathy

An understanding of intersubjectivity calls for an examination of embodied subjectivity. The very possibility of intersubjectivity is rooted in the bodily constitution of subjectivity. Many phenomenologists have also argued that a better understanding of the relation between subjectivity and world will increase our comprehension of intersubjectivity. More precisely, they have argued for intersubjectivity to be granted a place in the intentional relation between subjectivity and world, be it in the social character of tool-use, in the public nature of perceptual objects, or in the historicity of our understanding.

Let us begin with Heidegger, whose treatment of intersubjectivity is found in the context of his analysis of our being-in-the-world. More specifically, it is precisely in connection with an analysis of our practical engagement in the surrounding world that Heidegger addressed the issue of others, for, as he pointed out, the world we are engaged in is not a private world, but a public and communal one (Heidegger GA 20: 255).

According to Heidegger, the type of entities we encounter first and foremost in our daily life are not natural objects such as oaks and codfish, but artifacts or pieces of equipment, such as chairs, forks, shirts, pieces of soap, and so on. It is, however, a fundamental feature of such entities that they all contain references to other persons. This is because they are produced by others or because the work we are trying to accomplish with them involves others. In short, in our daily life of cares and concerns, we are constantly making use of entities that refer to others, and as Heidegger pointed out, this reference is frequently a reference to *indeterminate* others (Heidegger GA 20: 260–261). In fact, in utilizing tools or equipment Dasein is *being-with* (*Mitsein*) others, regardless of whether or not other persons are factually present (Heidegger GA 24: 414). That is, Dasein does not initially exist alone, and does not first acquire its being-with the moment another turns up; on the contrary, qua its engaged being-in-the-world, Dasein is essentially social from the start. If concrete and determinate others are absent, this simply means that Dasein's constitution as being-with does not attain its factual fulfilment. That is to say, one can, ultimately, only speak of others as "lacking," precisely because Dasein is fundamentally characterized by its being-with others. Heidegger even claimed that Dasein's being-with, the fact that sociality belongs to its very ontological structure, is the formal condition of possibility for any concrete experience of and encounter with others (Heidegger 1986, 120–125). As he wrote in *Sein und Zeit*:

The disclosedness of the *Mitda-sein* of others which belongs to being-with means that the understanding of others already lies in the understanding of being of Dasein because its being is being-with. This understanding, like all understanding, is not a knowledge derived from cognition, but a primordially existential kind of being which first makes knowledge and cognition possible. (Heidegger 1986, 123–124)

It is only because Dasein is itself social that human community and sociality is possible in all of its many shades and grades of authenticity and inauthenticity, permanence and transience (Heidegger GA 27: 141). Dasein does not first exist, in order then to make the step beyond itself to others or to worldly objects; rather, to exist always already means to step beyond, or better, to have stepped beyond:

Transcendence is not instituted by an object coming together with a subject, or a thou with an I, but the Dasein itself, as "being-a-subject," transcends. The Dasein as such is being-toward-itself, being-with others, and being-among entities handy and extant. (Heidegger GA 24: 427–428)

In this case, however, the problem of other minds, of how one isolated subject can encounter and understand another isolated subject, turns out to be an illusory problem. It is precisely one of those pseudo-problems that, according to Wittgenstein, has for far too long held philosophers spellbound. For the same reason, however, the empathic approach to intersubjectivity loses some of its attraction. As Heidegger wrote, if one seeks to understand intersubjectivity on the basis of empathy, one will remain committed to a serious misconception of the nature of the self:

If this word ["empathy"] is at all to retain a signification, then [it does so] only because of the assumption that the "I" is at first in its ego-sphere and must then subsequently enter the sphere of another. The "I" does not first break out . . . since it already is outside, nor does it break into the other, since it already encounters the other outside. (Heidegger GA 27: 145)

Even if the empathic approach does not commit the same mistakes as the argument from analogy, it still misconstrues the nature of intersubjectivity, since it takes it to be, first of all, a thematic encounter between individuals, wherein one is trying to grasp the emotions or experiences of the other (this connotation is particularly obvious in the German word for empathy: *Einfühlung*). However, the very attempt to thematically grasp the experiences of others is the exception rather than the rule. Under normal circumstances, we understand each other well enough through our shared engagement in the common world; it is only if this understanding for some reason breaks down that something like empathy becomes relevant. If this is so, then an investigation of intersubjectivity that takes empathy as its point of departure and constant point of reference is bound to lead us astray.

Heidegger was by no means the only phenomenologist to question the primacy of the empathic encounter. One finds related arguments in Gurwitsch, Husserl, and Merleau-Ponty as well.

Gurwitsch readily acknowledges the importance of expressive phenomena, but he criticized Scheler for having been too one-sided in his approach and argued that the realm of expressive phenomena is neither the only, nor the primary, dimension to be considered if we wish to understand what it is that enables us to encounter other human beings as humans (Gurwitsch 1979, 33). Ordinarily, we do not encounter others primarily as thematic objects of cognition. Rather, we encounter them in the world in which our daily life occurs or, to be more precise, we encounter others in a worldly situation and our way of being together and understanding each other is codetermined in its meaning by the situation at hand (Gurwitsch 1979, 35–36, 95, 106). To exemplify, Gurwitsch analyzed the situation where two workers are cobbling a street. In this (once) common work situation, one worker lays the stones while the other knocks them into place. Each worker is related to the other in his activity and comportment. When one worker understands the other, the understanding in question does not involve grasping some hidden mental occurrences. There is no problem of other minds. There is no problem of how one isolated ego gets access to another isolated ego. Rather, both workers understand each other in virtue of the roles they play in the common situation (Gurwitsch 1979, 104, 108, 112).

It is precisely within such common situations that expressive phenomena occur. When working or conversing with one's partner, he might shake his head or wrinkle his brow, but these facial expressions and bodily gestures are not unambiguous. They do not reveal psychological states either simply or uniformly. Each person has different countenances and facial habits, yet this is rarely a problem, since we do not encounter expressions in isolation. They always occur in a given context, and our understanding of the context, of what comes before and after, helps us understand the expression. As Gurwitsch pointed out, the "same" shaking of the head can take on different meanings in different situations. What an expressive phenomenon is and what it signifies in a particular case becomes comprehensible to me in the whole of the present situation (Gurwitsch 1979, 114; see also Sartre 1943, 396).

When considering Husserl and Merleau-Ponty, we must note that both of these authors also fully recognized that we are embedded in a living tradition and that the notion of empathy cannot account for the kind of intersubjectivity that is at play therein. As Husserl put it, I have been together with others for as long as I can remember, and my understanding and interpretation are, therefore, structured in accordance with the intersubjectively handed-down forms of apperception (Hua 15/136). I live in a world that is permeated by references to others, and which others have already furnished with meaning, and I typically understand the world (and myself) through a traditional linguistic conventionality. Thus, prior to Heidegger's analysis in *Being and Time*, Husserl pointed to the fact that, next to the tendencies originating from other persons, there also exist indeterminate general demands made by custom and tradition: "One" judges thus and thus, "one" holds the fork in such and such a way, and so on (Hua 4/269). I learn what counts as normal from others, and indeed, initially, and for the most part, from those closest to me, hence from those I grow up with, those who teach me, and those belonging to the most intimate sphere of my life (Hua 15/428–429, 569). I thereby participate in a communal tradition, which through a chain of generations stretches back into a dim past. I always already find myself a member of a community. I am born into it; I grow up in it. The historical is a living past handed down to me; it is a living force in me:

What I generate from out of myself (primally instituting) is mine. But I am a "child of the times"; I am a member of a we-community in the broadest sense—a community that has its tradition and that for its part is connected in a novel manner with the generative subjects, the closest and the most distant ancestors. And these have "influenced" me: I am what I am as an heir. (Hua 14/223)

At the same time, however, both Husserl and Merleau-Ponty also argued for intersubjectivity to have a place in the intentional relation to the world.

Instead of anchoring it exclusively in the social character of tool-use, as Heidegger tended to do, they also focused on the public nature of perceptual objects. As they put it, the subject is intentionally directed toward objects whose horizontal givenness bears witness to their openness for other subjects. My perceptual objects are not exhausted in their appearance for me; rather, each object always possesses a horizon of coexisting profiles, which although being momentarily inaccessible to me—I cannot see the front and the back of a chair simultaneously—could very well be perceived by other subjects. Since the perceptual object is always there for others too, whether or not such other subjects do, in fact, appear on the scene, the object refers to those other subjects and is for that reason intrinsically intersubjective.[4] It does not exist solely for me, but refers to intersubjectivity, and so does my intentionality whenever I am directed at intersubjectively accessible objects (Merleau-Ponty 1960a, 23, 215; Hua 6/468).[5] As Husserl wrote:

Thus everything objective that stands before me in experience and primarily in perception has an apperceptive horizon of possible experience, own and foreign. Ontologically speaking, every appearance that I have is from the very beginning a part of an open endless, but not explicitly realized totality of possible appearances of the same, and the subjectivity belonging to this appearance is open intersubjectivity. (Hua 14/289; see also Hua 9/394; 15/497)

My experience as mundane experience (that is already each of my perceptions) does not only entail others as mundane objects, but also and constantly (in existential co-validity) as co-subjects, as co-constituting, and both are inseparably intertwined. (Husserl Ms. C 17 36a)[6]

Consequently, even prior to my concrete *empathic* encounter with another subject, intersubjectivity is already present as cosubjectivity. This is what Husserl was referring to when he, in a still unpublished manuscript, wrote: "When empathy occurs, is perhaps sociality, intersubjectivity, likewise already there, and does empathy then merely accomplish the disclosure of it?" (Husserl Ms. C 17 84b).[7] He then went on to answer the question affirmatively.[8]

To sum up, the world we live in is a public and communal world, not a private one. Subjectivity and world are internally related, and since the structure of this world contains essential references to others, subjectivity cannot be understood except as inhabiting a world that it necessarily shares with others.

It is natural to conclude that a reflection on the intersubjective nature of tool-use, perception, and the historicity of understanding reveals that inter-subjectivity cannot be reduced to a thematic and concrete face-to-face encounter between two individuals. In other words, there are modalities of intersubjectivity that cannot be accounted for by means of a theory of empathy. However, as we have also seen, some have sharpened this criticism and gone on to claim that empathy is, in fact, a derived form of intersub-jectivity. That is, rather than first establishing intersubjectivity, empathy merely discloses an intersubjectivity already at work. Although this obser-vation might strike one as both perceptive and convincing, it has in fact given rise to one of the most hotly debated issues in the entire phenomenology of intersubjectivity: Which is more fundamental, the face-to-face encounter with the other, or our existence in a common world? Which has priority, the anonymous being-with-others, or the transcendence or *alterity* of the other? Is one the condition of possibility for the other?

IV The Transcendence of the Other

So far, we have seen that some phenomenologists regard the recognition and intentional analysis of empathy as the cornerstone of a phenomenological theory of intersubjectivity. Others in the tradition have gone further and attempted either to investigate the bodily preconditions for empathy or to argue that there are forms of intersubjectivity intrinsic to our very being-in-the-world that precede and found the concrete face-to-face encounter. Some phenomenologists, however, have criticized all of these attempts for failing to capture what really constitutes the core of intersubjectivity: the con-frontation with radical otherness. They have argued that it is essential to respect the irreducible difference between self and other. Let me in the fol-lowing briefly account for this criticism.

In his discussion of intersubjectivity in *L'être et le néant*, Sartre at first seemed to accept Heidegger's analysis of the social character of equipment. As he wrote (with an emphasis that reveals a characteristic lacuna in Heidegger's own account), it is undeniable that tools and artifacts contain references to a plurality of *embodied* others (Sartre 1943, 278, 389, 391). Just as Heidegger argued, Sartre consequently insisted that our daily activi-ties are intrinsically social; they reveal our existence in a community, even in the absence of concrete others:

To live in a world haunted by my fellowman is not only to be able to encounter the Other at every turn of the road; it is also to find myself engaged in a world in which instrumental-complexes can have a meaning which my free project has not first given to them. (Sartre 1943, 567 [1956, 509])

Despite this congruence, Sartre nevertheless ended up directing a pointed critique at Heidegger. According to Sartre, Heidegger's concept of being-with completely fails to capture our original and fundamental relation to others.

There are several steps in Sartre's criticism. At first, he simply pointed out that it would never occur to me to distinguish between a manufactured piece of equipment and a natural object unless I already had a prior experience of an other. It is precisely in and through my interaction with others that I learn to handle an object as a manufactured tool, as something that is designed for a specific purpose, or as something that *one* uses in a particular manner. For this very reason, the reference to others contained in tool-use is a *derived* reference. More generally, being-with, understood as a "lateral" relation to others, is not the most fundamental type of intersubjectivity. On the contrary, it presupposes a more original and quite concrete encounter with others (Sartre 1943, 478–479). As Sartre wrote, "The 'we' is a certain particular experience which is produced in special cases on the foundation of being-for-others in general. The being-for-others precedes and founds the *being-with-others*" (Sartre 1943, 465 [1956, 414]). Thus, according to Sartre, Heidegger made the mistake of interpreting our original relation to others as an oblique interdependence rather than as a frontal confrontation:

The empirical image which may best symbolize Heidegger's intuition is not that of a conflict but rather a *crew*. The original relation of the Other and my consciousness is not the *you* and *me*; it is the *we*. Heidegger's being-with is not the clear and distinct position of an individual confronting another individual; it is not *knowledge*. It is the mute existence in common of one member of the crew with his fellows, that existence which the rhythm of the oars or the regular movement of the coxswain will render sensible to the rowers and which *will be made manifest* to them by the common goal to be attained, the boat or the yacht to be overtaken, and the entire world (spectators, performance, *etc.*) which is profiled on the horizon. (Sartre 1943, 292 [1956, 246])

In contrast, as we will see in a moment, Sartre himself took intersubjectivity to be, first and foremost, a question of conflict and confrontation rather than of peaceful coexistence (Sartre 1943, 481).

In the second step of his criticism, Sartre took issue with Heidegger's attempt to understand being-with as an essential, intrinsic, and a priori determination of Dasein, rather than as a contingent and factual feature that shows up only in and through concrete encounters with others. According to Sartre, such a conception ignores what is most crucial in intersubjectivity, the relation to radical *otherness*. As Sartre pointed out, any "theory of intersubjectivity" that attempts to bridge the gap between the self and the other by emphasizing their similarity, undifferentiatedness, and a priori interconnectedness is not only in constant danger of relapsing into a monism that would be indistinguishable from solipsism, it is also losing sight of the real issue: our concrete encounter with this or that *transcendent* other. Sartre consequently argued that if solipsism is truly to be overcome, it will not do to neutralize the otherness of the other by positing intersubjectivity as an *a priori* feature of our being. On the contrary, our being-for-others must be understood as an existential dimension that only arises in and through concrete encounters with factual others (Sartre 1943, 293–295, 412).[9] In short, it is quite misleading to claim that the concrete encounter with another, rather than adding anything new, simply unfolds or articulates what was already there *a priori*.

Both the attempt to locate a form of internal *alterity* in the structure of embodied subjectivity and the argument that the encounter with the other is prepared by and made possible through an *alterity* internal to the self have been met with a similar criticism: Both downplay the difference between self and other, and, consequently, do not respect the otherness of the other. Obviously, the same criticism has been directed against the idea that the difference between self and other is a founded and derived difference, a difference arising out of a common and shared, undifferentiated, anonymous life. To speak of a fundamental anonymity prior to any distinction between self and other obscures what must be clarified, namely intersubjectivity understood as a relation between subjects. Properly speaking, it does not solve the problem of intersubjectivity, but dissolves it. On the level of radical anonymity there is neither individuation nor selfhood; but there is also no differentiation, *alterity*, or transcendence, and there is, consequently, room for neither subjectivity nor intersubjectivity. In other words, the radical anonymity thesis threatens not only our concept of the transcendent and irreducible other, it also threatens our concept of a self-given subject. It is consequently more than doubtful whether the notion of an undifferentiated anonymity with its latent solipsism can help us understand intersubjectivity. Rather, it seems to present us with one of those cases where the medicine turns out to be part of the sickness it was supposed to cure and, in the end, just as deadly.

As we have already seen, the empathic approach is characterized by its attempt to specify the particular intentional structure of empathy and distinguish it from other intentional acts such as perception, recollection, and imagination. Whereas the pertinent question for this approach has been how it is possible to experience the other in a way that preserves her subjectivity and otherness, Sartre took this line to be misguided, and instead proposed a reversal of the traditional direction of inquiry. According to Sartre, it is crucial to distinguish between the other, which I perceive, and the other, which perceives me, that is, it is crucial to distinguish between the other as object, and the other as subject. What is truly peculiar and exceptional about the other is not that I am experiencing a *cogitatum cogitans*, but that I am encountering somebody who is able to perceive and objectify me. The other is exactly the being for whom *I* can appear as an object. Thus, rather than focusing on the other as a specific object of empathy, Sartre argued that foreign subjectivity is revealed to me through my awareness of myself in the capacity of being-an-object for an other. It is when I experience my own objectivity, for and before a foreign subject, that I have experiential evidence for the presence of the other-as-subject (Sartre 1943, 302–303, 317).

This line of thought is effectively displayed in Sartre's renowned analysis of *shame*. According to Sartre, shame is not a feeling that I could elicit on my own. It presupposes the intervention of the other, not merely because the other is the one before whom I feel ashamed, but also, and more significantly, because the other is the one that constitutes that of which I am ashamed. I am ashamed not of myself qua being-for-itself, but of myself as I appear to the other. I exist not only for myself, but also for others, and this is precisely what shame undeniably reveals to me (Sartre 1943, 266).[10]

Compared to Heidegger's account, Sartre's treatment of intersubjectivity emphasizes the transcendent, ineffable, and elusive character of the other and rejects any attempt to bridge or downplay the difference between self and other. Sartre, however, was not the only phenomenologist to stress the importance of recognizing the transcendence of the other. Related considerations can be found in the writings of both Lévinas and Husserl.

Just like Sartre, Lévinas took the problem of intersubjectivity to be primarily a problem of radical otherness and explicitly denied that any form of intentionality, including empathy, will ever permit us to encounter the other in an authentic manner. Intentionality is a process of objectification that lets us meet the other only by reducing the other to something it is not, namely an object. To put it differently, although intentionality does relate me to that which is foreign, it is, in Lévinas's words, a nonreciprocal relationship. It never makes me leave home. On the contrary, the knowing subject acts like the famous stone of the alchemists that transmutes everything it touches; it absorbs the foreign and different, annuls its *alterity*, and transforms it into the familiar and same (Lévinas 1991, 52). In contrast, foreign subjectivity is exactly that which cannot be conceptualized or categorized: "If one could possess, grasp, and know the other, it would not be other" (Lévinas 1979, 83 [1987, 90]). My encounter with foreign subjectivity is, consequently, an encounter with an ineffable and radical exteriority. It is not conditioned by anything in my power, but has the character of a visitation, an epiphany, or a revelation. In a characteristic move, Lévinas then took the problem of justice and injustice to provide us with an original, nonreductionistic approach to the other. The authentic encounter with the other is not perceptual or epistemic, but *ethical* in nature. It is in the ethical situation where the other questions me and makes ethical demands of me, that is, it is when I have to assume responsibility for the other, that he is present as other (Lévinas 1961, 33).

This emphasis on the transcendence of the other is primarily associated with the writings of Sartre and Lévinas, but already in Husserl's work, one finds a concern with the same topic, although his interest was motivated by transcendental philosophical reasons. As we have already seen, Husserl argued that my perceptual experience is an experience of intersubjectively accessible being that does not exist for me alone, but for everybody. I *experience* objects, events, and actions as public, not as private. It is against this background that Husserl introduced his concept of *transcendental intersubjectivity* (Hua 15/110, 378). His idea was that objectivity is intersubjectively constituted and that a clarification of this constitution, accordingly, calls for an examination of my experience of other subjects. To be more specific, Husserl's thesis was that my experience of objective validity is mediated and made possible by my encounter with a transcendent other:

Here we have the only transcendence that is really worth its name, and anything else that is also called transcendent, such as the objective world, *depends* upon the transcendence of foreign subjectivity. (Hua 8/495)

Why is it that the other is a necessary condition of possibility for my experience of an objective world? Why is foreign subjectivity so central a condition of possibility for the constitution of objectivity? The explanation offered by Husserl is that objects cannot be reduced to being merely my own intentional correlates if they are experienceable by others. When I discover that the object I am currently experiencing is also perceived by an other, my relationship to the object changes. Only insofar as I experience that others experience the same objects as me do I really experience those objects as objective and real. The intersubjective experienceability of the object testifies to its real transcendence; or, in other words, that which is, in principle, incapable of being experienced by others cannot be ascribed transcendence and objectivity. My experience of this transcendence is, consequently, mediated by my experience of its givenness for another transcendent subject, that is, by my encounter with a foreign world-directed subject.[11] It is precisely for this reason that the other's transcendence is so vital. If the other were merely an intentional modification or an imaginative variation of myself, the fact that he experienced the same as me would be just as conclusive, to use an example of Wittgenstein's, as if one found the same report in several copies of the same newspaper.

Husserl continued his analyses by describing a special kind of experience of the other, namely those situations where I experience the other as experiencing myself.[12] This kind of "original reciprocal coexistence" in which I take over the other's objectifying apprehension of myself, that is, where my self-apprehension is mediated by the other, and I experience myself as other, is also construed to be of decisive importance for the constitution of an objective world. When I realize that I can be an *alter ego* for the other just as he can be one for me, a marked change in my own significance takes place: The absolute difference between self and other disappears. The other conceives of me as an other, just as I conceive of him as a self (Hua 13/243–244). I consequently come to the realization that I am only one among many and that my perspective on the world is by no means privileged (Hua 15/645).

When it comes to the constitution of objectivity, we are faced with an issue that transcends the horizon of the individual and calls for the contribution of other subjects. Objectivity is constitutively related to a plurality of subjects, and according to Husserl, the constitution of this objectivity takes place within the framework of a certain normality. For this reason, the phenomenological discussion of subjectivity, which is a discussion of the transcendental or constitutively functioning subject, turns out to be a discussion not simply of the I, but of the *we*. This is why Husserl ultimately argued that the transcendental subject is only what it is within intersubjectivity and that intersubjectivity must be taken into consideration if we wish to understand what it means to be a transcendental subject (Hua 15/74–75; 1/69; 6/275, 472; 9/245–246; 8/129). Thus, it is no coincidence that Husserl at times described his own project as a *sociological* transcendental philosophy (Hua 9/539) and in 1922 even wrote that the development of phenomenology necessarily implies the step from an " 'egological' . . . phenomenology into a transcendental sociological phenomenology having reference to a manifest multiplicity of conscious subjects communicating with one another" (Husserl 1981, 68).

V   A Multidimensional Approach

I have presented only a few facets from a wide-ranging and ongoing discussion, yet by now, it should have become clear that the phenomenological tradition, far from ignoring the issues of intersubjectivity and sociality, contains rich but quite diverse and even occasionally competing accounts. Four different phenomenological takes on the relation between self and other have crystallized over the course of my presentation:

- As we have seen, one possibility is to focus on the face-to-face encounter and try to account for it in terms of a specific mode of consciousness called "*Fremderfahrung*" or "empathy." The task then consists of analyzing the precise structure of empathy and spelling out the differences between empathy and other forms of intentionality, such as perception, imagination, and recollection. There is much of value in this approach as long as it does, in fact, involve a resolute showdown with the argument from analogy, that is, as long as it does not contain any reminiscences of the idea that an understanding of the other is based on projection or introjection. Nor must it assume any unfortunate dichotomy between mind and body. It should be emphasized, however, that this line of investigation is able to account for only some aspects of the self–other relation, and that it is debatable whether these aspects are the most crucial ones. In short, it remains questionable whether a theory of empathy can constitute the base and center of a theory of intersubjectivity.

• Another possibility is to begin by acknowledging the existence of empathy, yet insist that our ability to encounter others cannot simply be taken as a brute fact, but that it is, on the contrary, conditioned by a form of *alterity* internal to the embodied self, and for which reason the bodily interlacement of selfhood and otherness must be investigated. Insofar as the possibility of intersubjectivity is taken to be rooted in the bodily constitution of the self, we can, at this stage, witness a certain reluctance to simply equate intersubjectivity with the factual and concrete face-to-face encounter. This take on intersubjectivity also contains very valuable insights. It is crucial, however, to avoid conflating the *alterity* of the other and the *alterity* of the self, just as it is important to resist the temptation of assuming the distinction between self and other to be derivative and ultimately founded in a common anonymity.

• The third option goes one step further, since it quite explicitly denies that intersubjectivity can be reduced to a factual encounter between two individuals. On the contrary, such a concrete encounter is taken to presuppose the existence of another, more fundamental form of intersubjectivity that is rooted *a priori* in the very relation between subjectivity and world. By managing to disclose entirely new intersubjective dimensions bound to be overlooked by a narrow focus on empathy, this line of investigation is also very promising. Its main weakness is that it tends to belittle the relevance of the concrete face-to-face encounter, yet thereby it also ignores the significance of the *transcendence* of the other, and that is unsatisfactory.

• It is this failure that the fourth approach seeks to overcome. It rightly emphasizes that the confrontation with radical otherness is a crucial and nonnegligible aspect of what intersubjectivity is all about. As might be expected, however, the difficulty with this view is that it often tends to emphasize the transcendence and elusiveness of the other to such an extent that it not only denies the existence of a functioning cosubjectivity, but also the *a priori* status of intersubjectivity. The relation between self and other becomes a merely contingent relation. Moreover, in order to emphasize the absolute and radical *alterity* of the other, this approach has often denied that the encounter with the other is, in any way, prepared and conditioned by an *alterity* internal to the self, with the result that the encounter with the other is turned into a mystery (see Zahavi 2004g).

Most (but not all) phenomenologists have focused mainly on only one or two of the approaches at the expense of the others. This is particularly clear in the case of such authors as Scheler, Heidegger, Sartre, and Lévinas. In my own view, however, none of these approaches can be taken in isolation, and a systematic combination of the different accounts is therefore required; to what extent do they actually exclude each other, and to what extent do they simply complement each other? Ultimately, a convincing theory of inter-subjectivity must necessarily be multidimensional and draw on considerations taken from all four approaches.

Despite this diversity, it is still possible to uncover certain significant and quite distinctive features that are more or less common to all of the approaches. Let me conclude this chapter by briefly mentioning a few of them:

- Without ever denying the eminently intersubjective character of *language*, phenomenologists have often endeavored to unearth pre- or extralinguistic forms of intersubjectivity, be it in simple perception or in tool-use, in emotions, drives, or body-awareness. This emphasis constitutes one of the decisive differences between the phenomenological approach to intersubjectivity, and the approach that we find, for instance, in the writings of Habermas.
- Phenomenologists never conceive of intersubjectivity as an objectively existing structure in the world that can be described and analyzed from a third-person perspective. On the contrary, intersubjectivity is a relation between subjects and must be analyzed, as such, from a first-person and a second-person perspective. This also makes it clear that subjectivity and intersubjectivity, far from being competing alternatives, are, in fact, complementary and mutually interdependent notions. Thus, the introduction of intersubjectivity should not be taken to imply a refutation of the philosophy of subjectivity. On the contrary, it makes a genuine understanding of such a philosophy possible for the first time.
- One of the crucial insights that we find in phenomenology, particularly in Husserl, Heidegger, and Merleau-Ponty, is the idea that a treatment of intersubjectivity simultaneously requires an analysis of the relationship between subjectivity and world. That is, it is not satisfactory simply to insert intersubjectivity somewhere within an already established metaphysical framework; rather, the three dimensions "self," "others," and "world" belong together, they reciprocally illuminate one another, and can be fully understood only in their interconnection.[13] Thus, it does not matter which of the three one takes as a starting point, for one will still inevitably be led to the other two: the subjectivity that is related to the world gains its full relation

to itself, and to the world, only in relation to others, that is, in intersubjectivity. Intersubjectivity exists and develops only in relation between world-related subjects, and the world is brought to articulation only in the relation between subjects. As Merleau-Ponty would have written: The subject must be seen as a worldly incarnate existence, and the world must be seen as a common field of experience, if intersubjectivity is to be at all possible.

Much of what phenomenologists have had to say on the issue of intersubjectivity is of obvious relevance not only for related discussions in analytical philosophy of mind, but also for empirical disciplines, such as developmental psychology and psychiatry. In the final chapter, I will explore this interdisciplinary crossover in more detail.[14]

In recent years, most of the discussion on the nature of social cognition has taken place within the framework of the so-called theory of mind debate. The claim that an everyday understanding of minded beings, be it oneself or others, requires a theory of mind has found wide resonance in a number of empirical disciplines, not the least in the study of autism. Is it really plausible that the experiences of self and of others are theoretical, inferential, and quasi-scientific in nature? In this final chapter, I will point to some further problems in this explanatory model and then discuss how empirical evidence and descriptive analyses found in developmental psychology and phenomenology, respectively, might point to a different conception of intersubjectivity and self-experience and, thereby, also allow for a better understanding of autism.

I Theory of Mind

The term "theory of mind" was originally introduced by Premack and Woodruff in a seminal paper on intentionality in primates:

In saying that an individual has a theory of mind, we mean that the individual imputes mental states to himself and to others (either to conspecifics or to other species as well). A system of inferences of this kind is properly viewed as a theory, first, because such states are not directly observable, and second, because the system can be used to make predictions, specifically about the behavior of other organisms. (Premack and Woodruff 1978, 515)

The expression "theory of mind" has since been used as shorthand for our ability to attribute mental states to self and others and to interpret, predict, and explain behavior in terms of mental states such as intentions, beliefs, and desires. Premack and Woodruff took it for granted that it was the possession and use of a *theory* that provided an individual with the capacity to attribute mental states; thus, their choice of term was neither neutral nor innocent. The contemporary debate is split on the issue, however, and has been primarily divided between two opposing views, although it has recently become more common to argue for some kind of mixed approach.

On one side of the larger discussion, we find the *theory-theory of mind*, and on the other the *simulation theory of mind*. Theory-theorists claim that the ability to explain and predict behavior is underpinned by a folk-psychological theory dealing with the structure and functioning of the mind. We attribute beliefs to others by deploying our theoretical knowledge. We come to understand others by using principles like the following: "When an agent A acquires the belief that p and a rational thinker ought to infer q from the conjunction of p with other beliefs that A has, A comes to believe that q" (Botterill 1996, 116). There is, however, disagreement among theory-theorists about whether the theory in question is innate and modularized (Carruthers, Baron-Cohen), or whether it is acquired in the same manner as scientific theories (Gopnik, Meltzoff). The *theory-formation* theory can accept a certain nativism but such initial structures are taken to be defeasible. They can, and will, be changed by new evidence (Gopnik 1996, 171). Thus, for the theory-formation theory, there is a striking similarity between the acquisition of scientific knowledge and the child's increasing ability to adopt an intentional stance and "mind-read," that is, its ability to interpret behavior in terms of an agent's mental state. The same cognitive processes are responsible for both scientific progress and the development of the child's understanding of the mind (Gopnik 1996, 169). The child, consequently, can be viewed as a little scientist who is constructing and revising theories in the light of incoming data. In contrast, *modularists* claim that the core of the folk-psychological theory is hardwired. As they point out, if the theory is merely the product of scientific investigation, why is it culturally universal and why do all children reach the same theory at the same age (Carruthers 1996b, 23)? According to the modularists, the theory is forged by evolution and innately given, and although it may require experience as a trigger, the theory will not be modified by experience.

Whereas theory-theorists claim that our understanding of the mental is supported by a theory, simulationists claim that we possess no such theory, or at least none complete enough to uphold all our competence with psychological notions (Heal 1996, 75). Whereas theory-theorists make use of

Theory of Mind, Autism, and Embodiment | 181

what Gordon has called a cold methodology and argue that our understanding of others chiefly engages intellectual processes moving, by inference, from one belief to the other, simulationists employ a hot methodology and argue that our understanding of others exploits our own motivational and emotional resources (Gordon 1996, 11). Thus, in contrast to the theory-theory, the simulation theory would deny that what lies at the root of our mind-reading abilities is a sort of theory. At least one version of it would insist that our understanding of others is rooted in our ability to imagine, or project, ourselves into their situation. If, for instance, we witness an immigrant being harassed by a desk clerk, we would be able to grasp the immigrant's mental state by using ourselves as model. We could consider ourselves in his situation, imagine how we would feel and react under similar circumstances, and, on the basis of analogy, we could then infer that the foreigner is in a similar state.

In the following, my direct focus will be on the theory-theory. This focus should not be taken as an implicit endorsement of simulationism, since there are problems with the simulation theory as well. Its reliance on some type of argument from analogy has already been criticized (see chapter 6). Rather, it should be realized that there are available options outside the choice between theory-theory and simulation theory.

What precisely do the theory-theorists mean by theory? We have already seen that the views differ. Some take the theory of mind to be a theory in a very literal sense and compare it to scientific theory.[1] Others understand it in a more extended sense and compare it to a set of rules of symbol manipulation instantiated in an innate module. Some assume the theory in question to be explicit, to be something the agent is conscious of; others presume it to be more or less implicit and tacit, and to be something that operates on a subpersonal level.

Generally speaking, however, many theory-theorists have tended to construe theory in a rather loose sense in order to increase the plausibility of their own position. The danger they have thus run is to become vulnerable to what is known as the "promiscuity objection" (see Blackburn 1995): In the end, the notion of theory threatens to become vacuous since everything turns out to be theoretical or quasi-scientific, including cooking, gardening, and fishing. To avoid this, some theory-theorists have simply bitten the bullet, and accepted a strong definition of theory that entails much more than just some kind of semantic holism.

Botterill, for instance, has argued that every theory necessarily involves explanatory and predictive power along with counterfactual projection. He also mentions the introduction of unobservable entities and the implicit definition of concepts as a recurrent element. He concludes by arguing that theories are characterized by producing cognitive economy through the integration of information within a small number of general principles (Botterill 1996, 107–109).

The theory-theory claims that mastery of mental concepts is constituted by knowledge of a psychological theory. More specifically, our understanding of mental notions depends on our knowledge of the positions that these notions occupy within the theory. Thus, the notions are taken to receive their sense from the theory in which they are embedded, rather than from some form of direct acquaintance. This is one of the most characteristic features of the theory-theory. Since it considers the attribution of mental states to be a question of an inference to best explanation and prediction of behavioral data, it denies that we have any direct experience of such mental states as beliefs and desires, and instead argues that the concepts in question refer to unobservable and theoretically postulated entities. Thus, when the theory-theory argues that the attribution of mental states is theoretically mediated, the idea is not that we need the theory in order to be able to extract and comprehend the informational richness of what is already given, already present, like the wine connoisseur who is able to discern flavors and aromas imperceptible to others. It is not merely a question of emphasizing to what extent our observations might be influenced and enriched by former experiences; rather, the idea is that the employment of theory is what allows us to transcend the perceptually given. Some statements representative of this idea are:

One of the most important powers of the human mind is to conceive of and think about itself and other minds. Because the mental states of others (and indeed of ourselves) are completely hidden from the senses, they can only ever be inferred. (Leslie 1987, 139)

Normal humans everywhere not only "paint" their world with color, they also "paint" beliefs, intentions, feelings, hopes, desires, and pretenses onto agents in their social world. They do this despite the fact that no human has ever seen a thought, a belief, or an intention. (Tooby and Cosmides in Baron-Cohen 1995, xvii)

Although the postulation of mental states might allow us to explain and predict the behavior of human beings better than any other hypothesis currently available, there is no guarantee that this will remain the case in the future. As Churchland writes, "the hypothesis that a specific individual has conscious intelligence is . . . an explanatory hypothesis . . . plausible to the degree that the individual's continuing behavior is best explained and predicted in terms of desires, beliefs, perceptions, emotions and so on" (Churchland 1988, 71). Thus, one should not forget that to suggest that mental states and experiential episodes are theoretical entities is also to suggest that the (folk-psychological) theory that postulates them might be false and could be replaced by a better theory. According to the theory-theory, mental states are theoretically postulated entities comparable to the black holes of astrophysics, and many theory-theorists of an eliminativist persuasion would argue that black holes are considerably more real than mental states such as hopes, memories, intentions, and emotions.

II Theory-Theory of Self-Awareness

According to many theory-theorists (e.g., Gopnik, Carruthers, Frith and Happé), if we are to consider their statements at face value, we come to know our own beliefs and occurrent mental states just as we come to know the beliefs and experiences of others. In both cases, the same cognitive mechanism is in use; we are, in both cases, dealing with a process of mind-reading, with the application of a theory of mind. Thus, according to what might be labeled the theory-theory account of self-awareness, my access to my own mind depends on the same mechanisms that I use in attributing mental states to others. In both cases, the access, understanding, and knowledge are theory mediated, and the mediating theory is the same for self and for other (Carruthers and Smith 1996, 3; Gopnik 1993, 3; Frith and Happé 1999, 7). Even though we seem to perceive our own mental states directly, this direct perception is an illusion.

If this view is correct, there should be no significant difference in the development of our ability to attribute mental states to self and other. In other words, our ability to mind-read should be equally effective regardless of whether the task concerns our own mental states or the mental states of others.[2] The existence of an extensive parallelism could, as a result, provide empirical support for the theory-theory. Does such a parallelism, in fact, exist? To investigate the matter, an entire battery of tests has been employed.[3] Let me focus on the most well known of these tests: the *false-belief* tasks.

The two most frequently used false-belief tasks are the location change and content change tasks. The *Sally–Anne task*, a location change task, is set up in the following manner: The child is confronted with two dolls, Sally and Anne. Sally has a box and Anne has a basket. Sally puts a marble into her box and then goes for a walk. While she is away, Anne takes the marble from the box, and puts it into her own basket. Sally then returns and wants to play with her marble, but where will she look for it? When children four years and older are confronted with this question they will typically say that she will look inside her box, since that is where she (*falsely*) *believes* it to be hidden. Younger children, however, will often point to the basket, indicating that they think that Sally will look for the marble where it really is. They apparently fail to understand that other persons' beliefs could be false (Frith and Happé 1999, 3–4).

In the *Smarties task*, a content change task, children are shown a candy box. Based on its appearance, children first believe that the box contains sweets; the box is then opened and shown to contain pencils. The box is closed again, and the children are asked what other children, who have not yet looked inside the box, will think it contains. The typical four-year-old will answer that other children will think it contains candy, whereas younger children will answer pencils. Once again, the result seems to demonstrate that young children are unable to comprehend that other persons might have false beliefs.

Why this interest in children's ability to succeed on false-belief tasks? In order to make sense of Sally's behavior, for instance, the child has to understand that Sally is acting not on the basis of what is actually the case, but on the basis of a false belief about what is the case. Thus, in order to ascribe false beliefs to others (and to itself), the child is assumed to be able to understand that our beliefs might differ from, and thus be distinct from, real-world events and situations. The child's understanding that a person has a false belief consequently provides compelling evidence that the child is able to appreciate the distinction between world and mind, between reality and our beliefs about reality. In short, in order for the child to ascribe false beliefs to self or other, the child must have beliefs about beliefs. It must be in possession of a theory of mind.

To test the existence of a parallelism in the attribution of mental states to self and to other, a variation of the Smarties task was devised. Children were presented with the deceptive candy box full of pencils. They were first asked the above-mentioned questions, and then the following question was added: "When you first saw the box, before we opened it, what did you think was inside it?" Somewhat surprisingly, one-half to two-thirds of the three-year-olds said that they had originally thought that it contained pencils. They apparently failed to remember their own past false beliefs. Thus, as Gopnik argues, three-year-old children seem to have as much trouble understanding their own past false beliefs as they have in understanding the false beliefs of others (Gopnik 1993, 6–8).

According to Gopnik, this finding reveals a striking parallel between children's understanding of the psychological states of others and their understanding of their own immediately past psychological states. This parallelism, however, does not support our commonsense intuition that the process of discovering our own mental states is fundamentally different from the process of discovering someone else's states. According to the common-sense view, there is a phenomenological asymmetry between self and other. Whereas we observe the other's behavior and have to infer his beliefs and desires, we have direct access to our own beliefs and desires and can simply report them. We need not infer their existence; we do not need any theoretical model at all. For Gopnik, the existence of the parallelism challenges this view. When children can report and understand the psychological states of others, they can report having had those states themselves; when they cannot report and understand the psychological states of others, they report that they have not had those states themselves (Gopnik 1993, 1, 9; Gopnik, Meltzoff, and Kuhl 2001, 47). In short, there is little evidence that mental states are attributed to self before they are attributed to others, and vice versa. Thus, Gopnik is unequivocal in her dismissal of the traditional argument from analogy. It is incorrect to say that we have perceptual information about our own minds and about the bodies of others and use inference when it comes to gaining information about our own bodily appearance and the minds of others. Rather, we have information gained through perception as well as inference, and the situation in the case of self and other is much more symmetrical than traditionally assumed (Gopnik and Meltzoff 1994, 167).

If our acquisition of beliefs about our own mental states parallels our acquisition of beliefs about the mental states of others, and if the epistemic source is fundamentally the same in both cases, then why do we normally tend to believe that there is such a big difference between the two? The explanation offered by both Gopnik and Carruthers is that we have become experts on reading our own mind and, after having reached a certain expertise, we tend to see things at once, even though what we see is actually the result of a complex theoretical process. We draw on accumulated theoretical knowledge, but our expertise makes us unaware of the inferential processes and causes us to believe that our experience is immediate and non-inferential. Thus, self-knowledge or self-consciousness should be thought of on analogy with the theory-laden perception of theoretical entities in science. Just as a diagnostician can sometimes "see" a cancer in the blur of an X-ray, so, too, each of us can sometimes "see" that we are in a state accorded such-and-such a role by folk-psychological theory (Gopnik 1993, 11; Carruthers 1996b, 26; 1996c, 259–260).

When reading her article "How We Know Our Minds: The Illusion of First-Person Knowledge of Intentionality," one occasionally gets the impression that Gopnik wants to challenge first-person authority as such. On closer inspection, however, it becomes clear that she is actually prepared to distinguish between different types of mental states (Gopnik 1993, 2, 10), and that her main target is a particular type of complex beliefs, namely the beliefs that our psychological states are intentional. Thus, in contrast to what might be the case for simple sensations, Gopnik takes the idea of intentionality to be the result of a defeasible cognitive construction. It is not based on a direct first-person apprehension (Gopnik 1993, 10). For Gopnik, my beliefs about the intentionality of my own mental states share the same cognitive history as my beliefs about the intentionality of mental states belonging to others. This seems to suggest that Gopnik's concern is with metarepresentation or metacognition and that she is addressing the status of our higher-order beliefs and ideas about intentional states. However, Gopnik also writes that young children do not experience their own psychological states as intentional in the way adults do. She states that we first have psychological states, and observe the behaviors and experiences that they lead to in ourselves and others, then construct a theory about the causes of those behaviors and experiences that postulate intentionality, and *only* then experience the intentionality of those states (Gopnik 1993, 12). This indicates that Gopnik takes herself to be discussing not simply our beliefs about intentionality, but intentionality itself. Her view is apparently that intentionality, itself, is a theoretical construct and that we start to experience our mental states as intentional only after having acquired and applied a certain theory of mind.

Nichols and Stich have recently criticized Gopnik's position. As they point out, there are three ways to interpret it. First, it could be taken to involve the claim that the only information we have about our own mental states is the kind of evidence of which others are also in possession. In this sense, knowledge of self and knowledge of others would be completely analogous. They take this to be a form of pure behaviorism that is extremely implausible. Second, the theory could be taken to involve the concession that my access to my own mental states is based on information that is not available in the case of my access to the mental states of others. The problem, however, is that the theory never spells out what, exactly, this information is. Gopnik refers to first-person psychological experience as "the Cartesian buzz" (Gopnik 1993, 11), but as Nichols and Stich point out, this is not exactly an illuminating answer. Finally, the theory-theory of self-awareness might argue that the additional information that is available in my own case is information about my own mental states. But if this information is available to me from the outset, there is hardly any reason to introduce and involve any theory of mind mechanism (Nichols and Stich 2003, 169).[4]

The data provided by Gopnik are supposed to confirm the existence of a crucial parallelism in the attribution of intentional states to both others and to self. The most significant finding presented by Gopnik demonstrates the existence of a parallelism in the attribution of *current* false beliefs to others and *past* false beliefs to self. It is, however, unclear why these findings, puzzling and interesting as they are, should warrant the kind of general claim asserted by Gopnik. Her idea seems to be that unless you are able to appreciate that it is possible to have mistaken beliefs, you cannot understand what it means to have beliefs or intentional states, and as long as you lack this understanding, you cannot experience mental states as intentional (Gopnik 1993, 6). It is certainly reasonable to assume that if a child can understand what a false belief is, then it can also understand what a belief is. But is it also reasonable to conclude that unless a child can understand false beliefs it cannot understand beliefs? This makes good sense if we are talking of a full-fledged theoretical understanding of beliefs, that is, of an actual theory of beliefs. Such a theory must involve an understanding and explanation of the possibility of misrepresentation and error; if it did not, we would typically say that it was not really a theory of beliefs, or at best, that it was a very inadequate theory of beliefs. It is hardly surprising that we have high requirements for what a theory should entail. The question is whether it is also appropriate to apply the same strong requirements in the case of a young child, and to claim that the child does not experience itself as having intentional (i.e., object-directed) states unless it masters a theory of mind, unless it is capable of attributing false beliefs to self and others.

Defenders of the theory-theory occasionally present their findings as if they have provided evidence in favor of both the following claims:

1. Our access to our own mind depends on the same mechanisms we use in getting access to the minds of others. Thus, we come to know our own beliefs and occurrent mental states in much the same way we come to know the beliefs and experiences of others.

2. The access to the mind of self and other is theory mediated and inferential. Self-awareness (in the sense of having first-personal access to one's own experiential life) and the experience of others presuppose possession of a theory of mind, and they are, consequently, not acquired until around the age of four.

When pressed on the issue, however, some theory-theorists concede that infants do, in fact, understand (experience) psychological states such as emotions, perceptions, and desires in both self and other prior to the possession of a theory of mind. They then argue that what these infants lack is an understanding of *representational* mental states (see Wellman, Cross, and Watson 2001, 656, 677). However, since the term "representational mental state" is quite ambiguous, this admission does not clarify the situation much. At times, the term is used inclusively to cover all intentional states, including perceptions; at other times, it is used much more restrictively to cover only proper beliefs (thoughts). This vacillation makes the theory-theory into something of a moving target. It also threatens to leave it with an uncomfortable choice between only two options. It can either defend a very strong (some would say extreme) claim, according to which the infant has no first-personal access to any of its own mental episodes and no experience of other minded creatures prior to the acquisition of a theory of mind; or it can defend a much weaker (some would say trivial) claim by defining representational mental states in such narrow terms that it is no wonder that it takes a relatively high level of cognitive sophistication to be able to understand and attribute them to self and others.

To rephrase the criticism in slightly different terms: One can define a mental state as something purely interior and private, as something that is not visible in meaningful actions and expressive behavior. Given such a concept of a mental state, there are good reasons to believe that children will be able to master the concept and ascribe it to others and self only at a relatively late stage. However, the obvious and crucial question is why one would want to opt for such a narrow mentalistic understanding of the mind in the first place.

III Autism

The theory of mind hypothesis that our attribution of mental states to self and other is theoretical or quasi-scientific in nature has found extensive resonance within a variety of empirical disciplines, including developmental psychology, neuroscience, and psychiatry. It has also found use in research on autism.

What is autism? As the term *"autós"* indicates (the Greek word for self) it is a disorder affecting the self. According to the current DSM definition, autism is a pervasive developmental disorder characterized by (1) impaired social interaction, (2) impaired communication, and (3) a restricted repertoire of activities and interests. It is a spectrum disorder and the extreme forms differ greatly in severity. At one end of the spectrum is Kanner's syndrome, originally known as early infantile autism, which typically involves profound language deficits and below-normal IQ. A milder form is Asperger's syndrome, originally known as autistic psychopathy, where core language skills and IQ tend to be in the normal range. In both syndromes, one finds impairments of social functioning, though these, too, range in severity. It had previously been claimed that early infantile autism was a psychotic process with poor prognosis whereas autistic psychopathy was a personality disorder with good prognosis. The current view is that "Kanner's and Asperger's syndromes are best regarded as falling within the continuum of social impairment (of which they form only a part) but characterized, at least in the earlier years of childhood, by somewhat differing profiles of cognitive, language and motor functions" (Wing 1991, 115). Thus, Asperger's syndrome is generally seen as a high-functioning form of autism.

Here is a vignette from Kanner's original 1943 description of a six-year-old child with autism:

The most striking feature in his behaviour was the difference in his reactions to objects and to people. Objects absorbed him easily and he showed good attention and perseverance in playing with them. He seemed to regard people as unwelcome intruders to whom he paid so little attention as they would permit. When forced to respond, he did so briefly and returned to his absorption in things. When a hand was held out before him so that he could not possibly ignore it, he played with it briefly as if it were a detached object. He blew out a match with an expression of satisfaction with the achievement, but did not look up to the person who had lit the match. (Kanner 1943, 224)

A young adult with autism writes:

I really didn't know there were people until I was seven years old. I then suddenly realized that there are people. But not like you do. I still have to remind myself that there are people . . . I never could have a friend. I really don't know what to do with other people, really. (Cohen 1980, 388; ellipsis in original)

When attempting to engage with the autistic child as a social partner, one is struck by the lack of communication and responsiveness. There is a scarcity of facial expressions, poor eye contact, monotonous vocal intonation, and little or no use of gestures. Thus, a child with autism will typically fail to adopt a posture showing readiness and desire to be picked up. He might not look up when his name is called, or take much interest in people speaking to him; he might not look at objects that others are pointing to, or point out things for others to look at; and he may hardly react to other children when they try to play with him. If you throw him a ball, he might catch it, but will then be likely to throw it somewhere else rather than returning it. Impairments in communications will vary from an absence of any attempt to communicate at all, through communications of needs only, to repetitive questioning or lengthy monologues, regardless of the responses of the listener. One might get an answer to a specific question, but it will be difficult, if not impossible, to engage the child in a proper dialogue. Correspondingly, the child might initiate oddly repetitive one-sided approaches himself, he might passively accept being approached, or, and perhaps most strikingly, he might show aloof indifference to others, as if he were living in a glass cage, separated from others by an invisible wall. Thus, the autistic child's manner of relating to persons has occasionally been considered comparable to one that might be appropriate toward "pieces of furniture." Bosch recounts observing one autistic child who, while walking around the schoolyard, would simply push aside any child that stood in his way. He did not do this in a mean or vicious way, however, but, rather, in the manner one would push aside a chair that blocks the way (Bosch 1962, 5).

It is not that children with autism have poor attention, but it is an attention primarily directed at nonsocial objects, such as wheels, cars, empty detergent packs, tin lids, jugs, lamplights, train tables, and so on. Autistic children will also frequently engage in repetitive patterns of activities, show an anxiously obsessive desire for the preservation of sameness, and resist changes in their daily routines. Wing mentions one child who would spend hours running in circles with an object in his hand and who would scream if attempts were made to stop him (Wing 1991, 103).

The study of autism has been central to the theory of mind debate ever since it was discovered that autistic persons have problems passing theory of mind tasks. A dominant explanation, favored by Frith, Leslie, and Baron-Cohen, is that some of the cardinal symptoms in autism are the result of a failure in the development of the capacity to mind-read or "mentalize" (Baron-Cohen, Leslie, and Frith 1985; Frith 2003). Persons with autism lack an ability to understand mental states, they are *mindblind*, and this selective impairment is precisely explained by reference to a damaged or destroyed theory of mind mechanism. According to Frith, the theory of mind is not to be understood primarily as a consciously held scientific theory, but rather as an automatic and deeply unconscious computational mechanism sensitive to the invisible inner states of other people. It provides us with the ability to predict relations between external states of affairs and internal states of mind (Frith 2003, 77–80, 97). Accordingly, the problem facing persons with autism is that they are not automatically programmed to "mentalize," and in the most severe cases of autism, there will consequently not be any understanding of mental states at all. In the mildest cases, however, compensatory learning may lead to the acquisition of a theory of mind, and such individuals will be capable of attributing mental states to self and others. Since this acquired theory of mind is conscious, however, it lacks automaticity, and its use in everyday life will be slow and hence not quite sufficient for normal social communication (Frith 2003, 206).

In the following, I will focus on this *mindblindness hypothesis*, but it should be mentioned that even defenders of this approach now recognize that several different explanatory hypotheses might be needed in order to account for all the symptoms found in autism. Apart from the mindblindness hypothesis that addresses the impairments of social interaction, it has also become customary to speak of the *executive function hypothesis* and of the *central coherence hypothesis*. The former addresses the absence of higher-level attention and control of action in many people with autism and might be helpful in explaining repetitive behavior. The latter proposes that individuals with autism employ a style of information processing that focuses on details and disregards context (Frith 2003, 206–207).

As we have already seen, theory-theorists typically argue that a theory of mind is involved not only in the understanding of other people's mental states, but also in the access to one's own mental states. If this is true, it has some rather obvious implications. If autistic subjects lack a theory of mind, and if a theory of mind is required for self-awareness, then autistic persons should be "as blind to their own mental states as they are to the mental states of others" (Carruthers 1996c, 262; see also Frith and Happé 1999, 1, 7). If, by hypothesis, it is a theory of mind that provides the network of theoretical concepts and principles that enables us to understand mental states, the autist either will be unable to recognize his own mental states as such at all, or will be able to do so only through a slow and painstaking learning process (Carruthers 1996c, 260; Frith and Happé 1999, 2).

Are there any experimental data in support of this hypothesis? Both Baron-Cohen and Frith and Happé have argued that one can test the presence of self-awareness and introspection in autistic subjects by using classical theory of mind tasks, such as the false-belief task or the appearance–reality task (Baron-Cohen 1989, 581, 591; Frith and Happé 1999, 1, 5). As it turns out, even far older autistic children with good general cognitive capacities and high IQ scores answer the way normal three-year-olds do when confronted with theory of mind tasks. By contrast, nonautistic children with other mental handicaps perform relatively well on these tasks. When confronted with the Smarties task, autistic children have as much trouble remembering (self-ascribing) their own recent false beliefs as they have in attributing false beliefs to other people. Similarly, autistic children fail on the so-called appearance–reality task. In this task, children are presented with an object that appears to be one thing, but which is, in reality, something quite different. Typically, a sponge painted to look just like a rock has been used. The children are asked what the object looks like, and what it really is. Whereas normal four-year-olds are able to answer correctly, three-year-olds typically give the same answer to both questions: Either the object looks like a sponge and is a sponge, or the object looks like a rock and really is a rock (Gopnik 1993, 4; Baron-Cohen 1989, 591). In one setting, where autistic children with a mean verbal age of 8.48 years were confronted with fake plastic chocolates, they thought the objects both looked like chocolate and really were chocolate and apparently even persisted in trying to eat the fakes long after having discovered their plastic quality (Baron-Cohen 1989, 594). Since the ability to understand the appearance–reality distinction is taken to entail the ability to attribute mental states to oneself, failure to pass the task has, in turn, been interpreted as suggesting that autists lack awareness of their own mental states (Baron-Cohen 1989, 596; Carruthers 1996c, 260).

The study of autism is not merely an empirical enterprise; it also involves a good deal of conceptual analysis. Let us take a closer look at some of the arguments found in the work of Carruthers, Baron-Cohen, and Frith and Happé.

In order fully to understand the theory-theory perspective on self-awareness in autism, it is important to recall that theory-theorists are committed to some version of the higher-order account of consciousness. This commitment is rarely spelled out, but it is crucial to their general line of argumentation. If we return to Carruthers, we find an author who has not only undertaken the trouble of actually spelling out the link between the theory-theory of mind, the higher-order thought theory, and the issues of self-awareness and phenomenal consciousness, but who has also done so with characteristic bluntness. As we saw in chapter 1, Carruthers takes conscious mental states, that is, mental states with a distinctive subjective feel to them, mental states that it feels like something to be the subject of, to be mental states of which the subject is aware. He consequently argues that conscious mental states require reflective self-awareness, or, to put it differently, that reflective self-awareness is a conceptually necessary condition for phenomenal consciousness (Carruthers 1996a, 155). Carruthers considers the self-awareness in question to be a type of higher-order thinking, and he therefore argues that a creature must be able to think about and hence conceptualize its own mental states if these states are to feel like anything to the organism. Thus, in order to have a phenomenally conscious perception of a surface as green, the creature must entertain the higher-order thought "I am perceiving a green surface." Since mental concepts get their significance from being embedded in a folk-psychological theory dealing with the structure and functioning of the mind, what this ultimately means is that only creatures in possession of a theory of mind are capable of enjoying conscious experiences (Carruthers 1996a, 158; 2000, 194). Given this setup, Carruthers draws the obvious conclusion: Creatures who lack a theory of mind, such as most animals, young infants, and autistic persons, will also lack conscious experiences. As he writes, "if autistic subjects are blind to their own mental states, then that will mean they are incapable of self-directed HORs [higher-order representations]; which in turn will mean that they lack phenomenally conscious mental states" (Carruthers 2000, 202; see also Carruthers 1996a, 221).

To suggest, however, that autistic subjects do not feel pleasure, anxiety, or frustration and that there is nothing it is like for them to taste hot chocolate or to be scalded by boiling water is outrageous. It reduces them to zombies. Carruthers might be applauded for his clarity and consistency and for actually biting the bullet, but this does not make his theory any more plausible. Carruthers would find it scandalous to give people's intuitions any weight at all in this domain, let alone to think them sufficient to refute the higher-order theory of consciousness (Carruthers 2000, 199). In my view, however, the conclusion drawn by Carruthers is so counterintuitive that it can serve as a *reductio ad absurdum* of his own account of consciousness.

In the article "Are Autistic Children 'Behaviorists'?" Baron-Cohen suggests that autistic children who lack a theory of mind and are incapable of adopting the intentional stance will be forced to view the world exclusively in terms of behavioral and physical events (Baron-Cohen 1989, 580). Baron-Cohen presents different experimental data and writes that autistic children are unable to distinguish mental entities from physical entities; they simply seem unaware of the special nature of mental entities. In one example concerning dreaming, autistic children were asked where dreams are located, in the room or inside their head. Most would say in the room and, as Baron-Cohen writes, this finding suggests that autistic children simply do not understand the *concept* "dream" (Baron-Cohen 1989, 587). Baron-Cohen also argues that autistic children do not understand linguistic terms referring to thinking, pretending, and so on, and that their inability to distinguish appearance from reality reflects a lack of metacognition or metarepresentation (Baron-Cohen 1989, 596). All of these statements suggest that autists, according to Baron-Cohen, suffer from some defect in higher cognition. Their conceptual and linguistic skills are impaired and defective. At the same time, however, Baron-Cohen repeatedly makes assertions that can be construed as involving a much stronger claim, saying in turn that autistic children "appear oblivious to the existence of mental phenomena" (Baron-

Cohen 1989, 588); that "autistic subjects . . . appear to be largely unaware of the mental world" (Baron-Cohen 1989, 590); and that autistic subjects are "unaware of their own mental states" (Baron-Cohen 1989, 595).

Baron-Cohen concludes his article by denying that all internal (mental) states are beyond the comprehension of autistic subjects. In his view, they do, in fact, have an intact understanding of desires and simple emotions like happiness, sadness, and hunger. Thus, rather than saying that autistic persons are behaviorists, it would be better to call them "desire-psychologists." That is, autistic persons may be able to predict people's actions in terms of desires and physical causes, but they fail to develop a belief-desire psychology (Baron-Cohen, 1989, 597–598). How Baron-Cohen can reconcile the claim that autistic subjects understand certain emotions with his claim that they are oblivious to mental phenomena remains rather unclear.

Baron-Cohen takes the appearance–reality task to be a way of testing children's ability to represent the distinction between their perception of an object (its appearance) and their knowledge about it (its real identity), and, thus, as a way of testing their ability to attribute mental states to themselves (Baron-Cohen 1989, 591). Autistic children fail on this task, and this suggests, according to Baron-Cohen, that they lack awareness of their own mental states (Baron-Cohen 1989, 596). How is this argument actually supposed to work, and why should an inability to succeed on the appearance–reality task entail a lack of self-awareness? Although success on the appearance–reality task calls for some measure of access to one's own mental states, an argument to the effect that a person who fails this task will also lack such access is as valid as the argument that since writing one's autobiography requires possession of self-awareness, a person who is unable to write his memoirs lacks self-awareness. The argument is invalid, since it confuses necessary and sufficient conditions. Even if success on the appearance–reality task justifies ascribing self-awareness to the person in question, one cannot conclude that somebody who fails on the task will lack self-awareness. Such a conclusion would be warranted only if the ability to distinguish appearance and reality were a necessary requirement for possessing self-awareness, and no argument has yet been put forth to show that that should be the case. Furthermore, as Nichols and Stich have recently pointed out, even if the argument were valid, the experimental data do not at all support the conclusion drawn by Baron-Cohen, but rather the exact opposite one. As the example with the fake chocolates shows, autistic children have a tendency to fail on the appearance–reality task by being taken in by the *appearance* of the object, that is, by the way they *experience* the object. Had they had no access to their own mental states, this is not the kind of error they would have been expected to make; rather, they should have been very good at detecting what the object really is and should have had no access to its appearance (Nichols and Stich 2003, 179).

In their article "Theory of Mind and Self-Consciousness: What Is It Like to Be Autistic?" Frith and Happé argue that autism involves a kind of mind-blindness and they propose that autistic persons can only judge their own mental states by their actions (Frith and Happé 1999, 11). That is, they suggest that autistic persons do not have a direct, immediate, or noninferential access to their own mind, but that they, rather, come to know what transpires in their mind only by applying a theory of mind to their own behavior. Frith and Happé also write that the inability to attribute mental states to oneself is the same as not having introspective awareness and suggest that an autistic mind might contain only first-order representations of events and experiences (Frith and Happé 1999, 1, 8). As they stress, it is not that autistic persons lack mental states; it is only that they are unable to *reflect* on their mental states. Autists simply lack the cognitive machinery to represent their thoughts and feelings *as* thoughts and feelings (Frith and Happé 1999, 7); that is, they may not be able to conceptualize their own intentions *as* intentions (Frith and Happé 1999, 9). These statements, at first, seem to point in the same direction as some of Baron-Cohen's remarks, namely that autism might involve a defect in higher cognition, might involve defective conceptual skills. In the end, however, the article contains an ambiguity related to the one found in Baron-Cohen's contribution, since Frith and Happé not only speak of autism as involving an *impaired* self-consciousness, but also repeatedly write that autism involves a *lack* of self-consciousness (Frith and Happé 1999, 8). To have impaired self-consciousness and to lack self-consciousness are two very different things. The situation is not clarified by the fact that Frith and Happé never explain what, precisely, they mean by the term "self-consciousness." Is their claim that autistic subjects have mental states, but lack self-awareness in the sense of a first-personal (immediate and noninferential) access to these states, or is it, rather, that these states (perceptions, desires, beliefs, emotions) feel like something to the subjects, that there are experiences involved, but that autistic subjects simply have difficulties articulating these experiences reflectively and conceptually?[5]

IV A Critical Rejoinder

In my view, the theory-theory of mind is faced with a number of problems. Not only is there frequently a gap between the experimental data presented and the quite radical conclusions drawn from these data, but the position is also based on an inadequate and overly intellectualistic understanding of both self-consciousness and intersubjectivity. It is relatively uncontroversial that adults are in possession of some theoretical knowledge about other persons and about the workings of their own minds; the crucial question is whether this theoretical knowledge constitutes the whole of what we call upon when we understand others and ourselves.[6]

What I intend to do in the following is to challenge the theory-theory of mind. I will make use of the phenomenological insights obtained in the previous chapters, but I will also draw on recent developmental psychology. The relevance of the latter discipline for the present debate is obvious; if a theory of mind is required for the experience of minded beings, be it oneself or others, then any creature who lacks such a theory will also lack both self- and other-experience. According to the standard view, however, children gain possession of a theory of mind only when they reach the average age of four.[7] Thus, a direct implication of the theory-theory of mind is that young children will lack any understanding of self and other during the first three to four years of life. Is such a claim justified? In answering, I will discuss self-experience and other-experience, in turn, and then conclude by returning to the issue of autism.

Embodied Self-Experience

What does phenomenology say about self-experience? As we have already seen in the previous chapters, phenomenologists would insist that we have an innate and noninferential access to our own experiential life and that any investigation of consciousness that denies this first-personal access is seriously flawed. Moreover, phenomenologists would typically argue that it is legitimate to speak of a primitive type of self-experience or self-awareness whenever we are phenomenally conscious. This weak self-awareness does not exist apart from the ordinary conscious perception, feeling, or thought, as an additional mental act; it is not brought about by some kind of reflection or introspection, but is rather an intrinsic feature of the experience.

If this view is correct, it has obvious consequences for the ascription of self-awareness to infants, a topic that has lately attracted a lot of philosophical attention. Bermúdez, for instance, has recently criticized the attempt to reduce the question of self-awareness to a question of linguistic self-reference and successful mastery of the first-person pronoun. He has argued that a proper understanding of self-awareness must broaden its focus and acknowledge the existence of nonconceptual and prelinguistic forms of self-awareness that are "logically and ontogenetically more primitive than the higher forms of self-consciousness that are usually the focus of philosophical debate" (Bermúdez 1998, 274). We need to recognize the existence of forms of self-awareness that precede the mastery of language and the ability to form full-blown rational judgments and propositional attitudes. Such influential developmental psychologists as Stern, Neisser, and Rochat have also reached similar conclusions. They all argue that the infant is in possession of self-experience from birth, and all reject the view, originally defended by Piaget, that the infant initially lives in a kind of dualistic fusion where there is, as yet, no distinction between self, world, and other (Piaget and Inhelder 1969, 22). Thus, according to this once widely held view, the infant was supposed to exist in a "state of un-differentiation, of fusion with mother, in which the 'I' is not yet differentiated from the 'not-I' and in which inside and outside are only gradually coming to be sensed as different" (Mahler, Pine, and Bergman 1975, 44).

To begin with Stern: his argument has been that theory and language *transform* and *articulate* the infant's experience of self and other; they do not constitute it. As early as from birth onward the infant gains possession of different pre-reflective and prelinguistic "senses of self." Stern concedes that the sense of self initially available to the infant is basic, but he lists four types of experiences that he takes to be present at around three months of age. There is *self-agency*, that is, the sense of authorship of one's own actions; *self-coherence*, or, the sense of being an integrated, nonfragmented whole; and *self-affectivity*, the experience of subjective feelings. Finally, there is *self-history*, which is the having of a sense of endurance, of being in continuity with one's own past (Stern 1985, 71).

It would lead too far afield to discuss Stern's analyses of all four types of self-experience in detail, but let me focus on his account of self-agency or authorship of actions. How does the infant distinguish between its own movements/actions and the movements/actions of others, and what enables it to experience *itself* as an agent? Stern distinguishes two *experiential* invariants: (1) the sense of volition that precedes a motor act, and (2) the proprioceptive feedback that does or does not occur during the act (Stern 1985, 76). The infant will typically encounter three different types of action: self-willed action of self, other-willed action of other, and other-willed action of self, and it will be able to distinguish between the three precisely because of the presence or absence of the two invariants. If the experience of the action contains both volition and proprioceptive feedback, it is a self-willed action of self. If neither is present, it is an other-willed action of other; and if the proprioceptive feedback is present, but the experience of volition is absent, as when the mother moves the hand of the infant, we have an other-willed action of self.

In agreement with Stern, both Neisser and Rochat also reject the view that self-experience has a late developmental onset. In a well-known article from 1988, Neisser distinguished five selves: the ecological, interpersonal, extended, private, and conceptual self (Neisser 1988, 35). The most basic and primitive of these is the ecological self, that is, the individual understood as an active agent in the immediate environment. When and how are we aware of the ecological self? According to Neisser, whenever we perceive. Continuing a Gibsonian line of thought, Neisser takes perception to involve information about the relation between the perceiver and the environment. All perception involves a kind of self-sensitivity; all perception involves a coperception of self and of environment (see Gibson 1979/1986, 126). As perceivers, we are embedded and embodied agents. We see with mobile eyes, set in a head that can turn and attached to a body that can move from place to place; in this sense, a stationary point of view is only the limiting case of a mobile point of view (Gibson 1986, 53, 205). Every movement of the perceiver produces a systematic flow pattern in the visual field that provides her with awareness of her own movements and postures, and thereby with a weak, or primitive, form of ecological self-awareness.

Adopting Gibson's notion of affordance, Neisser writes that any given situation affords some actions and not others. We see at a glance whether objects are within reach, whether doors are wide enough to walk through, or chairs the right height to sit on. Moreover, this perception is "body-scaled," that is, the distance that matters is not measured in centimeters, but in relation to our own bodily dimensions and capabilities (Neisser 1993, 8). For instance, an infant as young as a few weeks can discriminate between objects that are within its reach and objects that are just outside its reach. The infant is far less inclined to reach out for an object that is just outside its reach. Of course, for the infant to be able to make this distinction is for the infant to be aware of the position of the object in relation to *itself*. This is not to say, however, that infants are already, at this stage, in possession of an explicit representation of self; rather, they are able to perceive a distinctive kind of affordance—they are in possession of *self-specifying information*. Even very young infants pick up the information that specifies the ecological self. They respond to optical flow, discriminate between themselves and other objects, and easily distinguish their own actions and their immediate consequences from events of other kinds. They are able to perceive themselves, among other things; where they are, how they are moving, what they are doing, and whether a given action is their own or not. These achievements appear in the very first weeks and months of life and testify to the existence of a primitive and irreducible form of self-awareness (Neisser 1993, 4).

All healthy infants have an innate rooting response. When the corner of the infant's mouth is touched, the infant turns her head and opens her mouth toward the stimulation. By recording the frequency of rooting in response to either external tactile stimulation or tactile self-stimulation, it was discovered that newborns (24 hours old) showed rooting responses almost three times more frequently in response to external stimuli. This made Rochat conclude that even newborns can discriminate double touch stimulation combined with proprioception and single touch of exogenous origin. That is, they can pick up the intermodal invariants that specify self- versus non-self-stimulation, and, thereby, have the ability to develop an early sense of self (Rochat 2001, 40–41).

Infants are in possession of proprioceptive information from birth, and as Rochat argues, proprioception is "the modality of the self par excellence" (Rochat 2001, 35). Thus, long before they are able to pass any mirror self-recognition tasks, not to speak of any false-belief tasks, infants have a sense of their own bodies as organized and environmentally embedded entities and, hence, an early perceptually based sense of themselves. Following in the footsteps of Neisser and Gibson, Rochat calls this early sense of self the infant's ecological self (Rochat 2001, 30–31, 41).

For Rochat, the ecological self is clearly a bodily self. He argues that the infant's self-experience is initially a question of the infant's experience of its own embodied self. It is through their early explorations of their own bodies that infants specify themselves as differentiated agents in the environment, eventually developing an explicit awareness of themselves. More precisely, infants have an inborn inclination to investigate their own bodies. This inclination forms the cradle of self-perception and constitutes the developmental origin of self-knowledge (Rochat 2001, 29, 39, 74).

At around the age of fifteen to eighteen months, the child becomes able to perform symbolic actions and acquires some linguistic competence. That the child becomes able to assume a more detached perspective on itself can be seen from its use of names and pronouns to designate itself and from its behavior before a mirror. Prior to this age, the infant presumably does not realize that it sees itself in the mirror. If one marks the face of the infant with rouge without its knowledge and it subsequently looks in a mirror, a younger child will point to the mirror and not to itself. After the age of eighteen months, however, the child will touch the rouge on its own face. Since the confrontation with the mirror motivates a *self-directed* behavior, it is assumed that the child now recognizes what it sees in the mirror as its own reflection (Lewis and Brooks-Gunn 1979, 33–46; Stern 1985, 165).

The ability to recognize one's own mirror image is linked to an increasing ability to assume a detached perspective on oneself, an increasing ability to recognize the perspectives of others on oneself. The mirror permits the child to see itself as it is seen by others. As Merleau-Ponty wrote: "To recognize his image in the mirror is for him to learn that *there can be a viewpoint taken on him.* . . . I am no longer what I felt myself, immediately, to be. . . . I leave the reality of my lived *me* in order to refer myself constantly to the ideal, fictitious, or imaginary *me*, of which the specular image is the first outline. In this sense, I am torn from myself, and the image in the mirror prepares me for another still more serious alienation, which will be the alienation by others" (Merleau-Ponty 1960b, 55–56 [1964, 136]).[8]

Although this recognition of one's own mirror image testifies to the existence of self-experience, its absence certainly does not imply the lack of every kind of self-experience. The recognition of one's own reflection is, by no means, a primitive and basic type of self-experience; on the contrary, we are dealing with a rather sophisticated type of representationally mediated self-identification where the self-experience in question takes place across distance and separation. We identify "that other" as ourselves. Moreover, the child would not be able to perform this identification, which presumably takes place through a detection of the perfect cross-modal match between its own bodily movements and the movements of the mirror image, if it were not already aware of its *own* bodily movements. In short, to recognize oneself in the mirror, one must already be in possession of bodily self-awareness.

There are good reasons, philosophical as well as empirical, for maintaining that body-awareness constitutes genuine self-experience. Unfortunately, however, and contrary to expectations, the accounts offered by Rochat, Neisser, and Stern are not always sufficiently clear on this.

In the introduction to his book *The Infant's World*, Rochat suggests that there are three fundamentally different classes of experiences: the experience of self, of objects, and of other people (Rochat 2001, 27). I wholeheartedly agree with this division, which very much fits the received view in phenomenology. Unfortunately, however, Rochat does not entirely respect his own division. He soon begins to talk of the body as an object of exploration and of self-perception as a question of differentiating one's own body from *other* objects in the environment (Rochat 2001, 34, 37). We find the very same take in the work of Neisser, who repeatedly speaks of the self as an object (Neisser 1988, 35, 39, 40). Although Neisser concedes that the ecological self is not per se an object of thought, he nevertheless considers it to be an object of perception (Neisser 1988, 41, 56).

If we return to Stern's multifaceted analysis of the infant's self-experience, we come across a similar objectivistic strain. Stern occasionally makes it sound as if the infant's self-experience is a result of its ability to discriminate itself from others and that this is merely an instance of its general ability to discriminate between different entities. He claims that the infant, far from being a *tabula rasa*, is predesigned to perceive the world in a highly structured fashion. Just as, very early, it is able to perceive and organize various stimuli into different natural categories, the infant has inborn capabilities that enable it to discriminate incongruous gestalt constellations of stimuli in such a way that it can keep self and other separate. When the infant sees the face of the father, hears the voice of the mother, and feels its own hand, it is not overwhelmed by a surge of unstructured sensations, but is able to distinguish between itself, the father, and the mother as three distinct entities. It recognizes that the behavior of different persons is differently structured; it distinguishes one agent from another (Stern 1983, 56–62) and is, thereby, ultimately able to discriminate the invariant structure that characterizes its own self-generated actions and experiences from the patterns belonging to the movement and actions of particular others (Stern 1985, 7, 65, 67).

This way of describing and accounting for self-experience, however, is beset with a major problem. Even if an infant is able to distinguish between different entities in such a way that no confusion takes place, this does not answer the key question: How does the infant sense that one of these experiential configurations is *itself*? The answer given is not satisfactory. Although both Stern and Rochat acknowledge that the infant's (direct and immediate) experience of proprioception and volition is of crucial importance (Rochat 2001, 89; Stern 1983, 65), they still present it as if self-experience is a question of discriminating correctly between two different objects. This is to commit the mistake of equating self-experience with object-identification, as if the infant were first confronted with certain experiences that it then, in a subsequent move, succeeded in identifying as its own.

As we have seen in previous chapters, however, it is problematic to conceive of the (embodied) self as an object, and of (embodied) self-experience as a kind of object-awareness. To put it quite simply: For something to be given as an object is for it to be given as something that transcends the merely subjective. For something to be given as an object of experience is for it to differ from the subjective experience itself. However, if this is so, if object-awareness always involves a kind of epistemic divide, a distinction between the subject and the object of experience, it cannot help us understand self-experience. After all, self-experience is precisely supposed to acquaint us with our own subjectivity; it is not merely to acquaint us with yet another object of experience. Perhaps it could be objected that there are surely cases where I am first confronted with a certain object and then recognize that the object in question is, in fact, myself. This is true, of course, but this kind of objectified self-recognition can never constitute the most fundamental form of self-experience. In order for me to recognize a certain object as myself, I need to hold something true of it that I already know to be true of myself. The only way to avoid an infinite regress is to accept the existence of a nonobjectifying self-experience. To quote Shoemaker:

The reason one is not presented to oneself "as an object" in self-awareness is that self-awareness is not perceptual awareness, i.e., is not a sort of awareness in which objects are presented. It is awareness of facts unmediated by awareness of objects. But it is worth noting that if one were aware of oneself as an object in such cases (as one is in fact aware of oneself as an object when one sees oneself in a mirror), this would not help to explain one's self-knowledge. For awareness that the presented object was ϕ, would not tell one that one was oneself ϕ, unless one had identified the object as oneself; and one could not do this unless one already had some self-knowledge, namely the knowledge that one is the unique possessor of whatever set of properties of the presented object one took to show it to be oneself. Perceptual self-knowledge presupposes non-perceptual self-knowledge, so not all self-knowledge can be perceptual. (Shoemaker 1984, 105)

The problem with the account offered by Stern, Rochat, and Neisser is that they conceive of the embodied self as an object, and of embodied self-experience as a kind of object-awareness. In contrast, phenomenology has insisted that first-personal experience presents me with an immediate, nonobjectifying and nonobservational access to myself. In other words, the phenomenological analysis complements the argumentation provided by developmental psychologists since it explicitly tackles an issue they remain largely silent about, that of the nature of experience and phenomenal consciousness. Most of the evidence presented by Stern, Rochat, and Neisser is obviously behavioral in nature. However, in order for a creature to be in possession of self-experience, it is not sufficient that the creature in question behaves in a certain way. It must also be in possession of phenomenal consciousness and behave as it does because it has the experiences it has. Any reasonable ascription of self-experience cannot bypass a discussion of the relationship between phenomenal consciousness and self-experience. This is precisely what the phenomenological tradition can provide. To put it differently, the phenomenological defense of a one-level account of consciousness can provide strong support for the existence of prelinguistic forms of self-experience. Of course, this is not to deny that there are also more advanced forms of self-awareness that do, in fact, presuppose the use of language, but the primitive self-awareness entailed by phenomenal consciousness is independent of such conceptual sophistication. The newborn does not have to master the words and concepts "pain," "hunger," "frustration," and "mine," in order to feel the *mineness* of the pain, the hunger, and the frustration. To put it another way, the question of self-awareness is not primarily a question of a specific *what*, but of a unique *how*. It does not concern the specific content of an experience, but its unique mode of givenness. This is why the infant, even prior to any conceptual discrimination between self and world or self and other, can be self-aware. It is a self-awareness rooted in the first-personal givenness of its experiences, in the intrinsic self-manifesting character of its experiential life.

In addition, phenomenology has also investigated the nature of embodiment in detail. As Michel Henry once pointed out, a phenomenological clarification of the body must take its departure in the original givenness of the body (Henry 1965, 79). How, precisely, is the body originally given? When I am watching a football match, I normally pay no attention to the turn of my head as I follow the motions of the players, or to the narrowing of my eyes when I attempt to discern the features of the goalkeeper. When I give up and reach for my binoculars, the movements of my hand remain outside the focus of my consciousness. When I am occupied with objects, my perceptual acts and their bodily roots are generally passed over in favor of the perceived, that is, my body tends to efface itself on its way to its intentional goal. This is fortunate, for were we aware of our bodily movements in the same way in which we are aware of objects, our body would make such high demands on our attention that it would interfere with our daily life. When I execute movements without thinking about them, this is not necessarily because the movements are nonconscious, mechanical, or involuntary; rather, they might simply be part of my functioning intentionality, they might be immediately and pre-reflectively felt, as both Henry and Merleau-Ponty argued (Henry 1965, 128; Merleau-Ponty 1945, 168). Even if my movements are absent as thematic intentional objects, this does not entail that they are experientially absent in any absolute sense.[9]

Under normal circumstances, I do not need to perceive my arm visually in order to know where it is. If I wish to catch a frisbee, I do not first have to search for the hand, since it is always with me. Whereas I can approach or move away from any object in the world, the body itself is always present as my very perspective on the world. That is, rather than being simply yet another perspectivally given object, the body itself, as Sartre and Merleau-Ponty argued, is precisely that which allows me to perceive objects perspectivally (Sartre 1943, 378; Merleau-Ponty 1945, 107). The body is present not as a permanent perceptual object, but as myself. Usually, I do not have any consciousness *of* my body as an intentional object. I do not perceive it; *I am it*. Sartre even wrote that the lived body is invisibly present precisely because it is existentially lived rather than known (Sartre 1943, 372). This is also why Husserl repeatedly emphasized how important it is to distinguish

206 | Chapter 7

between *Leib* and *Körper*, that is, between the pre-reflectively lived body, or, the body as an embodied first-person perspective, and the subsequent thematic experience *of* the body as an object (Hua 14/57). To view the body as an objective piece of nature is to engage in a process of abstraction.

In short, phenomenologists typically take pre-reflective body-awareness to be a question of how an embodied self is given, not as an *object*, but as a *subject*. Whereas Bermúdez has recently claimed that "somatic proprioception is a form of perception" that takes "the embodied self as its object" (Bermúdez 1998, 132), phenomenologists would argue that *primary* body-awareness is not a type of object-consciousness—it is not a perception of the body as an object at all (see Gallagher 2003b). They would insist, rather, that it constitutes a genuine form of subjective self-experience.[10]

Primary and Secondary Intersubjectivity

Classical phenomenology and recent developmental psychology have both pointed to a dimension of bodily self-experience that is in place long before the infant is capable of solving any theory of mind tasks. However, the theory-theory of mind defends a double thesis. It claims not only that self-experience is theoretically mediated, but also that intersubjectivity is theoretically mediated. After all, the whole idea is that any reference to minded beings involves a process of mind-reading, involves an application of a theory of mind. Given this situation, it is natural to ask whether the theory-theory treatment of intersubjectivity might not be beset with related empirical and conceptual difficulties.

According to the theory-theory, our understanding of other people is, in principle, like our understanding of trees, rocks, and clouds. Other people are just complex objects in our environment whose behavior we attempt to predict and explain, but whose causal innards are hidden to us. This is part of the reason that we must make appeal to theory and postulate "unobservables" such as beliefs and desires (Heal 1986, 135). But could it not be argued that our understanding of other people differs in fundamental ways from our understanding of inanimate objects? Could it not be argued that other people are subjects like ourselves, and that this makes the epistemic situation completely different? Could it not be argued that knowledge of bodies as minded is fundamentally different from knowledge of bodies as physical objects? We can access the feelings, desires, and beliefs of others through their expressive behavior; expressive and meaningful behavior is a visible manifestation of the life of the mind (see chapter 6). Moreover, when we seek to understand others, we do not normally first attempt to classify their actions under lawlike generalizations; rather we seek to make sense of them. The question is whether this process of sense-making is theoretical or quasi-scientific in nature, or whether it rather involves some kind of embodied (emotional and perceptual) skill or practice (Gallagher 2001, 85). Our conviction that we are, in daily life, engaging with other minded creatures is, in any case, quite unlike any ordinary theoretical hypothesis. In ordinary life (exclusive of both various forms of pathological conditions, as well as philosophical thought experiments), we are never faced with the choice about whether or not we wish to take the people we are meeting in the street or conversing with as real people or mere automatons. Where does this deep-rooted certainty, which far exceeds our confidence in well-confirmed scientific hypotheses, come from? Should it be dismissed as simply an irrational instinct or fallacious reasoning (Gurwitsch 1979, 10–11)?

The crucial question is not whether we can predict and explain the behavior of others, and if so, how that happens, but rather whether such prediction and explanation constitute the primary and most fundamental form of intersubjectivity. As Heidegger famously argued, the very attempt to grasp the mental states of others is the exception rather than the rule. Under normal circumstances, we understand each other well enough through our shared engagement in the common world (Heidegger GA 20: 334–335). It is only if this understanding for some reason breaks down, for instance, if the other behaves in an unexpected and puzzling way, that other options of inferential reasoning, or some kind of simulation, kick in and take over. Because we conform to shared norms, much of the work of understanding one another does not really have to be done by us. The work is already accomplished (McGeer 2001, 119).

According to the theory-theory of mind, my access to the mind of another is always inferential in nature, is always mediated by his bodily behavior. As we have repeatedly seen, however, this way of raising and tackling the problem of intersubjectivity presupposes a highly problematic dichotomy between inner and outer, between experience and behavior. If we start with a radical division between a perceived body and an inferred mind we will never, to use Hobson's phrase, be able to "put Humpty Dumpty together again" (Hobson 1993, 104). When it comes to my own experiential episodes, the claim that they are hidden, unobservable, theoretically postulated entities seems highly counterintuitive, to put it mildly. The assumption is also highly questionable when it comes to the experience of others.

Whereas, in adult life, we occasionally make inferential attributions of mental states to other people, such attributions cannot be considered the basis of the smooth and immediate interpersonal interaction, often called *primary intersubjectivity*, found in young infants (Trevarthen 1979). In some of his writings, Merleau-Ponty called attention to the fact that an infant will understand the affective meaning of a smile long before it has seen its own face in a mirror; it will understand threatening gestures long before it has itself executed any. If an adult takes one of the infant's fingers between his teeth and pretends to bite it, the infant will open its mouth. Why does it do that? There is no obvious resemblance between its own felt but unseen mouth and the seen but unfelt mouth of the adult. As Merleau-Ponty suggested, the infant might be able to cross the gap between the visual appearance of the other's body and the proprioceptive appearance of its own body precisely because its lived body has an outside and contains an anticipation of the other. The infant does not need to carry out any process of inference. Its body schema is characterized by a transmodal openness that immediately allows it to understand and imitate others (Merleau-Ponty 1942, 169; 1945, 165, 404–405; 1960a, 213, 221).

Merleau-Ponty's observation has recently been substantiated by a number of empirical studies concerned with infant imitation. A series of experiments conducted by Meltzoff and Moore demonstrated successful facial imitation in newborn babies, the youngest being forty-two minutes, the oldest seventy-two hours (Meltzoff and Moore 1995).[11] It may have been natural to assume that this early imitation should be classified as automatic, reflexive, stimulus-driven behavior, but a number of findings suggest differently and indicate that the imitation is a question of early social interaction and social cognition. Using slightly older babies (twelve to twenty-one days), Meltzoff and Moore demonstrated that the facial imitation of this group was highly differentiated. They were able to imitate a number of different types of actions (tongue protrusion, mouth opening, and lip protrusion), and the range and specificity of these imitative acts suggest that they were considerably more sophisticated than mere reflexlike mechanisms. Moreover, it was shown that infants are able to imitate across temporal gaps, something that mere reflexes cannot do. Another experiment demonstrated that when six-week-old babies were shown an unusual gesture of large tongue protrusion to the side, they were at first unable to imitate it, but gradually corrected and improved their imitative attempts until success was obtained. The imitation involved effort and progressive approximation; infants that were unable to imitate the gesture became frustrated and cried. All of these findings suggest that the facial imitation in young infants is a goal-directed, intentional activity, and not merely an automatic reflex.

How "do babies 'know' that they have a face or facial features? How do they 'know' that the face they see is anything like the face they have? How do they 'know' that specific configurations of that other face, as only seen, correspond to the same specific configurations in their own face as only felt, proprioceptively, and never seen?" (Stern 1985, 51). Meltzoff and Moore suggest that early imitation involves a kind of cross-modal matching. Infants seem to have a primitive body schema that allows them to unify the visual and proprioceptive information into one common "supramodal," "cross-modal," or "amodal" framework, that is, they seem to have an innate capacity to translate information received in one sensory modality into another sensory modality.[12] It is this innate capacity to detect cross-modal equivalences between own felt movements and the visually perceived movements of others that forms the foundation for later, more sophisticated interpersonal understanding. Thus, Meltzoff and Moore end up reaching a conclusion rather similar to Merleau-Ponty's view:

One interesting consequence of this notion of supramodality is that there is a primordial connection between self and other. The actions of other humans are seen as like the acts that can be done at birth. This innate capacity has implications for understanding people, since it suggests an intrinsic relatedness between the seen bodily acts of others and the internal states of oneself (the sensing and representation of one's own movements). A second implication of young infants' possessing a representation of their own bodies is that it provides a starting point for developing objectivity about themselves. This primitive self-representation of the body may be the earliest progenitor of being able to take perspective on oneself, to treat oneself as an object of thought. (Meltzoff and Moore 1995, 53–54)[13]

In short, if the infant is to experience other embodied subjects, it must be in possession of a type of bodily self-experience that undercuts the gap between interiority and exteriority.

Imitation implies detection of similarities between self and other. Indeed, one reason typical infants might attend preferentially to other people rather than objects might be their sense that others are "like me." This not only provides evidence for the presence of a bodily based, minimal sense of self;

as Stawarska has pointed out, the infant's ability to monitor and correct gestures through practice in order to attain the closest possible match also indicates that the infant has a sense of its own body as *distinct* from the perceived body of the other, that is, imitation does not indicate lack of differentiation (Stawarska 2003, 141). Moreover, infants are not only able to imitate adults; they are also able to recognize that they themselves are being imitated by adults. They can do so before they are able to pass any mirror self-recognition task. In one experiment involving fourteen-month-old infants, an infant and two experimenters would sit across each other. One of the experimenters would imitate the actions of the infant, while the other experimenter would perform other nonmatching actions from within the same range of movements. The infant would consistently look, smile, and direct more testing behavior at the imitating adult (Gopnik and Meltzoff 1994, 168–173). That children in the second year of life already recognize that they are the object of others' attention is also evident from their display of affective forms of self-consciousness (shyness, coyness, embarrassment, etc.) when looked at.

Eye contact and facial expressions are of paramount importance to the young infant, who, shortly after birth, is able to distinguish its mother's face from the face of a stranger. Initially, the infant has very little command over its own locomotion, but it has an almost fully developed control over its eye-movements and can function as a social partner through its gaze. By controlling its own direction of gaze, it can regulate the level and amount of social stimulation. Through such gaze behaviors as averting its gaze, shutting its eyes, staring past, becoming glassy-eyed, and so on, it can to a large extent initiate, maintain, terminate, and avoid social contact (Stern 1985, 21).

A two- to three-month-old infant will engage in "protoconversations" with other people by smiling and vocalizing, and will demonstrate a capacity to vary the timing and intensity of communication with its partner. The purpose of this early interaction seems to be the interaction itself with the participants affectively resonating to one another (Fivaz, Favez, and Frascarolo 2004). When a mother mirrors the infant's affects, the infant will reciprocate and show sensitivity to the affective mirroring of the mother. In fact, infants clearly expect people to communicate reciprocally with them in face-to-face interactions, and to work actively with them in order to sustain and regulate the interaction. If the mother remains immobile and unresponsive to the infant's attempts to engage her, the infant will react by ceasing to smile, and will exhibit distress and attempt to regain her participation.

Infants are not only able to pick up information about their partners that enable them to respond correspondingly and coherently, but, as numerous experiments have demonstrated, they are also very sensitive to the character of the ongoing interaction itself. In one experimental setup, for instance, mothers and their six- to eight-week-old infants were placed in separate rooms but kept in contact via double closed-circuit television. Thus, each partner saw and heard a full-face, life-size video image of the other. The first minute of interaction was videotaped, and the tape of the mother was then rewound and replayed on the infant's screen. As long as the video presentation was "live," the interaction proceeded normally. During the replay segment, although the infants saw the same mother, the same gestures, and the same displays of affection as they had seen a moment ago, their reactions changed dramatically. Whereas the infants had been happy and actively engaged during the initial, real-time interaction, they now exhibited signs of distress, turning away from the mother's image, frowning and grimacing. The infants' distress during the replay was evidently produced by some kind of mismatch between their mothers' responses and their own; the infants were obviously able to detect that the interactions were out of tune (Neisser 1993, 17).

Infants clearly differentiate objects and other people from the very start. Whereas objects are simply toys to be looked at and manipulated, the faces, voices, and bodily movements of other people are treated as special social parameters (Legerstee 1999, 217, 220–221). There is nothing inferential or theoretical about this early social interaction; rather it is a form of intersubjectivity rooted in the infant's intuitive grasp of the expressive gestures of other individuals.

When the infant reaches the age of nine months, a change occurs. Whereas the early interaction that had no topic other than the interaction itself has been called *primary intersubjectivity*, we are now faced with a *secondary intersubjectivity* that involves triangulation. The infants' interactions with other persons start to have reference to the world around them, to the objects and events that can be shared with others.

Infants of nine months can follow the eye-gaze or pointing finger of another person and, when they do so, they often look back at the person and appear to use the feedback from his or her face to confirm that they have, in fact, reached the right target. In other words, they seek to validate whether joint *attention* has been achieved. Similarly, they might show objects to others, often looking to the other person's eyes, to check whether he or she is attending. The sharing of *intentions* is most obvious in protolinguistic requests for help. Such requests suggest that the infant apprehends the other as someone who can comprehend and satisfy its own intentions. Similarly, they might respond to simple verbal requests by others or shake the head to express refusal. Thus, intentions have become shareable experiences (Stern 1985, 129–131). Finally, new forms of *affective* sharing can also be witnessed. If the infant is placed in a situation that is bound to generate uncertainty—for instance, the presence of a new, unusual, and highly stimulating object such as a beeping and flashing toy—it will look toward the mother for her emotional reaction, to see what it should feel in order to help resolve its own uncertainty. If the mother shows pleasure by smiling, the infant will continue its exploration; if she shows fear, the infant will turn back from the object and perhaps become upset (Stern 1985, 132).

A vivid example of this sort of interaction is the famous "visual cliff" experiment. Infants aged twelve months are placed on one side of a "visual cliff," an apparent sudden drop beneath a transparent surface. On the other side of the drop-off, the infant's mother and an attractive toy are placed. When the infant notices the drop-off it will typically look spontaneously at the mother's face. If the mother poses a happy face, most infants will cross to the other side; if the mother poses a fearful expression, the infants will freeze or even actively retreat. As Hobson points out, it is noteworthy that the mother's mere presence is not enough; rather it is her emotional reaction, as perceived through her expressions and behavior, that has a decisive influence (Hobson 1991, 47). In other words, the infant appears to recognize that another person's expression has meaning with reference to an environment common to both of them. The infant is not living in a solipsistic world, a world that has the meaning it has solely because of how it is taken by the infant. Rather, the world has also meaning for others, and the meaning it has for others affect the meaning it has for the infant. Thus, the gestures and utterances of the caretaker are perceived as being both emotionally expressive and directed to something in the infant's world (Hobson 1993, 38, 140–141; 2002, 73). This makes Hobson conclude that infants "have direct perception of and natural engagement with person-related meanings that are apprehended in the expressions and behavior of other persons. It is only gradually, and with considerable input from adults, that they eventually come to conceive of 'bodies' on the one hand, and 'minds' on the other" (Hobson 1993, 117). Needless to say, this is a conclusion that ties in rather nicely with the phenomenological analyses in chapter 6.

Although there are culturally specific rules regarding the public expression of basic emotions, such as happiness, fear, or disgust, extensive empirical research suggests that the expressions themselves are cross-cultural and universal (Ekman 2003, 4, 10, 58). That basic emotional expressions are innate is further indicated by the fact that even congenitally blind children display such facial expressions normally.

Hobson recounts a number of incidents that suggest that children in the second year of life already experience other people as individuals who feel distress or desire, who can be comforted or provoked, and for whom objects have personal significance. One example concerns an eleven-month-old girl who saw another child fall and cry:

At first she stared at the hurt child, looking as though she was about to cry herself. Then she put her thumb in her mouth and buried her head in her mother's lap, which is what she would do if she hurt herself. (Hobson 2002, 82)

Another example concerns a fifteen-month-old boy who was fighting with a friend over a toy, when the friend started to cry:

Michael appeared disturbed and let go, but the friend continued to cry. Michael paused, then offered his teddy bear to the friend. When this did not work, Michael paused, went to fetch his friend's security blanket from the next room, and gave it to him. At this point, the friend stopped crying. (Hobson 2002, 82)

A final example concerns Marcy, a twenty-month-old girl who wanted a toy her sister was playing with:

When she asked for it, her sister refused. Marcy paused as if reflecting on what to do, and then went straight to her sister's rocking horse—a favourite toy that her sister never allowed anyone to touch—climbed on it, and began yelling, "Nice horsey! Nice horsey!", keeping a watchful eye on her sister. Her sister put down the toy Marcy wanted and came running angrily, whereupon Marcy immediately climbed down from the horse, ran directly to the toy, and grabbed it. (Hobson 2002, 82–83)

To state the obvious: All of this happens long before the toddlers are capable of solving theory of mind tasks, that is, long before the children should be in possession of a theory of mind, which according to the theory-theory of mind is what first permits them to mind-read and engage with others as minded individuals.

In his book *Mindblindness*, Baron-Cohen introduces three mechanisms that he considers precursors to a theory of mind. First, there is what he calls an *Intentionality Detector*. This detector is a device that interprets motion stimuli in terms of primitive volitional mental states. It is very basic, works through the senses, and provides the infant with a direct and nontheoretical understanding of the intentionality of the other (Baron-Cohen 1995, 32–34). Second, there is what Baron-Cohen calls an *Eye-Direction Detector*. This device works through vision; it detects the direction of the eyes of others, and interprets gaze as seeing (Baron-Cohen 1995, 39). Finally, there is the *Shared-Attention Mechanism* that enables the infant to become aware that another is attending the same object as itself (Baron-Cohen 1995, 44–45). According to Baron-Cohen, these three mechanisms, which all become available in the first year of life, enable the infant to understand two crucial intentional properties, namely aboutness and aspectuality (Baron-Cohen 1995, 56). This may still fall short of a full understanding of the representational powers of the mind, but it is nevertheless striking that even Baron-Cohen, a prominent defender of the theory-theory of mind, concedes that infants are in possession of a nontheoretical understanding of some features of intentionality. The question, then, is whether these basic abilities constitute a constant operative basis, or whether they are, as Baron-Cohen claims, simple precursors to a theory of mind (Baron-Cohen 2000, 1251). In my view, Gallagher is exactly right when he, articulating an insight found among many of the classical phenomenologists, writes as follows:

Primary, embodied intersubjectivity is not primary simply in developmental terms. Rather it remains primary across all face-to-face intersubjective experiences, and it subtends the occasional and secondary intersubjective practices of explaining or predicting what other people believe, desire or intend in the practice of their own minds. (Gallagher 2001, 91)

Once again, the theory-theory seems to be confronted with a dilemma. It can opt for an inclusive definition of mind-reading and adhere to the idea that every experience and understanding of other minded creatures involves a process of mind-reading. Given the available evidence, it must then concede that infants can mind-read long before they can pass theory of mind tests. Alternatively, it can opt for an exclusive definition of mind-reading. It can argue that mind-reading, in the proper sense of the term, is present only when the child is capable of false beliefs ascriptions, and that it ultimately involves an inference to unobservable, theoretically postulated entities. In this case, it would make sense to maintain that theory of mind tasks are currently our best way of measuring whether children are able to mind-read. Even if young children were unable to mind-read, however, it would then be necessary to concede, given the evidence, that they possess ways of understanding the emotions and intentions of others that are much more fundamental and immediate. Theorizing about other minded creatures does not establish intersubjectivity or sociality. It does not establish access to the embodied minds of others. It is the exception rather than the rule.

V Autism Revisited

The theory-theory approach views autism primarily as a cognitive disorder. The selective impairment on mind-reading tasks is explained by reference to a damaged or destroyed theory of mind module, that is, by reference to some malfunctioning computational mechanism. This explanatory hypothesis is, however, confronted with a number of difficulties. Some of these are related to the general question concerning whether we do, in fact, need a theory in order to experience and understand self and others. Other difficulties are more specifically related to the study of autism. Since I have already discussed the former issue, let me now turn to the latter.

Given the experimental data presented by the theory-theorists, there is nothing to substantiate the claim that autistic persons lack phenomenal consciousness. There is nothing to suggest that they lack first-personal access to their own occurrent experiences, perceptions, desires, thoughts, and emotions. This fact, however, does not rule out that many autistic persons suffer from a basic self-estrangement, nor does it preclude many of them from having an impaired propositional self-knowledge as a result of widespread deficits in their cognitive and linguistic capabilities. In other words, the findings presented by Baron-Cohen and by Frith and Happé are compatible with the view that although autistic persons are *self-aware* in a primitive, pre-reflective sense, many may have difficulties achieving a more robust and comprehensive interpersonal, conceptual, and narrative type of self-understanding (see Raffman 1999). This is precisely a suggestion that phenomenology has the conceptual resources to develop further.

Given the equivocal nature of the term "self-awareness," much will depend on the definition in use. For instance, young children with autism can pass the mirror-recognition test. They will remove the mark from their faces when they perceive it in the mirror, and they consequently display the kind of self-directed behavior that some take to indicate the first presence of self-awareness. However, as Hobson has pointed out, when facing a mirror, autistic children do not show the signs of coyness so typical of nonautistic children. Nor do they more generally display many signs of embarrassment. They do not seem much concerned with the way they appear to others; in fact, they seem to have great difficulties conceiving of themselves as selves in the minds of others (Hobson 2002, 89). According to a classical definition of self-consciousness, famously advocated by Mead, self-consciousness is precisely a question of becoming an object to oneself in virtue of one's social relations to others, that is, self-consciousness is constituted by adopting the perspective of the other toward oneself (Mead 1962, 164, 172). As Mead wrote in *Mind, Self, and Society*:

> The individual experiences himself as such, not directly, but only indirectly, from the particular standpoints of other individual members of the same social group, or from the generalized standpoint of the social group as a whole to which he belongs. For he enters his own experience as a self or individual, not directly or immediately, not by becoming a subject to himself, but only in so far as he first becomes an object to himself just as other individuals are objects to him or in his experience; and he becomes an object to himself only by taking the attitudes of other individuals toward himself within a social environment or context of experience and behavior in which both he and they are involved. (Mead 1962, 138)

When it comes to this type of self-awareness, there is good reason to think that it is, at the very least, severely limited in autistic persons. Again, this does not imply or suggest that they also lack the minimal kind of self-awareness that is part and parcel of the experiential dimension.

As we have already seen, Baron-Cohen and Frith and Happé argue that one can test the presence of self-awareness in autistic subjects by using classical theory of mind tasks, such as the false-belief task or the appearance–reality task. According to the prevailing view, the capacity to attribute false beliefs to others presupposes a capacity for metarepresentation. Why should a capacity for metarepresentation be required in order to have first-personal access to one's own experiential life? Why should the absence of higher-order intentionality imply that the autistic subject lacks phenomenal consciousness? The argument is obvious if one, like Carruthers, defends a higher-order account of consciousness, but highly questionable if one rejects such an account.

When discussing the merits of the mindblindness hypothesis, it is worth remembering that young infants and many learning-disabled people lack a theory of mind without thereby being autistic. In fact, children with Down's syndrome, who are noticeably deficient in theoretical abilities, do have the psychological competence necessary to understand others. At the same time, people with Asperger's syndrome, so-called high-functioning, are autistic although they do, in fact, have a theory of mind and succeed relatively well when it comes to false-belief tasks (Boucher 1996, 233). Strictly speaking, the lack of a theory of mind consequently seems to constitute neither a sufficient nor a necessary condition for autism. This conclusion is corroborated by the fact that infants with autism display socio-affective abnormalities long before the supposed emergence of a theory of mind; it is generally agreed that the earliest signs of autism begin to appear during the first year of life. Recently, this has made even theory-theorists identify deficient precursors of a theory of mind, rather than the lack of a theory of mind itself, as the primary cause of autism (see Baron-Cohen 2000, 1251).

What are the first signs of autism? They include deficits in very basic early infantile forms of I–thou relatedness, expressed in poor eye contact, a scarcity of coordinated affective and motoric exchanges with other people, and a more general failure to attend to and respond to others (see p. 190 above). There is a marked absence of joint-attention behavior, but also a lack of *emotional* engagement or contact with others. As Kanner pointed out in the paper that established autism as a diagnostic category: "We must, then, assume that these children have come into the world with innate inability to form the usual, biologically provided affective contact with people, just as other children come into the world with innate physical or intellectual handicaps" (Kanner 1943, 250).

In one experiment, a group of autistic children and a control group of nonautistic children were presented with photos of faces and asked to identify the emotions expressed by the faces. To increase the difficulty of the task, the foreheads and mouths of the faces were blanked out, leaving only the eyes by which to judge the emotion. Whereas nonautistic children could pass the test, autistic children were unable to sort the emotions in these blanked-out photos. As a final test, four full-faced photos were placed upside-down, and the two groups were then asked to sort the photos. Remarkably, the performance of the children with autism markedly improved. In fact, they even scored significantly higher than the control group when asked to sort the emotions in these upside-down photos. As Hobson points out, however, when faces are presented upside-down, emotions are no longer recognizable as emotions. The task is then transformed into one of (emotionally meaningless) pattern or feature recognition, and here the children with autism performed better than children without autism (Hobson 2002, 246–248).

The emotional responsiveness of twenty-month-old children with autism was tested in yet another experiment. An investigator pretended to hit his thumb with a hammer while he and the child were playing with plastic toys. He cried out with pain and displayed facial expressions of distress. In the meantime, the child's reactions were videotaped in order to see whether the child would show facial concern, whether he would look at the investigator's face, at his hand, or stop playing with the toys. Out of ten children with autism, no one showed any facial concern and only four looked at the investigator's pained face. In a control group of normal developing children, thirteen out of nineteen showed facial concerns and everyone looked at the investigator's face (Hobson 2002, 45–46).

What is suggested by these tests is how very differently people with autism might perceive other persons. They may be able to detect fine details in their faces, but they have great difficulties picking up the emotional dimension of the other's facial expression. This is particularly so for more complex social emotions, like embarrassment, jealousy, guilt, or pride. If we understand each other primarily by way of emotional contact and interchange, and if intersubjectivity crucially involves the intuitive ability to grasp the emotionally expressive gestures and utterances of others, then it is, perhaps, not so strange that people who lack this ability might also have difficulties interacting with and understanding other minded creatures (Hobson 2002, 59–60).

In his classical paper on autism, Asperger made the following observation: "When we talk to someone we do not only 'answer' with words, but we 'answer' with our look, our tone of voice and the whole expressive play of face and hands. A large part of social relationships is conducted through eye gaze, but such relationships are of no interest to the autistic child. Therefore, the child does not generally bother to look at the person who is speaking" (Asperger 1991, 69). Asperger might be quite right about the importance of expression in ordinary communication. A large part of the responses we look for do, in fact, depend on facial expression and animation. But is he right in saying that autistic children ignore the facial display because they are disinterested, or is it rather, as Cole has recently suggested, a question of active avoidance (Cole 1998, 81)? First-person descriptions by autistic subjects indicate that they might actively avoid eye contact because the facial expression of the other is too complex for them to decipher, too overwhelming in its subtle interweaving of movement, behavior, and feeling. Some have even expressed a fear of losing their own fragile sense of self in the encounter with the otherness of the other (Cole 1998, 4, 88, 90, 117). This interpretation matches rather well with suggestions made by some of the few phenomenologically oriented psychiatrists who have worked on autism. Bosch, for instance, has argued that autism involves a specific and fundamental impairment in the comprehension and understanding of expressions (Bosch 1962/1970, 101).

The very term "autism" was originally introduced into psychiatry by Bleuler in his discussion of schizophrenia (Bleuler 1911/1950), and it was, at one point, suggested that autism might be a childhood variant of schizophrenia (Wing 1991, 106). For a variety of reasons, this suggestion has since been abandoned, one of them being that very few, if any, people with infantile autism go on to develop clinically recognizable adult schizophrenia (Wing 1991, 116). Nevertheless, it can still be illuminating to compare certain features of autism to certain features of schizophrenia (see Frith 1994, 150; Frith 2003, 68–69). This is particularly so, since some of the insights obtained in phenomenologically oriented work on schizophrenia are of direct relevance for the current discussion.

In his classical study *La Schizophrénie* from 1927, Minkowski described schizophrenia as involving a *lack* of a "vital contact with reality" (Minkowski 1927, 82). For Minkowski, this vital contact consists in a basic, nonreflective attunement between self and world. It involves the ability to "resonate with the world," the ability to immerse oneself in the intersubjective world and empathize with others. Schizophrenia is, consequently, characterized by a limited grasp of social meaning and a compensatory reliance on reflective inferential reasoning, a cognitive style traditionally labeled as "morbid rationalism" (see Minkowski 1927, 104; Parnas, Bovet, and Zahavi 2002).

This approach to schizophrenia was subsequently taken up by Blankenburg, who argued that schizophrenia was marked by a "pathology of common sense" or a "loss of natural evidence" (Blankenburg 1971). This natural evidence does not refer to a set of propositionally articulated beliefs about the world, such as "one has to wear clothes when dining in a restaurant," or "winter follows fall." Rather, it concerns an implicit grip of the "rules of the game," a sense of proportion, a taste for what is adequate and appropriate, likely and relevant. It refers to a skillful coping, or an intuitive grasp of the significance of objects, situations, events, and other people. Because of this loss, schizophrenic patients might be captured and puzzled by matters that seem obvious to normal people. They may have a heightened awareness of aspects, structures, or processes of action and experience that, for a normal person, would simply be presupposed and remain taken for granted and unnoticed. A young female schizophrenic patient described the situation in the following way:

What is it that I really lack? Something so small, so comic, but so unique and important that you cannot live without it. . . . I find that I no longer have footing in the world. I have lost a hold in regard to the simplest, everyday things. . . . What I lack really is the "natural evidence." . . . It has simply to do with living, how to behave yourself in order not to be pushed outside society. But I cannot find the right word for that which is lacking in me. . . . It is not knowledge . . . It is something that every child is equipped with. It is these very simple things a human being has the need for, to carry on life, how to act, to be with other people, to know the rules of the game. (Quoted in Blankenburg 1971, 42–43)

The similarity to the following description given by a person with autism is striking:

I always felt there was something I didn't really understand. Even when I understood quite a lot, there was always something left—the actual way it all hung together. I made a huge effort . . . The world was an ever-changing mystery, things happened suddenly. How? Why? (Quoted in Frith 2003, 158–159)

We have repeatedly seen that the theory-theorists emphasize the inferential, theory-driven nature of the intersubjective encounter. One way to assess the plausibility of this conjecture is to look for first-person accounts, where autistic persons describe their own experience of interpersonal relations. In her conversations with Oliver Sacks, Temple Grandin provides an illuminating account:

She was at pains to keep her own life simple, she said, and to make everything very clear and explicit. She had built up a vast library of experiences over the years, she went on. They were like a library of videotapes, which she could play in her mind and inspect at any time—"videos" of how people behaved in different circumstances. She would play these over and over again and learn, by degrees, to correlate what she saw, so that she could then predict how people in similar circumstances might act. She had complemented her experience by constant reading, including reading of trade journals and the *Wall Street Journal*—all of which enlarged her knowledge of the species. "It is strictly a logical process," she explained. . . . When she was younger, she was hardly able to interpret even the simplest expressions of emotion; she learned to "decode" them later, without necessarily feeling them. . . . What is it, then, I pressed her further, that goes on between normal people, from which she feels herself excluded? It has to do, she has inferred, with an implicit knowledge of social conventions and codes, of cultural presuppositions of every sort. This implicit knowledge, which every normal person accumulates and generates throughout life on the basis of experience and encounters with others, Temple seems to be largely devoid of. Lacking it, she has instead to "compute" others' intentions and states of mind, to try to make algorithmic, explicit, what for the rest of us is second nature. She herself, she infers, may never have had the normal social experiences from which a normal social knowledge is constructed. (Sacks 1995, 248, 257–258)

What we are confronted with here is not a lack of a theory of mind, but with a lack of an immediate, pre-reflective, or implicit understanding of emotional expressions and the unwritten rules of social interaction. These deficits are then compensated by an intellectual, theory-driven approach. This clinical picture, however, contradicts the claims made by some proponents of the mindblindness hypothesis. In fact, it seems that Grandin's compensatory way of understanding others resembles how *normal* intersubjective understanding is occasionally portrayed by the proponents of the theory-theory of mind. To put it somewhat ironically, there is evidence suggesting that autistic persons, provided they posses a sufficiently high IQ, might be more characterized by an excessive reliance on a theory of mind, in the proper sense of the word, than by a lack of such a theory. They seem to have to rely on algorithms and formulas if they are to understand other persons. Whereas nonautistic people do not need a "theory of mind" in order to know that others are minded individuals, autistic people demonstrate what it is like to need recourse to such a theory. This is not to deny, of course, that autistic persons have difficulties passing theory of mind tasks. Rather the point is that they have these difficulties not because of theoretical deficits, but because of socio-affective deficiencies. In this sense, it really is question begging to label false-belief tasks or appearance–reality tasks as "theory of mind" tasks; it prejudges the issue by suggesting that psychological competence consists in the possession and use of a theory.

Is this critical appraisal premature? After all, Frith readily concedes that there are different ways to achieve knowledge of other minds and that explicit logical inference is one such way. In fact, she even states that autistic persons who lack the theory of mind module that allows for an intuitive and automatic attribution of mental states to others might acquire a conscious theory of mind by way of compensation (Frith 2003, 94–95, 206, 218). Does this imply that the dispute is terminological rather than substantial? I think not. For Frith, the decisive difference between autistic and nonautistic people is not that autistic people have to employ a theory of mind, whereas nonautistic people can do without. For her, the difference is that autistic people have to employ a conscious and explicit theory of mind, whereas nonautistic people can make do with a nonconscious, automatic, and implicit theory of mind. In my view, it would have been better to avoid using the term "theory" when speaking of a nonconscious information-processing mechanism. Moreover, I find it rather misleading to designate such nonconscious inferential processes as *intuitive*, as Frith repeatedly does (Frith 2003, 15, 94, 120, 206, 218). These minor qualms aside, however, the decisive issue is the following: According to the theory-theory, mental states, be they our own or those of others, are unobservable and theoretically postulated entities. To argue in such a fashion is, however, to ignore the first-personal givenness of the experiential dimension and to disregard the way in which the life of the mind of others is visible in their expressive behavior and meaningful action.[14]

Notes

Introduction

1. This is (or was) supposedly Metzinger's view (see the editorial in *Journal of Consciousness Studies* 4/5–6, 1997, 385).

2. The phenomenologists themselves have always vigorously denied that they should be engaged in some kind of introspective psychology. For some representative statements, see Gurwitsch 1966, 89–106; Hua 5/38, 25/36 (throughout, "Hua" refers to *Husserliana*); Merleau-Ponty 1945, 69–70. One simple argument is that phenomenology must be appreciated as a form of transcendental philosophy; it is not a kind of empirical psychology. Another related argument is that introspection is typically understood as a mental operation that enables us to report about and describe our own mental states. Strictly speaking, however, phenomenology is not concerned with or based on operations like this. Rather, phenomenology is concerned with structures of meaning. It investigates phenomena, appearances, structures of the life-world and their conditions of possibility. Phenomenologists would typically argue that it is a metaphysical fallacy to locate this phenomenal realm within the mind and to suggest that the way to access and describe it is by turning the gaze inward (*introspicio*). The entire facile divide between inside and outside is phenomenologically suspect, but this divide is precisely something that the term "introspection" buys into and accepts (see Zahavi 2003b; 2004c).

3. Let me add that my focus in the following will be on insights to be found in concrete phenomenological analyses. I will only to a much lesser extent deal with the more metaphilosophical and methodological aspects of phenomenology. However, for a discussion of these important issues, see Zahavi 2003c and 2006.

Chapter 1

1. When quoting Husserl, the reference is to the critical *Husserliana* edition where possible, cited by volume number, with the page number(s) following a slash—e.g., Hua 8/188. Where an English translation exists, several different conventions are

used. In cases where the English edition includes the Husserliana page numbers in the margin, only the German page numbers are provided. But where the marginal page numbers in the English refer to a different edition or no marginal page numbers are provided, the corresponding English page number is added in square brackets immediately following the Husserliana citation—e.g., Hua 19/375 [2001, II/93]. (The same principle has also been applied in those cases where I am quoting from authors other than Husserl, e.g., Nietzsche, Heidegger, Merleau-Ponty, and so on.) For the most part, I have used the standard English translations of Husserl's works. Where no English translation was available, I have provided one myself (with the help of numerous colleagues), and in all cases where Husserl's unpublished manuscripts are quoted, the original German text can be found in the notes. When referring to these latter manuscripts the last number always refers to the original shorthanded page.

2. When quoting Heidegger, the reference is to the *Gesamtausgabe* (Collected Works), cited by volume number, with the page number(s) following a colon—e.g., Heidegger GA 20: 45. The only exception to this will be references to *Sein und Zeit*, which will be to the 1986 Max Niemeyer edition.

3. For a comparison of the phenomenological approach to self-awareness with the semantic and indexical analysis of the first-person pronoun found in the writings of Perry, Shoemaker, Castañeda, and Anscombe, see Zahavi 1999.

4. A word of caution: When I, in the following, speak of our first-personal access to our own experiences, I will be referring to the first-personal givenness or manifestation of our experiential life. Thus, my use of the term "access" has nothing to do with Block's notion of *access consciousness*, which is precisely defined as a nonphenomenal notion of consciousness (Block 1997).

5. Block has recently argued that mental states that are phenomenally conscious often seem to have a "me-ishness" about them, i.e., that the phenomenal content often represents the state as a state of me. However, he then goes on to deny that this should warrant the reduction of phenomenal consciousness to self-consciousness. The argument is simple: The "me-ishness" is the same in states whose phenomenally conscious content is different, and that precludes any straightforward identification (Block 1997, 390). I wholeheartedly agree, and I will in fact argue along similar lines in chapters 3 and 5. But, of course, there is a difference between upholding the view that phenomenal consciousness can be reduced to self-consciousness and defending the view that phenomenal consciousness entails self-consciousness. It is the latter view that I currently defend.

6. For some critical comments to the more specific details of Kriegel's account, see Zahavi 2004b.

7. For an informative comparison of the HOT and HOP models, see Van Gulick 2000.

8. In the following, I will not distinguish terminologically between "self-consciousness," "self-awareness," and "self-experience," but rather use the terms interchangeably.

9. Although Carruthers is, in general, quite unequivocal about denying conscious experiences to young infants (see Carruthers 1996a, 221; 2000, 202–203), he occasionally leaves a door open for a different conclusion. As he writes at one point, it might be that infants are capable of discriminating between their experiences (and hence be capable of enjoying conscious experiences) even while still being incapable of conceptualizing them (Carruthers 1996a, 222).

10. Of course, one should distinguish the view that consciousness is intrinsic to those states that possess it from the more radical view that consciousness is intrinsic to all mental states (see Thomasson 2000, 197).

11. Whereas early on Sartre spoke of an irreflective or nonreflective self-awareness, he later increasingly opted for the term "pre-reflective self-awareness."

12. For a more extensive discussion of Sartre's account of self-consciousness, see Zahavi 1999.

13. In making this claim, Rosenthal explicitly refers to the work of Castañeda, Chisholm, Lewis, and Perry (Rosenthal 1997, 750).

14. On some occasions, Rosenthal has argued that a higher-order thought might occur in the absence of the mental state it is purportedly about. He even writes that "a case in which one has a higher-order thought along with the mental state it is about might well be subjectively indistinguishable from the case in which the higher-order thought occurs but not the mental state" (Rosenthal 1997, 744). This might make Rosenthal's HOT position safe from the objection just outlined, but it also turns his theory into a rather strange type of higher-order theory. If one can have a higher-order thought about a first-order state even when the first-order state does not exist, consciousness is not really explained in terms of a relation between two different states, nor does it really make sense to say that intransitive consciousness is a relational property that the first-order state acquires if one is transitively conscious of it. In fact, since there can be phenomenal consciousness even in the absence of a first-order mental state, it looks as if the higher-order thought itself is sufficient for phenomenal consciousness (see also Byrne 1997, 123).

Chapter 2

1. There are two editions of *Logische Untersuchungen*. The first edition was published in 1900 (volume 1) and 1901 (volume 2), and the second revised edition in 1913 (volume 1 and volume 2, part I) and 1921 (volume 2, part II). Originally, Husserl's plan for the reissue was to rework *Logische Untersuchungen* so that the entire text could match the phenomenology of *Ideen I* (Hua 18/9). Owing to the scale

of the work, this goal soon proved unrealizable, and since Husserl refused to simply issue a reprint of the first edition, owing in part to what he took to be its many equivocations (Hua 18/10), some sort of compromise had to be found. In effect, the different investigations ended up being revised to quite different extents (for a meticulous account see Panzer's introduction in *Husserliana* 19/1). Broadly speaking it is possible to distinguish three types of changes: 1. There are changes of a purely stylistic nature. This includes corrections of misprints, etc. 2. There are changes that reflect what Husserl took to be a more precise rendering of the line of thought that was already contained in the first edition. 3. Finally, there are changes that quite clearly express Husserl's own change of mind. The second edition of the Fifth Investigation contains changes of all three types, and since my goal will be to analyze Husserl's original position, all references will be to the first edition of *Logische Untersuchungen*, unless otherwise noted.

2. See, however, Scanlon 1971 and Bernet 1994, 300–303.

3. Sartre referred, in passing, to Husserl's investigations of time-consciousness in *Zur Phänomenologie des inneren Zeitbewußtseins* (see chapter 3), but he did not elaborate on this (Sartre 1936, 22).

4. In the second edition of *Logische Untersuchungen*, Husserl explicitly referred to the process of temporalization (Hua 19/369).

5. Whether Brentano actually succeeded in avoiding an infinite regress is another issue. Gurwitsch, Henrich, Pothast, and Cramer have all argued that Brentano's theory, while avoiding one type of regress, gives rise to another. They also claim that this results from the fact that Brentano remained committed to viewing self-awareness as a special form of object-consciousness (Gurwitsch 1979, 89–90; Henrich 1970, 261; Pothast 1971, 75; Cramer 1974, 581; see also Zahavi 1999).

6. In the second edition of *Logische Untersuchungen*, Husserl's appraisal was slightly more positive. For a careful discussion of this change of view, see Lohmar 1998, 194.

7. Incidentally, this seems to be Searle's view. Searle speaks of the mistake involved in claiming that all our states of consciousness involve self-awareness. One version of this mistake would be to argue that every conscious state, apart from intending a certain object, also has itself as its own intentional object, i.e., in the case of a perception of a red sports car, we would have a perceptual awareness of the sports car and an additional second-order awareness of the perception (Searle 1998, 73). Since Searle denies that this is the case for all conscious states, he can conclude that it is a mistake to say that they all involve self-awareness. If one rejects Searle's definition of self-awareness as being excessively narrow, there is no reason to accept his conclusion.

8. For a more elaborate account of these different egological levels, see Zahavi 1999, 138–156.

9. This chapter incorporates revised material from my article "The Three Concepts of Consciousness in *Logische Untersuchungen*," originally published in *Husserl Studies* 18, 2002, 51–64. I am grateful to Springer Science and Business Media for their kind permission to allow me to reuse the material.

Chapter 3

1. I am grateful to the Director of the Husserl-Archives in Leuven, Prof. Rudolf Bernet, for permitting me to consult and quote from Husserl's unpublished manuscripts. Following standard practice, I will append the original German text in those cases where I quote from the manuscripts (the translations are my own): "Wann immer ich reflektiere, finde ich mich 'in bezug auf' Etwas, als Affiziertes bzw. Aktives. Das, worauf ich bezogen bin, ist erlebnismäßig bewusst—es ist für mich etwas schon als 'Erlebnis,' damit ich mich darauf beziehen kann" (Husserl Ms. C 10 13a).

2. Let me, from the outset, emphasize that my focus will be on Husserl's theory of inner time-consciousness *to the extent* that it throws light on his theory of self-awareness. I will consequently have to disregard many aspects of his analysis of time per se.

3. Of course, it could be argued along Kantian lines that the transcendental condition is not itself given, is not itself a phenomenon. Since such a conclusion would exclude the possibility of a transcendental phenomenology and, therefore, a phenomenological investigation of transcendental subjectivity, it was not really an option for Husserl.

4. Husserl's favored term was "primal impression" (*Urimpression*). In his recently published *Bernauer Manuskripte über das Zeitbewusstsein*, however, he used the term "primal presentation" (*Urpräsentation*) (Hua 33/116–117). This is a better and less equivocal term, and I will consequently use it in the following.

5. As Proust illustrated in his famous Madeleine example in the beginning of *Remembrance of Things Past*, there are, of course, also recollections that arise quite unbidden.

6. This apparent preoccupation with objects also comes to the fore in a slightly different context. In text number 15, Husserl wrote that every immanent object has a peculiar relation to a prominent object, namely the I, and that this I is also an object for itself (Hua 33/284). One page later, Husserl modified this statement and wrote that the I is not an object in exactly the same way as other objects. In fact, it is precisely a subject for whom everything else is an object. Regardless of this correction, Husserl still insisted that the I can be an I only insofar as it can become an object for itself (Hua 33/285). Husserl was apparently still not quite satisfied with the phrasing and a few pages later he wrote, "Its being is however completely different from the being of any objects. It is precisely the being of a subject" (Hua 33/287). Once again,

it is possible to detect a patent indecision in Husserl's text. In my view, this indecision should have long been resolved. One should bear in mind, of course, that the texts in question are so-called research manuscripts. They are not texts that were intended for publication, but texts that Husserl wrote in order to obtain insights through the very process of writing.

7. For a classical account of the relation between thematic and marginal consciousness, see Gurwitsch 1974 and 1985, where he argues that pre-reflective self-awareness should be understood as a kind of marginal, inattentive object-consciousness (Gurwitsch 1974; 339–340; 1985, 4).

8. Perhaps it could be argued that in text number 6 (and elsewhere) Husserl was simply playing with certain ideas in an attempt to see where they would lead him. If this charitable interpretation is correct, which it very well could be, one might wonder whether the text really deserved to be published (see note 6). For a more extensive discussion of the *Bernau Manuscripts*, see Zahavi 2004d.

9. For a more extensive discussion of these issues, see Zahavi 1999.

10. "Aber meine thematische Erfahrung vom Ich und Bewusstsein ist in ihrer Art selbst Stiftung einer Fortgeltung—eines bleibenden Seins, des Seins des Immanenten" (Husserl Ms. C 12 3b).

11. "Aber das bloße Strömen wird eben erst durch das Betrachten etc. gegenständlich und durch die Vermöglichkeiten des Immer-Wieder" (Husserl Ms. C 16 59a).

12. This is why Derrida's argumentation contains a puzzling tension. On one hand, Derrida wanted to stress the intimate connection and continuity between the primal presentation and the retention. It is a falsifying abstraction to speak of them in isolation and separation. On the other hand, however, he also wanted to describe the retention as different from and foreign to the primal presentation. Only this allowed him to speak of impressional consciousness as being mediated and constituted by the *alterity* of the retention.

13. Fink spoke of retention and protention in terms of an "*Entgegenwärtigung*" (Fink 1966, 22).

14. An earlier version of some of the material in this chapter originally appeared in my article "Inner Time-Consciousness and Pre-reflective Self-Awareness," in D. Welton (ed.), *The New Husserl: A Critical Reader* (Indiana University Press, 2003), 157–180.

Chapter 4

1. Let me anticipate a critical rejoinder. Is it not true that one of Heidegger's aims was to overcome the traditional philosophy of subjectivity, and is it not, for that reason, rather dubious to suggest that he should have shown interest in the very ques-

tion of how to investigate subjectivity? In contrast to this widespread reading, I would defend the view that Heidegger's own notion of Dasein must be interpreted as an ontologically clarified concept of subjectivity. Thus, what Heidegger was opposed to was precisely the *traditional* concept of subjectivity in the sense of a worldless, self-contained substance and not the notion of subjectivity as such. This interpretation can find support in, for instance, *Sein und Zeit, Die Grundprobleme der Phänomenologie* (1927), *Einleitung in die Philosophie*, and *Kant und das Problem der Metaphysik*. In these works, Heidegger called for an analysis of the being of the subject, and wrote that it was necessary to commence a phenomenological investigation of the subjectivity of the finite subject. He also argued that his own thematization of the ontology of Dasein was an ontological analysis of the subjectivity of the subject, and that an ontological comprehension of the subject would lead us to the existing Dasein (Heidegger 1986, 24, 366, 382; Heidegger GA 3: 87, 219; GA 24: 207, 220; GA 27: 72, 115). For an extensive discussion of the role of subjectivity in *Sein und Zeit*, see Øverenget 1998 and Overgaard 2004.

2. One of Heidegger's most extensive discussions of Natorp can be found in the lecture course *Phänomenologie der Anschauung und des Ausdrucks* from 1920. The first section of the second part of the lecture, which covers more than fifty pages, is entitled "Die destruierende Betrachtung der Natorpschen Position."

3. It is worth mentioning that it was Natorp who introduced the distinction between a *static* and a *genetic* investigation (Natorp 1912, 285) that Husserl was, subsequently, to make famous among phenomenologists. Husserl read *Allgemeine Psychologie* carefully in September 1918. Ultimately, it might be asked whether Natorp's reconstructive method is all that different from Husserl's genetic phenomenology and from his notion of an "*Abbaureduktion*." If it should turn out that they are similar, would this not make Husserl himself vulnerable to a phenomenological criticism of Natorp? To investigate the relation between Husserl and Natorp in detail would lead too far afield, but allow me to point out that there is a decisive difference between arguing for the value of a reconstructive (or genetic) method and arguing that such a method provides the only kind of access to lived subjectivity. Husserl would never have defended the latter view. In fact, as he remarked in one of his research manuscripts after having summarized Natorp's reconstructive method: "I really cannot approve of this. The true task will be lost of sight" (quoted in Kern 1964, 367–368). For an extensive discussion of Husserl's appraisal of Natorp, see Kern 1964, 326–373.

4. Heidegger's stance might here be compared to Husserl's view. As Husserl wrote in his 1906–1907 lecture course *Einleitung in die Logik und Erkenntnistheorie*: "If consciousness ceases to be a human or some other empirical consciousness, then the word loses all psychological meaning, and ultimately one is *led back to something absolute that is neither physical nor psychical being in a natural scientific sense*. In the phenomenological perspective this is the case throughout the field of givenness. It is precisely the apparently obvious thought that everything given is either physical or psychical that must be abandoned" (Hua 24/242). Thus, Husserl was keen to

emphasize that the realm of givenness, or phenomenality, is prior to any traditional distinction between the psychical and the physical, between the inner and outer. In fact, one of the decisive merits of his work is its discovery of a new nonmentalistic notion of phenomenon. This, of course, is yet another reason why it is highly misleading to suggest that Husserl's phenomenology is a kind of introspectionism or internalism (see also Zahavi 2004e).

5. See Dilthey 1905, 326. For an interesting and rather polemic attack on views found in both Dilthey and Heidegger, see Rickert 1922.

6. Heidegger introduced the notion of *formal indication* (*formale Anzeige*) in order to point to the unique phenomenological or hermeneutical conceptuality that runs counter to the theoretical and objectifying way in which normal concepts function. As Heidegger argued, the concepts found in phenomenology are of an altogether different kind than the objectifying, ordering concepts found in and utilized by the positive sciences (Heidegger GA 58: 262–263). Phenomenological concepts cannot communicate their full content, but only indicate it, and it is up to the phenomenologizing individual to actualize the concepts and their content. The final determination is not to be given in the definition, but to be realized in the phenomenological activity itself. What is given formally in a definition becomes authentically given only through the concrete enactment of the interpreter, i.e., in application (see Granberg 2003).

7. In a rather unique passage at the end of the same lecture course, Heidegger delineated in further detail the different steps involved in a phenomenological understanding of life: 1. The first stage simply consists in an unprejudiced selection of and reference to a specific sphere of factic life. 2. Then follows what Heidegger called the gaining of a foothold in the lived experience. This entails neither a seizing of the life nor a stilling of its stream, but simply a going along with, or rather a being carried along with the very stream of life. 3. The third stage involves a "*Vorschauen*," a "*Vorausspringen*" in the horizons and tendencies of the lived experience itself. 4. This is followed by an articulation and accentuation of the different moments of the phenomenon. 5. The fifth step consists in an interpretation thereof. 6. Finally, there follows a unification of what has been phenomenologically intuited; a bringing together of that which has been torn through the articulation. Heidegger also described these stages as the different moments of the phenomenological method, and it is interesting to notice that he explicitly mentioned that the articulation involves a critical *destruction* of the objectifications that are distorting the phenomenon (Heidegger GA 58: 254–255).

8. Heidegger would later express dissatisfaction with this tripartition since he took it to express an undue emphasis on the self-world (see Heidegger GA 20: 333; GA 58: 197–198).

9. This was Heidegger's *terminus technicus* for subject or self.

10. The English translation has been corrected so that it now corresponds to the amended German text (see Kisiel 1995, 378, 546).

11. As Stolzenberg has argued, however, although Heidegger might have acknowledged the existence of an immediate pre-reflective self-acquaintance, he apparently also considered it so fundamental that he never attempted to analyze its inner structure any further (Stolzenberg 1995, 293).

12. The change of language is striking, and Heidegger's choice of words in *Sein und Zeit* makes one wonder whether he did, after all, recognize the methodological need for some kind of phenomenological epoché. It would lead too far to investigate this question in any detail here, but for some interesting reflections see Tugendhat 1970, 262–264; Caputo 1992; and in particular Courtine 1990, 207–247.

13. For more on Sartre's concept of pure reflection, see Monnin 2002.

14. It must be emphasized that this suggestion by no means entails that the phenomenological reflection can make do without a preliminary effectuation of the phenomenological epoché and reduction. For a more extensive discussion, see Zahavi 2003c.

15. Does this signal the demise of phenomenology as a philosophy of reflection? Are we witnessing the dramatic failure of the phenomenological enterprise, or rather facing an unavoidable but quite harmless impasse? Let me give one reason for taking the latter to be the case. It is true that reflection cannot apprehend the anonymous life in its very functioning, but neither is it supposed to. The aim of reflection is to lift the naïveté of pre-reflective experience, not to reproduce it. It could be retorted that the anonymously functioning subjectivity is bound to remain a problem for Husserlian phenomenology as long as the latter adheres to the principle of principles, i.e., the principle put forth in §24 of *Ideen I*, which states that phenomenology is to base its considerations exclusively on that which is given intuitively in phenomenological reflection. How can this principle be upheld the moment it is acknowledged that reflection is always too late to grasp functioning subjectivity? I think that at least two replies are appropriate. First of all, it must be emphasized that we do, in fact, encounter the elusiveness and unthematizability of pre-reflective experience every time we try (and fail) to catch it in reflection, i.e., reflection points toward that which both founds it and eludes it. These features are not deficiencies to overcome, but rather the defining traits of its pre-reflective givenness. Second, Husserl himself eventually conceded that the intentional activity of the subject is founded upon and conditioned by an obscure and blind passivity, i.e., by drives and associations. He even argued that there are constitutive processes of an anonymous and involuntary nature taking place in the underground or depth-dimension of subjectivity that cannot be seized by direct reflection, but only through an elaborate "archeological effort" (Hua 4/266–277; 11/125; see also Mishara 1990). In fact, as Husserl famously declared in *Analysen zur passiven Synthesis*, his investigation of the problem of passivity could

well carry the title "a phenomenology of the unconscious" (Hua 11/154). For some of Husserl's rare references to psychoanalysis, see Hua 4/222; 6/240.

16. Going one step further than the authors mentioned here, Lévinas has argued that the unnatural movement of reflection is conditioned and made possible by the encounter with an other. Reflection is a suspension of the natural spontaneity. It makes my thought detach from itself and then rejoin itself as if it were another. This movement cannot, however, arise out of nothing; it needs an impulse from without. This impulse comes from the other, who interrupts and disrupts my dogmatic slumber by putting me into question (Lévinas 1991, 61; 1992, 224).

17. Contrary to Heidegger, however, authors like Husserl or Merleau-Ponty insisted that even the merely accentuating form of reflection involves a moment of alteration or transformation and that this is something to appreciate.

18. See also Rinofner-Kreidl 2001.

19. See Zahavi 2001, 2002b, and 2003c.

20. This chapter incorporates revised material from my article "How to Investigate Subjectivity: Natorp and Heidegger on Reflection" originally published in *Continental Philosophy Review* 36/2, 2003, 155–176. I am grateful to Springer Science and Business Media for their kind permission to allow me to reuse the material.

Chapter 5

1. By introducing ethics into the equation, Ricoeur can maintain that selfhood entails a dialectical relationship with otherness. As he puts it at one point: "the selfhood of oneself implies otherness to such an intimate degree that one cannot be thought of without the other" (Ricoeur 1990, 14 [1992, 3]). Ricoeur is thereby broaching a topic that for a long time has been in the center of Lévinas's thinking. Thus, in *Autrement qu'être ou au-dela de l'essence*, we find Lévinas defending the claim that *ipseity* depends on *alterity*. One of the arguments given by Lévinas is that I become a subject exactly by being addressed and accused by the other. It is when the other makes an irrefutable appeal to me and when I am charged with an unsubstitutable and irreplaceable responsibility that I am provided with a true self-identity and individuality. Thus, according to Lévinas, subjectivity is ultimately a question of subjection to responsibility (Lévinas 1974, 26, 29, 141, 183, 216–217).

2. Using quite Husserlian jargon, Siewert has recently spoken of *noetic phenomenal features* (Siewert 1998, 284).

3. However, this does not entail that two experiences that differ in their "what it is like" cannot intend the same object, nor does it entail that two experiences that are alike in their "what it is like" must necessarily intend the same object.

4. In *Logische Untersuchungen*, Husserl also criticized the view that accompanying visualizations might constitute the very meaning of the thought, i.e., the suggestion

that to understand what is being thought is to have the appropriate "mental image" before one's inner eye (Hua 19/67–72). The arguments he employed bear a striking resemblance to some of the ideas that were subsequently used by Wittgenstein in *Philosophical Investigations*. These were: 1. From time to time, the thoughts we are thinking, for instance thoughts like "every algebraic equation of uneven grade has at least one real root," will, in fact, not be accompanied by any imagery whatsoever. If the meaning were actually located in the "mental images," the thoughts in question would be meaningless, but this is not the case. 2. Frequently, our thoughts, such as the thought that "the horrors of World War I had a decisive impact on postwar painting," will in fact evoke certain visualizations, but visualizations of quite unrelated matters. To suggest that the meanings of the thoughts are to be located in such images is, of course, absurd. 3. Furthermore, the fact that the meaning of a thought can remain the same although the accompanying imagery varies also precludes any straightforward identification. 4. The thought of a square circle is not meaningless, but it can never be accompanied by a matching image, since a visualization of a square circle is, in principle, utterly impossible. 5. Finally, referring to Descartes' famous example in the *Sixth Meditation*, Husserl pointed out that we can easily distinguish thoughts like "a chiliagon is a many-sided polygon," and "a myriagon is a many-sided polygon," although the images that accompany both thoughts might be indistinguishable. Thus, as Husserl concludes, although imagery might function as an aid to the understanding, it is not what is understood and does not constitute the meaning of the thought (Hua 19/71).

5. As Siewert points out, Wittgenstein has "long warned us off the error of assimilating thought and understanding to mental imagery. But we ought not to correct Humean confusion on this point, only to persist in the empiricist tradition's equally noxious error of supposing thought and understanding to be *experiential*, only if *imagistic*" (Siewert 1998, 305–306). For further recent attempts to argue in defense of a broader notion of phenomenal consciousness, see Smith 1989; Flanagan 1992; Goldman 1997; Van Gulick 1997.

6. This also happens to be Putnam's view (see Putnam 1999, 156). For a discussion of some of the affinities between Putnam's recent reflections and views found in phenomenology, see Zahavi 2004f.

7. To speak of worldly properties in this context should not be misunderstood; it does not entail any metaphysical claims concerning the subject-independent existence of said properties. The claim being made is merely that the properties in question are properties of the experienced objects and not of the experience of the objects.

8. For a more elaborate argument, see Zahavi 2001.

9. Although Henry might in fact be read as defending a kind of immanentism, I would take exception to this aspect of his position (see Zahavi 1999).

10. For an extensive discussion of the way in which self-awareness and otherness is intertwined, see Zahavi 1999.

11. This is why it is also slightly odd to argue against an egological theory of self-awareness by pointing out that pre-reflective self-awareness is a passive, given state that precedes all egological initiative (Henrich 1970, 276). The very same thing can be said about our selfhood. To be a self in the most basic sense is a gift, the result of a happening (*Ereignis*) and not something that we decide to become (Henry 1966, 31).

12. More specifically, Strawson has argued that the phenomenological investigation can proceed in several ways. One possibility is to investigate what ordinary human self-experience involves, and another is to investigate the minimal form of self-experience. What is the least you can have and still call a(n experience of) self? Strawson is mainly interested in this latter question. His conclusion, which he calls the *pearl view*, is that minimal self-experience involves the experience of oneself as (1) a subject of experience that is a (2) single, (3) mental (4) thing that exists during any gap-free period of experience. By contrast, he considers issues like personality, agency, and long-term diachronic persistency to be inessential features. They may be important when it comes to human self-experience, but something can lack them and still be a self(-experience). As for the metaphysical question, Strawson concedes that the self is real if, by self, we understand a minimal self with the four listed properties, i.e., the self in the sense of a short-term bare locus of consciousness void of any personality. When it comes to the more persisting kind of personal self, he is considerably more skeptical (Strawson 2000, 44–48).

13. Whereas Husserl was prepared to ascribe a first-person perspective to (some) animals, he was ambiguous about whether they can also be persons. He alternately denied and affirmed it (see Hua 15/177; 3/73; 1/101).

14. In its emphasis on the *invariant* aspect of the self, the phenomenological notion of self differs from the *pearl view* recently defended by Strawson (see note 12 above). According to Strawson, all there is, metaphysically speaking, is a simple succession of transient minimal selves (each of which has duration of 2–3 seconds). Thus, Strawson would deny the existence of an experiential flow. In his view, the so-called stream of consciousness is, in reality, a series of isolated short-term experiential episodes, i.e., brief episodes that are constantly broken by fissures and white noise. In this sense, consciousness might be said to be continually restarting; it is one of many repeated returns into consciousness from a state of complete unconsciousness (Strawson 1997, 421–422).

There are problems with this proposal, however. First, it is natural to ask how Strawson can know about the states of complete unconsciousness that are supposed to repeatedly disrupt our experiential episodes, since these states, by definition, must be inaccessible from a first-person perspective. For obvious reasons, we can never experience the absence of experience. Second, although Strawson might be right about the fragmentary nature of our *thinking*, our occurrent propositional thoughts do not occur in isolation but always against a relatively constant phenomenal background made up of peripheral bodily, emotional, and perceptual experiences (see Dainton 2000, 118). If there is anything to the arguments in the previous chapters, this phenomenal field is characterized by an invariant quality of mineness. Finally, one implication of Strawson's view is that the distinction between my current minimal self and "my" previous minimal self is as absolute as the distinction between my current minimal self and the current minimal self of somebody else. To put it mildly, this implication seems rather implausible.

15. Damasio also speaks of a *proto-self*, which is the nonconscious biological precedent to, or forerunner of, the consciously experienced levels of self. The proto-self is *"a coherent collection of neural patterns which map, moment by moment, the state of the physical structure of the organism in its many dimensions"* (Damasio 1999, 154).

16. For a sustained criticism, see Wilkes 1988.

17. One might take issue with the terminology, however. To speak of ownership suggests that the self is the owner of, and therefore distinct and separate from, the different experiences. As we have already seen (see p. 100 above), there are problems with this view.

18. It has also been suggested that the phenomenon of thought insertion constitutes an exception to Shoemaker's thesis about first-person experience ascription being immune to the error of misidentification, since a patient who supposes that someone else has inserted thoughts into his mind is clearly mistaken about whose thoughts they are. If the analysis given above is correct, however, there is good reason to believe that the immunity principle remains intact even in cases of inserted thoughts. Since the afflicted subject does not confuse thoughts occuring in foreign minds with foreign thoughts occuring in his own mind it is doubtful whether any invalidating misidentification has taken place. As Gallagher writes:

When the schizophrenic reports that certain thoughts are not his thoughts, that someone else is generating these thoughts, he is also indicating that these thoughts are being manifested, not "over there" in someone else's head, but within *his own* stream of consciousness, a stream of consciousness for which he claims ownership. . . . The sense of ownership is still intact, despite the feeling that he is no longer the agentive cause of the thoughts. . . . His phenomenology is this: he has a sense of ownership for the stream of consciousness which is impossible to misidentify (and is, in fact, in no need of identification, since it is his own), but into which are inserted thoughts for which he has no sense of agency. His judgment that it is *he* who is being subjected to these thoughts is immune to error through misidentification, even if he is completely wrong about who is causing his thoughts. (Gallagher 2000b, 230–231)

19. See Parnas and Sass 2001, and Parnas 2004.

20. If this is true, it has some rather obvious consequences for the attribution of both self and self-consciousness to animals. It is also obvious, of course, that there are higher and more complex forms of self-consciousness that most, if not all, nonhuman animals lack. As for the question of where to draw the line, i.e., whether it also

makes sense to ascribe a sense of self to lower organisms such as birds, amphibians, fish, beetles, worms, etc., this is a question that I will leave for others to decide. All I will say is that *if* a certain organism is in possession of phenomenal consciousness, *then* it must also be in possession of both a primitive form of self-consciousness and a core self. For an interesting discussion of different types of self-consciousness in animals, see Mitchell 1994 and Sheets-Johnstone 1999.

Chapter 6

1. As Dancy points out, any pain you can conceive of as hurting, in just the same way as *your* pain hurts, must be conceived of as hurting you; thus a pain conceived of as being in another body is not yet conceived of as hurting another person (Dancy 1985, 70). To put it another way, the argument from analogy runs afoul of the conceptual problems of other minds (see pp. 159–160 above). If we start out by accepting the conceptual separation of the mental from the behavioral, we will never come to understand what it is for others to have mental states. That is, if we start from our own case alone, and from an understanding of mental states that is independent of behavior, we will not be able to move from our understanding of ourselves as subjects of experience to an understanding of other subjects of experience.

2. It could be objected that although this might hold true for humans, it does not necessarily hold true for all intelligent life. Would it, for instance, be nonsensical to imagine intersubjectivity between brains-in-vats or disembodied angels? Is the very idea of telepathy incoherent? (Thanks to Galen Strawson for this objection.) I am, however, not all that convinced that it is legitimate to draw substantial philosophical conclusions from the fact that certain scenarios are imaginable. Is our imagination always trustworthy; does it always attest to metaphysical possibility, or might imaginability occasionally reflect nothing but our own ignorance (see pp. 140–141 above)? Furthermore, if something like intersubjectivity is possible between brains-in-vats or angels, it would certainly be a kind of intersubjectivity that is utterly different from the one we are familiar with.

3. It is questionable whether Merleau-Ponty ever fully embraced this view himself. On one hand, he seems to have had misgivings about the position; misgivings that, for instance, come to the fore in his criticism of Scheler, whom he accused of having held a position similar to the one in question here (Merleau-Ponty 1988, 41–44). On the other hand, he occasionally admitted that there is an experiential dimension that remains unique for each individual. I can never be aware of an other's experiences in the same way as he is himself, nor can he be aware of mine (Merleau-Ponty 1945, 408–412, 418, 514).

4. In *L'être et le néant*, Sartre nicely summed up Husserl's position in the following manner: "Thus each object far from being constituted as for Kant, by a simple relation to the *subject*, appears in my concrete experience as polyvalent; it is given orig-

inally as possessing systems of reference to an indefinite plurality of consciousnesses; it is *on* the table, *on* the wall that the Other is revealed to me as that to which the object under consideration is perpetually referred—as well as on the occasion of the concrete appearances of Pierre or Paul" (Sartre 1943, 278 [1956, 233]).

5. For a more extensive presentation of this line of argumentation, see Zahavi 1997 and 2001.

6. "Meine Erfahrung als Welterfahrung (also jede meiner Wahrnehmungen schon) schließt nicht nur Andere als Weltobjekte ein, sondern beständig (in seinsmäßiger Mitgeltung) als Mitsubjekte, als Mitkonstituierende, und beides ist untrennbar verflochten" (Husserl Ms. C 17 36a).

7. "Wenn Einfühlung eintritt, ist etwa auch da schon die Gemeinschaft, die Intersubjektivität da und Einfühlung dann bloß enthüllendes Leisten?" (Husserl Ms. C 17 84b).

8. Husserl's discussion of intersubjectivity contains quite a number of different suggestions. To mention a further issue that, incidentally, illustrates an aspect of Husserl's thought still virtually unknown outside the narrow circles of Husserl scholars: "Here I can only briefly point out that it is not only through social acts that such connectedness can be brought about. Just as individual subjects develop their activity on the basis of an obscure, blind passivity, so the same also holds of social activity. But passivity, the instinctual life of drives, can already bring about intersubjective connection. Thus at the lowest level, a sexual community is already established through the instinctual sexual life, even though it may only disclose its essential intersubjectivity when the instinct is fulfilled" (Hua 9/514).

9. As a curiosity, it can be mentioned that Heidegger, in a letter to Sartre from October 28, 1945, wrote as follows: "I am in agreement with your critique of 'being-with' and with your insistence on being-for-others, as well as in partial agreement with your critique of my explication of death" (quoted in Towarnicki 1993, 84).

10. In his discussion of the emotional life of humans, Darwin writes, "It is not the simple act of reflecting on our own appearance, but the thinking of what others think of us, which excites a blush" (Darwin 1998, 324).

11. Whereas the guarantee is, in every single case, fallible—what I take to be a valid experience of another could turn out to be a hallucination—this is not the case when it comes to the fundamental connection between intersubjective experienceability and objectivity.

12. See p. 95 above.

13. This idea is not unique to phenomenology. As Davidson writes, "There are three basic problems: how a mind can know the world of nature, how it is possible for one mind to know another, and how it is possible to know the contents of our own minds

without resort to observation or evidence. It is a mistake, I shall urge, to suppose that these questions can be collapsed into two, or taken in isolation" (Davidson 2001, 208).

14. An earlier version of some of the material in this chapter originally appeared in my article "Beyond Empathy: Phenomenological Approaches to Intersubjectivity," *Journal of Consciousness Studies* 8/5–7, 2001, 151–167.

Chapter 7

1. Gopnik and Wellman have compared the transition that occurs between a three-year-old and four-year-old child's understanding of mind to the transition between Copernicus' *De revolutionibus* and Kepler's discovery of elliptical orbits (Gopnik and Wellman 1995, 242).

2. Occasionally, some theory-theorists have been cautious enough to admit that this parallelism might not hold true for all kinds of mental states, but there is no general agreement about what should count as relevant exceptions.

3. For an informative overview of these tests, see Baron-Cohen 2000.

4. Nichols and Stich further argue that mind-reading skills should be divided into two categories, detecting and reasoning. Roughly put, the idea is that different mechanisms are active in detecting (attributing, having access to) mental states and reasoning about (explaining) them (Nichols and Stich 2003, 158). This distinction appears quite reasonable, and so does the natural inference that only the process of reasoning involves a theory of mind. However, Nichols and Stich also argue that in order to be in possession of self-awareness all that is needed is a monitoring mechanism that "takes the representation p in the Belief Box as input and produces the representation *I believe that p* as output. This mechanism would be trivial to implement. To produce representations of one's own beliefs, the monitoring mechanism merely has to copy representations from the Belief Box, embed the copies in a representation schema of the form: *I believe that—*, and then place the new representations back in the Belief Box" (Nichols and Stich 2003, 170). Whether this attempt to account for the structure of self-awareness and solve the classical problems concerning *first-person reference* is successful, is, however, another question. It is in my view highly unlikely that it would succeed.

5. In the recent edition of her book *Autism: Explaining the Enigma*, Frith readily concedes that autistic subjects can describe their inner states, feelings, and bodily sensations in remarkable details and with extraordinary vividness. Autistic persons who do acquire a conscious theory of mind might consequently attain an extensive degree of self-knowledge. According to Frith, however, it would remain a completely self-directed type of self-knowledge. It would provide the autistic subject with an awareness of himself, but it would not allow him to understand that there are other selves; he would still lack knowledge of the minds of others (Frith 2003, 208–209, 213).

6. As Heal has pointed out, our theoretical knowledge is much too general and abstract to cover everything. Only a small part of our know-how can be reflected and articulated in a theoretical "know-that"; by arguing the way they do, the theory-theorists are basically facing the same problem that research in artificial intelligence has also faced and failed to solve, namely the so-called frame problem: the problem of providing a general theory of relevance (Heal 1996, 78, 81; see also Dreyfus 1992).

7. This is also granted by modularity nativism. Although this version of the theory-theory argues that the theory is innate, it still concedes that the theory needs a certain amount of experience as a trigger.

8. In one of his research manuscripts, Husserl stated that empathy is a precondition for the recognition of one's own mirror-image (Hua 14/509). There might be some empirical evidence in support of this idea. Chimpanzees are also able to pass the mirror-recognition task, but as Lewis and Brooks-Gunn write, chimpanzees reared in social isolation have been unable to exhibit self-directed behavior in a mirror situation even after extensive exposure. "As a further test of the importance of social experience, two of the original chimpanzees were given three months of group experience, after which time self recognitory responses began to appear" (Lewis and Brooks-Gunn 1979, 220).

9. When performing habitual or skillful acts (brushing our teeth, walking, typing, dancing, etc.) we are usually unable to thematize the performance without obstructing its very flow, and afterward we are rarely, if ever, able to recall each of the single movements. Should this not make us pause, and force us to acknowledge that although proprioception might provide vital and essential information about the body, it is information that is generally processed nonconsciously? But although we might be unable to thematize and recall each of our movements, this does not necessarily make the movements nonconscious. When I am typing, I do not pay attention to the movements of each digit, but I am certainly aware that they are moving. It is consequently important not to confuse different levels of bodily awareness. Pre-reflective body-awareness might be relatively undifferentiated—as Merleau-Ponty wrote, our functioning body is primarily given as an undivided and unified bodily field (Merleau-Ponty 1945, 114)—but this does not make it negligible. The following example by Merleau-Ponty may help illustrate the idea: If I stand in front of my desk and lean on it with both hands, only my hands are stressed, but the whole of my body trails behind them like the tail of a comet. It is not that I am unaware of the whereabouts of my shoulders or back, but they are simply swallowed up in the awareness of my hands (Merleau-Ponty 1945, 116, 168).

10. For a more extensive overview of different phenomenological investigations of the body, see Zaner 1964; Leder 1990; and Waldenfels 2000.

11. The timetable has changed drastically, however. Merleau-Ponty was referring to a fifteen-month-old child, and he even maintained that the child lacked the neurological capacity to perceive external objects until after the process of myelinization

had occurred between the third and sixth month of life (Merleau-Ponty 1988, 313).

12. As Merleau-Ponty pointed out, the connection between the visual and tactile experience of the body is not forged gradually. I do not translate the "data of touch" into the language of "seeing" or vice versa. There is an immediate awareness of the correspondence (Merleau-Ponty 1945, 175–177, 262, 265).

13. For a recent attempt to relate the findings of Meltzoff and Moore to ideas found in Husserl's posthumously published research manuscripts, see Smith 2003, 239–247.

14. An earlier version of some of the material in this chapter originally appeared in my article "The Embodied Self-Awareness of the Infant: A Challenge to the Theory of Mind?" in D. Zahavi, Th. Grünbaum, and J. Parnas (eds.), *The Structure and Development of Self-Consciousness: Interdisciplinary Perspectives*, John Benjamins, Amsterdam and Philadelphia, 2004, 35–63.

References

Armstrong, D. M. (1968). *A Materialist Theory of the Mind*. London: Routledge and Kegan Paul.

Asemissen, H. U. (1958/1959). "Egologische Reflexion." *Kant-Studien 50*, 262–272.

Asperger, H. (1991). "Autistic psychopathology in childhood." In U. Frith (ed.), *Autism and Asperger Syndrome* (37–92). Cambridge: Cambridge University Press.

Avramides, A. (2001). *Other Minds*. London: Routledge.

Baker, L. R. (2000). *Persons and Bodies*. Cambridge: Cambridge University Press.

Baron-Cohen, S. (1989). "Are Autistic Children 'Behaviorists'? An Examination of Their Mental–Physical and Appearance–Reality Distinctions." *Journal of Autism and Developmental Disorders 19*, 579–600.

Baron-Cohen, S. (1995). *Mindblindness: An Essay on Autism and Theory of Mind*. Cambridge, Mass.: MIT Press.

Baron-Cohen, S. (2000). "The Cognitive Neuroscience of Autism: Evolutionary Approaches." In M. S. Gazzaniga (ed.), *The New Cognitive Neurosciences*, second edition (1249–1257). Cambridge, Mass.: MIT Press.

Baron-Cohen, S., A. Leslie, and U. Frith (1985). "Does the Autistic Child Have a 'Theory of Mind'?" *Cognition 21*, 37–46.

Bernet, R. (1994). *La vie du sujet*. Paris: PUF.

Bermúdez, J. L. (1998). *The Paradox of Self-Consciousness*. Cambridge, Mass.: MIT Press.

Berrios, G. E., and I. S. Marková (2003). "The Self and Psychiatry: A Conceptual History." In T. Kircher and A. S. David (eds.), *The Self in Neuroscience and Psychiatry* (9–39). Cambridge: Cambridge University Press.

Blackburn, S. (1995). "Theory, Observation, and Drama." In M. Davies and T. Stone (eds.), *Folk Psychology: The Theory of Mind Debate* (274–290). Oxford: Blackwell.

Blankenburg, W. (1971). *Der Verlust der natürlichen Selbstverständlichkeit. Ein Beitrag zur Psychopathologie symptomarmer Schizophrenien.* Stuttgart: Enke.

Bleuler, E. (1911/1950). *Dementia Praecox or the Group of Schizophrenias.* Transl. J. Zinkin. New York: International Universities Press.

Block, N. (1997). "On a Confusion about a Function of Consciousness." In N. Block, O. Flanagan, and G. Güzeldere (eds.), *The Nature of Consciousness* (375–415). Cambridge, Mass.: MIT Press.

Bosch, G. (1962/1970). *Infantile Autism: A Clinical and Phenomenological-Anthropological Approach Taking Language as the Guide.* New York: Springer-Verlag.

Botterill, G. (1996). "Folk Psychology and Theoretical Status." In P. Carruthers and P. K. Smith (eds.), *Theories of Theories of Mind* (105–118). Cambridge: Cambridge University Press.

Boucher, J. (1996). "What Could Possibly Explain Autism?" In P. Carruthers and P. K. Smith (eds.), *Theories of Theories of Mind* (223–241). Cambridge: Cambridge University Press.

Brentano, F. (1874/1924). *Psychologie vom empirischen Standpunkt* I. Hamburg: Felix Meiner; *Psychology from an Empirical Standpoint.* Trans. A. C. Rancurello, D. B. Terrell, and L. L. McAlister. London: Routledge and Kegan Paul, 1973.

Brook, A. (1994). *Kant and the Mind.* Cambridge: Cambridge University Press.

Bruzina, R. (1993). "The Revision of the Bernau Time-Consciousness Manuscripts: *Status Questionis*—Freiburg, 1928–1930." *Alter* 1, 357–383.

Byrne, A. (1997). "Some Like It HOT: Consciousness and Higher-Order Thoughts." *Philosophical Studies* 86, 103–129.

Campbell, J. (1994). *Past, Space, and Self.* Cambridge, Mass.: MIT Press.

Caputo, J. D. (1992). "The Question of Being and Transcendental Phenomenology: Reflections on Heidegger's Relationship to Husserl." In C. Macann (ed.), *Martin Heidegger—Critical Assessments I* (326–344). London: Routledge.

Carruthers, P. (1996a). *Language, Thoughts, and Consciousness: An Essay in Philosophical Psychology.* Cambridge: Cambridge University Press.

Carruthers, P. (1996b). "Simulation and Self-Knowledge: A Defence of Theory-Theory." In P. Carruthers and P. K. Smith (eds.), *Theories of Theories of Mind* (22–38). Cambridge: Cambridge University Press.

Carruthers, P. (1996c). "Autism as Mind-Blindness: An Elaboration and Partial Defence." In P. Carruthers and P. K. Smith (eds.), *Theories of Theories of Mind* (257–273). Cambridge: Cambridge University Press.

Carruthers, P. (1998). "Natural Theories of Consciousness." *European Journal of Philosophy* 6/2, 203–222.

Carruthers, P. (2000). *Phenomenal Consciousness: A Naturalistic Theory.* Cambridge: Cambridge University Press.

Carruthers, P., and Smith, P. K. (1996). "Introduction." In P. Carruthers and P. K. Smith (eds.), *Theories of Theories of Mind* (1–8). Cambridge: Cambridge University Press.

Cassam, Q. (1997). *Self and World.* Oxford: Clarendon Press.

Cassirer, E. (1954). *Philosophie der symbolischen Formen III.* Darmstadt: Wissenschaftliche Buchgesellschaft; *The Philosophy of Symbolic Forms III.* Trans. R. Manheim. New Haven and London: Yale University Press, 1957.

Castañeda, H.-N. (1967). "The Logic of Self-Knowledge." *Noûs* 1, 9–22.

Chalmers, D. J. (1996). *The Conscious Mind: In Search of a Fundamental Theory.* New York: Oxford University Press.

Churchland, P. M. (1988). *Matter and Consciousness: A Contemporary Introduction to the Philosophy of Mind.* Cambridge, Mass.: MIT Press.

Churchland, P. S. (2002). *Brain-Wise: Studies in Neurophilosophy.* Cambridge, Mass.: MIT Press.

Cohen, D. J. (1980). "The Pathology of the Self in Primary Childhood Autism and Gilles de la Tourette Syndrome." *Psychiatric Clinics of North America* 3, 383–402.

Cole, J. (1998). *About Face.* Cambridge, Mass.: MIT Press.

Conrad, K. (1958/2002). *Die beginnende Schizophrenie: Versuch einer Gestaltsanalyse des Wahns.* Bonn: Psychiatrie-Verlag.

Courtine, J.-F. (1990). *Heidegger et la phénomenologie.* Paris: Vrin.

Cramer, K. (1974). " 'Erlebnis.' Thesen zu Hegels Theorie des Selbstbewusstseins mit Rücksicht auf die Aporien eines Grundbegriffs nachhegelscher Philosophie." In H.-G. Gadamer (ed.), *Stuttgarter Hegel-Tage 1970* (537–603). Beiheft 11. Bonn: Hegel-Studien.

Crowell, S. G. (2001). *Husserl, Heidegger, and the Space of Meaning.* Evanston, Ill.: Northwestern University Press.

Dainton, B. (2000). *Stream of Consciousness: Unity and Continuity in Conscious Experience.* London: Routledge.

Damasio, A. (1999). *The Feeling of What Happens.* San Diego: Harcourt.

Dancy, J. (1985). *An Introduction to Contemporary Epistemology.* Oxford: Basil Blackwell.

Darwin. C. (1998). *The Expression of the Emotions in Man and Animals.* New York: Oxford University Press.

Davidson, D. (2001). *Subjective, Intersubjective, Objective.* Oxford: Oxford University Press.

Dennett, D. C. (1981). "Reflections." In D. R. Hofstadter and D. C. Dennett (eds.), *The Mind's I: Fantasies and Reflections on Self and Soul* (230–231). London: Penguin.

Dennett, D. C. (1991). *Consciousness Explained.* Boston: Little, Brown.

Dennett, D. C. (1992). "The Self as the Center of Narrative Gravity." In F. S. Kessel, P. M. Cole, and D. L. Johnson (eds.), *Self and Consciousness: Multiple Perspectives* (103–115). Hillsdale, N.J.: Erlbaum.

Derrida, J. (1967a). *La voix et le phénomène.* Paris: PUF; *Speech and Phenomena and Other Essays on Husserl's Theory of Signs.* Trans. D. B. Allison. Evanston: Northwestern University Press, 1973.

Derrida, J. (1967b). *De la grammatologie.* Paris: Les Éditions de Minuit.

Derrida, J. (1990). *Le problème de la genèse dans la philosophie de Husserl.* Paris: PUF.

Dilthey, W. (1905). "Studien zur Grundlegung der Geisteswissenschaften." *Sitzungsbericht der Königlichen Preußischen Akademie der Wissenschaften* 5, 322–343.

Dokic, J. (2003). "The Sense of Ownership: An Analogy between Sensation and Action." In J. Roessler and N. Eilan (eds.), *Agency and Self-Awareness* (321–344). Oxford: Oxford University Press.

Dretske, F. (1995). *Naturalizing the Mind.* Cambridge, Mass.: MIT Press.

Dreyfus, H. L. (1992). *What Computers Still Can't Do: A Critique of Artificial Reason.* Cambridge, Mass.: MIT Press.

Drummond, J. (2004). " 'Cognitive Impenetrability' and the Complex Intentionality of the Emotions." *Journal of Consciousness Studies* 11/10–11, 109–126.

Ekman, P. (2003). *Emotions Revealed: Understanding Faces and Feelings.* London: Weidenfeld and Nicolson.

Evans, C. O. (1970). *The Subject of Consciousness.* London: George Allen and Unwin.

Fink, E. (1966). *Studien zur Phänomenologie 1930–1939.* Den Haag: Martinus Nijhoff.

Fink, E. (1987). *Existenz und Coexistenz.* Würzburg: Königshausen und Neumann.

Fink, E. (1992). *Natur, Freiheit, Welt.* Würzburg: Königshausen und Neumann.

Fivaz-Depeursinge, E., N. Favez, and F. Frascarolo (2004). "Threesome Intersubjectivity in Infancy." In D. Zahavi, T. Grünbaum, and J. Parnas (eds.), *The Structure and Development of Self-Consciousness: Interdisciplinary Perspectives* (221–234). Amsterdam: John Benjamins.

Flanagan, O. (1992). *Consciousness Reconsidered.* Cambridge, Mass.: MIT Press.

Frank, M. (1984). *Was ist Neostrukturalismus?* Frankfurt am Main: Suhrkamp.

Frank, M. (1986). *Die Unhintergehbarkeit von Individualität.* Frankfurt am Main: Suhrkamp.

Frank, M. (1991a). "Fragmente einer Geschichte der Selbstbewußtseins-Theorie von Kant bis Sartre." In M. Frank (ed.), *Selbstbewußtseinstheorien von Fichte bis Sartre* (413–599). Frankfurt am Main: Suhrkamp.

Frank, M. (1991b). *Selbstbewußtsein und Selbsterkenntnis.* Stuttgart: Reclam.

Frith, C. D. (1992). *The Cognitive Neuropsychology of Schizophrenia.* Hove: Lawrence Erlbaum.

Frith, C. D. (1994). "Theory of Mind in Schizophrenia." In A. David and J. Cutting (eds.), *The Neuropsychology of Schizophrenia* (147–161). Hillsdale, N.J.: Erlbaum.

Frith, C. D., and E. C. Johnstone (2003). *Schizophrenia: A Very Short Introduction.* Oxford: Oxford University Press.

Frith, U. (2003). *Autism: Explaining the Enigma.* Oxford: Blackwell.

Frith, U., and F. Happé (1999). "Theory of Mind and Self-Consciousness: What Is It Like to Be Autistic?" *Mind and Language* 14, 1–22.

Gallagher, S., and J. Shear (eds.) (1999). *Models of the Self.* Thorverton: Imprint Academic.

Gallagher, S. (2000a). "Philosophical Conceptions of the Self: Implications for Cognitive Science." *Trends in Cognitive Science* 4/1, 14–21.

Gallagher, S. (2000b). "Self-Reference and Schizophrenia: A Cognitive Model of Immunity to Error through Misidentification." In D. Zahavi (ed.), *Exploring the Self* (203–239). Amsterdam: John Benjamins.

Gallagher, S. (2001). "The Practice of Mind: Theory, Simulation, or Interaction." *Journal of Consciousness Studies* 8/5–7, 83–108.

Gallagher, S. (2003a). "Self-Narrative in Schizophrenia." In T. Kircher and A. David (eds.), *The Self in Neuroscience and Psychiatry* (336–357). Cambridge: Cambridge University Press.

Gallagher, S. (2003b). "Bodily Self-Awareness and Object Perception." *Theoria et Historia Scientiarum* 7, 53–68.

Gendler, T. S. (1999). "Exceptional Persons: On the Limits of Imaginary Cases." In S. Gallagher and J. Shear (eds.), *Models of the Self* (447–465). Thorverton: Imprint Academic.

Gethmann, C. F. (1986–87). "Philosophie als Vollzug und als Begriff." *Dilthey Jahrbuch* 4, 27–53.

Gibson, J. J. (1979/1986). *The Ecological Approach to Visual Perception*. Hillsdale, N.J.: Erlbaum.

Gloy, K. (1998). *Bewusstseinstheorien. Zur Problematik und Problemgeschichte des Bewusstseins und Selbstbewusstseins*. Freiburg: Alber.

Goldman, A. I. (1997). "Consciousness, Folk Psychology, and Cognitive Science." In N. Block, O. Flanagan, and G. Güzeldere (eds.), *The Nature of Consciousness* (111–125). Cambridge, Mass.: MIT Press.

Gopnik, A. (1993). "How We Know Our Minds: The Illusion of First-Person Knowledge of Intentionality." *Behavioral and Brain Sciences* 16, 1–14.

Gopnik, A. (1996). "Theories and Modules: Creation Myths, Developmental Realities, and Neurath's Boat." In P. Carruthers and P. K. Smith (eds.), *Theories of Theories of Mind* (169–183). Cambridge: Cambridge University Press.

Gopnik, A., and A. N. Meltzoff (1994). "Minds, Bodies, and Persons: Young Children's Understanding of the Self and Others as Reflected in Imitation and 'Theory of Mind' Research." In S. Parker and R. Mitchell (eds.), *Self-Awareness in Animals and Humans* (166–186). New York: Cambridge University Press.

Gopnik. A., A. N. Meltzoff, and P. K. Kuhl (2001). *The Scientist in the Crib: What Early Learning Tells Us about the Mind*. New York: Perennial.

Gopnik, A., and H. M. Wellman (1995). "Why the Child's Theory of Mind Really *Is* a Theory." In M. Davies and T. Stone (eds.), *Folk Psychology: The Theory of Mind Debate* (232–258). Oxford: Blackwell.

Gordon, R. M. (1996). " 'Radical' Simulationism." In P. Carruthers and P. K. Smith (eds.), *Theories of Theories of Mind* (11–21). Cambridge: Cambridge University Press.

Granberg, A. (2003). "Mood and Method in Heidegger's *Sein und Zeit*." In D. Zahavi, S. Heinämaa, and H. Ruin (eds.), *Metaphysics, Facticity, Interpretation* (91–113). Dordrecht: Kluwer Academic.

Gurwitsch, A. (1941). "A Non-egological Conception of Consciousness." *Philosophy and Phenomenological Research* 1, 325–338.

Gurwitsch, A. (1966). *Studies in Phenomenology and Psychology*. Evanston, Ill.: Northwestern University Press.

Gurwitsch, A. (1974). *Das Bewußtseinsfeld*. Berlin: de Gruyter.

Gurwitsch, A. (1979). *Human Encounters in the Social World*. Trans. F. Kersten. Pittsburgh: Duquesne University Press.

Gurwitsch, A. (1985). *Marginal Consciousness*. Athens: Ohio University Press.

Habermas, J. (1981). *Theorie des kommunikativen Handelns II*. Frankfurt am Main: Suhrkamp.

Habermas, J. (1984). *Vorstudien und Ergänzungen zur Theorie des kommunikativen Handelns*. Frankfurt am Main: Suhrkamp.

Habermas, J. (1988). *Nachmetaphysisches Denken*. Frankfurt am Main: Suhrkamp.

Hart, J. G. (1992). *The Person and the Common Life*. Dordrecht: Kluwer Academic.

Heal, J. (1996). "Simulation, Theory, and Content." In P. Carruthers and P. K. Smith (eds.), *Theories of Theories of Mind* (75–89). Cambridge: Cambridge University Press.

Heidegger, M. (1986). *Sein und Zeit*. Tübingen: Max Niemeyer; *Being and Time*. Trans. J. Stambaugh. Albany: SUNY, 1996.

Heidegger's Gesamtsausgabe (GA)

Gesamtausgabe Band 3: *Kant und das Problem der Metaphysik*. Frankfurt am Main: Vittorio Klostermann, 1991.

Gesamtausgabe Band 9: *Wegmarken*. Frankfurt am Main: Vittorio Klostermann, 1976.

Gesamtausgabe Band 20: *Prolegomena zur Geschichte des Zeitbegriffs*. Frankfurt am Main: Vittorio Klostermann, 1979; *History of the Concept of Time: Prolegomena*. Trans. Th. Kisiel. Bloomington, Ind.: Indiana University Press, 1985.

Gesamtausgabe Band 24: *Die Grundprobleme der Phänomenologie*. Frankfurt am Main: Vittorio Klostermann, 1989; *The Basic Problems of Phenomenology*. Trans. A. Hofstadter. Bloomington, Ind.: Indiana University Press, 1982.

Gesamtausgabe Band 27: *Einleitung in die Philosophie*. Frankfurt am Main. Vittorio Klostermann, 2001.

Gesamtausgabe Band 56/57: *Zur Bestimmung der Philosophie*. Frankfurt am Main: Vittorio Klostermann, 1999.

Gesamtausgabe Band 58: *Grundprobleme der Phänomenologie (1919/1920)*. Frankfurt am Main: Vittorio Klostermann, 1993.

Gesamtausgabe Band 59: *Phänomenologie der Anschauung und des Ausdrucks*. Frankfurt am Main: Vittorio Klostermann, 1993.

Gesamtausgabe Band 61: *Phänomenologische Interpretationen zu Aristoteles. Einführung in die phänomenologische Forschung*. Frankfurt am Main: Vittorio Klostermann, 1994.

Heal, J. (1986). "Replication and Functionalism." In J. Butterfield (ed.), *Language, Mind, and Logic* (135–150). Cambridge: Cambridge University Press.

Henrich, D. (1966). "Fichte ursprüngliche Einsicht." In D. Henrich and H. Wagner (eds.), *Subjektivität und Metaphysik. Festschrift für Wolfgang Cramer* (188–232). Frankfurt am Main: Klostermann.

Henrich, D. (1970). "Selbstbewußtsein, kritische Einleitung in eine Theorie." In R. Bubner, K. Cramer, and R. Wiehl (eds.), *Hermeneutik und Dialektik* (257–284). Tübingen: Mohr.

Henrich, D. (1982). *Selbstverhältnisse*. Stuttgart: Reclam.

Henry, M. (1963). *L'essence de la manifestation*. Paris: PUF.

Henry, M. (1965). *Philosophie et phénoménologie du corps*. Paris: PUF; *Philosophy and Phenomenology of the Body*. Trans. G. Etzkorn. The Hague: Martinus Nijhoff, 1975.

Henry, M. (1966). "Le concept d'âme a-t-il un sens?" *Revue philosophique de Louvain* 64, 5–33.

Henry, M. (2003). *De la subjectivité*. Paris: PUF.

Herrmann, F.-W. von (2000). *Hermeneutik und Reflexion. Der Begriff der Phänomenologie bei Heidegger und Husserl*. Frankfurt am Main: Vittorio Klostermann.

Hobson, R. P. (1991). "Against the theory of 'Theory of Mind.'" *British Journal of Developmental Psychology* 9, 33–51.

Hobson, R. P. (1993). *Autism and the Development of Mind*. Hove: Psychology Press.

Hobson, R. P. (2002). *The Cradle of Thought*. London: Macmillan.

Hume, D. (1888). *A Treatise of Human Nature*. Oxford: Clarendon Press.

Husserl, E. (1981). *Shorter Works*. Edited by P. McCormick and F. A. Elliston. Notre Dame, Ind.: University of Notre Dame Press.

Husserl, E. (1994). *Briefwechsel II*. Husserliana Dokumente III/1–10. Dordrecht: Kluwer Academic.

Husserliana (Hua)

Husserliana 1: *Cartesianische Meditationen und Pariser Vorträge*. Den Haag: Martinus Nijhoff, 1950.

Husserliana 3: *Ideen zu einer reinen Phänomenologie und phänomenologischen Philosophie. Erstes Buch. Allgemeine Einführung in die reine Phänomenologie*. Den Haag: Martinus Nijhoff, 1976.

Husserliana 4: *Ideen zu einer reinen Phänomenologie und phänomenologischen Philosophie. Zweites Buch. Phänomenologische Untersuchungen zur Konstitution*. Den Haag: Martinus Nijhoff, 1952.

Husserliana 5: *Ideen zu einer reinen Phänomenologie und phänomenologischen Philosophie. Drittes Buch: Die Phänomenologie und die Fundamente der Wissenschaften.* Den Haag: Martinus Nijhoff, 1952.

Husserliana 6: *Die Krisis der europäischen Wissenschaften und die transzendentale Phänomenologie. Eine Einleitung in die phänomenologische Philosophie.* Den Haag: Martinus Nijhoff, 1954.

Husserliana 7: *Erste Philosophie (1923/24). Erster Teil. Kritische Ideengeschichte.* Den Haag: Martinus Nijhoff, 1956.

Husserliana 8: *Erste Philosophie (1923/24). Zweiter Teil. Theorie der phänomenologischen Reduktion.* Den Haag: Martinus Nijhoff, 1959.

Husserliana 9: *Phänomenologische Psychologie. Vorlesungen Sommersemester 1925.* Den Haag: Martinus Nijhoff, 1962; *Phenomenological Psychology: Lectures, Summer Semester, 1925.* Trans. John Scanlon. The Hague: Martinus Nijhoff, 1977.

Husserliana 10: *Zur Phänomenologie des inneren Zeitbewusstseins (1893–1917).* Den Haag: Martinus Nijhoff, 1966; *On the Phenomenology of the Consciousness of Internal Time (1893–1917).* Trans. John Barnett Brough. Dordrecht: Kluwer Academic, 1991.

Husserliana 11: *Analysen zur passiven Synthesis. Aus Vorlesungs- und Forschungsmanuskripten 1918–1926.* Den Haag: Martinus Nijhoff, 1966; *Analyses Concerning Passive and Active Synthesis. Lectures on Transcendental Logic.* Trans. Anthony J. Steinbock. Dordrecht: Kluwer Academic, 2001.

Husserliana 13: *Zur Phänomenologie der Intersubjektivität. Texte aus dem Nachlass. Erster Teil: 1905–1920.* Den Haag: Martinus Nijhoff, 1973.

Husserliana 14: *Zur Phänomenologie der Intersubjektivität. Texte aus dem Nachlass. Zweiter Teil: 1921–1928.* Den Haag: Martinus Nijhoff, 1973.

Husserliana 15: *Zur Phänomenologie der Intersubjektivität. Texte aus dem Nachlass. Dritter Teil: 1929–1935.* Den Haag: Martinus Nijhoff, 1973.

Husserliana 16: *Ding und Raum. Vorlesungen 1907.* Den Haag: Martinus Nijhoff, 1973.

Husserliana 17: *Formale und transzendentale Logik. Versuch einer Kritik der logischen Vernunft.* Den Haag: Martinus Nijhoff, 1974; *Formal and Transcendental Logic.* Trans. Dorion Cairns. The Hague: Martinus Nijhoff, 1969.

Husserliana 18: *Logische Untersuchungen. Erster Band. Prolegomena zur reinen Logik.* Den Haag: Martinus Nijhoff, 1975; *Logical Investigations.* 2 vols. Trans. J. N. Findlay. London: Routledge and Kegan Paul, 1970, 41–247.

Husserliana 19: *Logische Untersuchungen. Zweiter Band. Untersuchungen zur Phänomenologie und Theorie der Erkenntnis.* Den Haag: Martinus Nijhoff, 1984; *Logical Investigations.* 2 vols. Trans. J. N. Findlay. London: Routledge & Kegan Paul, 1970, 248–869.

Husserliana 23: *Phantasie, Bildbewußtsein, Erinnerung.* Dordrecht: Kluwer Academic, 1980.

Husserliana 24: *Einleitung in die Logik und Erkenntnistheorie. Vorlesungen 1906/07.* Dordrecht: Martinus Nijhoff, 1984.

Husserliana 25: *Aufsätze und Vorträge (1911–1921).* Dordrecht: Martinus Nijhoff, 1987.

Husserliana 29: *Die Krisis der europäischen Wissenschaften und die transzendentale Phänomenologie. Ergänzungsband. Texte aus dem Nachlass 1934–1937.* Dordrecht: Kluwer Academic, 1993.

Husserliana 33: *Die "Bernauer Manuskripte" über das Zeitbewußtsein 1917/18.* Dordrecht: Kluwer Academic, 2001.

Husserl's unpublished manuscripts: Ms. C 10 (1931); Ms. C 12 (no date); Ms. C 16 (1931–1933); Ms. C 17 (1930–1932).

James, W. (1890). *The Principles of Psychology I–II.* London: Macmillan.

Jaspers, K. (1959). *Allgemeine Psychopathologie.* Berlin: Springer.

Jopling, D. A. (2000). *Self-Knowledge and the Self.* London: Routledge.

Journal of Consciousness Studies 4/5–6, 1997, 385–388. (Editorial.)

Kanner, L. (1943). "Autistic Disturbances of Affective Contact." *Nervous Child* 2, 217–250.

Kant, I. (1956). *Kritik der reinen Vernunft.* Hamburg: Felix Meiner.

Kern, I. (1964). *Husserl und Kant.* Den Haag: Martinus Nijhoff.

Kern, I. (1975). *Idee und Methode der Philosophie.* Berlin: de Gruyter.

Kern, I. (1989). "Selbstbewußtsein und Ich bei Husserl." In G. Funke (ed.), *Husserl-Symposion Mainz 1988* (51–63). Stuttgart: Akademie der Wissenschaften und der Literatur.

Kircher, T., and David, A. (eds.) (2003). *The Self in Neuroscience and Psychiatry.* Cambridge: Cambridge University Press.

Kisiel, T. (1995). *The Genesis of Heidegger's "Being and Time."* Berkeley: University of California Press.

Klawonn, E. (1991). *Jeg'ets ontologi.* Odense: Odense Universitetsforlag.

Kortooms, T. (2002). *Phenomenology of Time: Edmund Husserl's Analysis of Time-Consciousness.* Dordrecht: Kluwer Academic.

Kriegel, U. (2003). "Consciousness as Intransitive Self-Consciousness: Two Views and an Argument." *Canadian Journal of Philosophy* 33/1, 103–132.

Kriegel, U. (2004). "Consciousness and Self-Consciousness." *Monist* 87/2, 185–209.

Laing, R. D. (1960/1990). *The Divided Self.* Harmondsworth: Penguin Books.

Leder, D. (1990). *The Absent Body.* Chicago: University of Chicago Press.

Legerstee, M. (1999). "Mental and Bodily Awareness in Infancy." In S. Gallagher and J. Shear (eds.), *Models of the Self* (213–230). Thorverton: Imprint Academic.

Leslie, A. M. (1987). "Children's Understanding of the Mental World." In R. L. Gregory (ed.), *The Oxford Companion to the Mind* (139–142). Oxford: Oxford University Press.

Lévinas, E. (1961/1990). *Totalité et infini.* Dordrecht: Kluwer Academic.

Lévinas, E. (1974). *Autrement qu'être ou au-dela de l'essence.* Den Haag: Martinus Nijhoff.

Lévinas, E. (1979). *Le temps et l'autre.* Paris: Fata Morgana; *Time and the Other.* Trans. R. A. Cohen. Pittsburgh: Duquesne University Press, 1987.

Lévinas, E. (1991). *Cahier de l'Herne.* Ed. C. Chalier and M. Abensour. Paris: L'Herne.

Lévinas, E. (1992). *De Dieu qui vient à l'idée.* Paris: Vrin.

Lewis, M., and J. Brooks-Gunn (1979). *Social Cognition and the Acquisition of Self.* New York: Plenum Press.

Lewis, M. (2003). "The Development of Self-Consciousness." In J. Roessler and N. Eilan (eds.), *Agency and Self-Awareness* (275–295). Oxford: Oxford University Press.

Lohmar, D. (1998). *Erfahrung und kategoriales Denken.* Dordrecht: Kluwer Academic.

Lycan, W. G. (1987). *Consciousness.* Cambridge, Mass.: MIT Press.

Lycan, W. G. (1997). "Consciousness as Internal Monitoring." In N. Block, O. Flanagan, and G. Güzeldere (eds.), *The Nature of Consciousness* (754–771). Cambridge, Mass.: MIT Press.

MacIntyre, A. (1985). *After Virtue: A Study in Moral Theory.* London: Duckworth.

Mahler, M. S., F. Pine, and A. Bergman (1975). *The Psychological Birth of the Human Infants: Symbiosis and Individuation.* New York: Basic Books.

Marbach, E. (1974). *Das Problem des Ich in der Phänomenologie Husserls.* Den Haag: Martinus Nijhoff.

Marcel, A. (2003). "The Sense of Agency: Awareness and Ownership of Action." In J. Roessler and N. Eilan (eds.), *Agency and Self-Awareness* (48–93). Oxford: Clarendon Press.

McCulloch, G. (2003). *The Life of the Mind: An Essay on Phenomenological Externalism.* London: Routledge.

McDowell, J. (1998). *Meaning, Knowledge, and Reality.* Cambridge, Mass.: Harvard University Press.

McGeer, V. (2001). "Psycho-Practice, Psycho-Theory, and the Contrastive Case of Autism." *Journal of Consciousness Studies* 8/5–7, 109–132.

McIntyre, R. (1999). "Naturalizing Phenomenology? Dretske on Qualia." In J. Petitot, F. J. Varlea, B. Pachoud, and J.-M. Roy (eds.), *Naturalizing Phenomenology* (429–439). Stanford: Stanford University Press.

Mead, G. H. (1962). *Mind, Self, and Society: From the Standpoint of a Social Behaviorist.* Chicago: University of Chicago Press.

Meltzoff, A. N., and M. K. Moore (1995). "Infants' Understanding of People and Things: From Body Imitation to Folk Psychology." In J. L. Bermúdez, A. Marcel, and N. Eilan (eds.), *The Body and the Self* (43–69). Cambridge, Mass.: MIT Press.

Merleau-Ponty, M. (1942). *La structure du comportement.* Paris: PUF.

Merleau-Ponty, M. (1945). *Phénoménologie de la perception.* Paris: Éditions Gallimard; *Phenomenology of Perception.* Trans. C. Smith. London: Routledge and Kegan Paul, 1962.

Merleau-Ponty, M. (1960a). *Signes.* Paris: Éditions Gallimard; *Signs.* Trans. R. C. McCleary. Evanston, Ill.: Northwestern University Press, 1964.

Merleau-Ponty, M. (1960b). *Les relations avec autrui chez l'enfant.* Paris: Centre de Documentation Universitaire; *The Child's Relation with Others.* Trans. W. Cobb. In Merleau-Ponty, *The Primacy of Perception.* Evanston, Ill.: Northwestern University Press, 1964, 96–155.

Merleau-Ponty, M. (1964). *Le visible et l'invisible.* Paris: Tel Gallimard; *The Visible and the Invisible.* Trans. A. Lingis. Evanston, Ill.: Northwestern University Press, 1968.

Merleau-Ponty, M. (1966/1996). *Sens et non-sens.* Paris: Èditions Gallimard; *Sense and Nonsense.* Transl. H. L. Dreyfus and P. A. Dreyfus. Evanston, Ill.: Northwestern University Press, 1964.

Merleau-Ponty, M. (1988). *Merleau-Ponty à la Sorbonne.* Grenoble: Cynara.

Metzinger, T. (2003a). *Being No One*. Cambridge, Mass.: MIT Press.

Metzinger, T. (2003b). "Phenomenal Transparency and Cognitive Self-Reference." *Phenomenology and the Cognitive Sciences* 2/4, 353–393.

Minkowski, E. (1927). *La schizophrénie. Psychopathologie des schizoïdes et des schizophrènes*. Paris: Payot.

Minkowski, E. (1997). *Au-delà du rationalisme morbide*. Paris: Éditions l'Harmattan.

Mishara, A. (1990). "Husserl and Freud: Time, Memory, and the Unconscious." *Husserl Studies* 7, 29–58.

Mitchell, R. W. (1994). "Multiplicities of Self." In S. T. Paker, R. W. Mitchell, and M. L. Boccia (eds.), *Self-Awareness in Animals and Humans* (81–107). Cambridge: Cambridge University Press.

Moland, L. L. (2004). "Ideals, Ethics, and Personhood." In H. Ikäheimo, J. Kotkavirta, A. Laitinen, and P. Lyyra (eds.), *Personhood* (178–184). Jyväskylä: University of Jyväskylä Press.

Monnin, N. (2002). "Une réflexion pure est-elle possible?" *Alter* 10, 201–227.

Moran, R. (2001). *Authority and Estrangement: An Essay on Self-Knowledge*. Princeton: Princeton University Press.

Nagel, T. (1974). "What Is It Like to Be a Bat?" *Philosophical Review* 83, 435–450.

Natorp, P. (1912). *Allgemeine Psychologie*. Tübingen: J. C. B. Mohr.

Neisser, U. (1988). "Five Kinds of Self-knowledge." *Philosophical Psychology* 1/1, 35–59.

Neisser, U. (1993). "The Self Perceived." In U. Neisser (ed.), *The Perceived Self: Ecological and Interpersonal Sources of Self-Knowledge* (3–21). New York: Cambridge University Press.

Ni, L. (1998). "Urbewußtsein und Reflexion bei Husserl." *Husserl Studies* 15, 77–99.

Nichols, S., and S. Stich. (2003). "How to Read Your Own Mind: A Cognitive Theory of Self-Consciousness." In Q. Smith and A. Jokic (eds.), *Consciousness: New Philosophical Perspectives* (157–200). Oxford: Oxford University Press.

Nietzsche, F. (1960) *Werke III*. Munich: Carl Hanser Verlag.

Nietzsche, F. (1968). *The Will to Power*. Ed. Walter Kaufmann. London: Weidenfeld and Nicolson.

Øverenget, E. (1998). *Seeing the Self: Heidegger on Subjectivity*. Dordrecht: Kluwer Academic.

Overgaard, S. (2004). *Husserl and Heidegger on Being in the World*. Dordrecht: Kluwer Academic.

Overgaard, S. (2005). "Rethinking Other Minds: Wittgenstein and Levinas on Expression." *Inquiry* 48/3, 249–274.

Parfit, D. (1987). *Reasons and Persons*. Oxford: Clarendon Press.

Parnas, J. (2003). "Self and Schizophrenia: A Phenomenological Perspective." In T. Kircher and A. David (eds.), *The Self in Neuroscience and Psychiatry* (217–241). Cambridge: Cambridge University Press.

Parnas, J. (2004). "Belief and Pathology of Self-Awareness: A Phenomenological Contribution to the Classification of Delusions." *Journal of Consciousness Studies* 11/10–11, 148–161.

Parnas, J., P. Bovet, and D. Zahavi (2002). "Schizophrenic Autism: Clinical Phenomenology and Pathogenetic Implications." *World Psychiatry* 1/3, 131–136.

Parnas, J., and L. A. Sass (2001). "Self, Solipsism, and Schizophrenic Delusions." *Philosophy, Psychiatry, Psychology* 8/2–3, 101–120.

Piaget, J., and B. Inhelder (1969). *The Psychology of the Child*. New York: Basic Books.

Pothast, U. (1971). *Über einige Fragen der Selbstbeziehung*. Frankfurt am Main: Vittorio Klostermann.

Premack, D., and G. Woodruff (1978). "Does the Chimpanzee Have a Theory of Mind?" *Behavioral and Brain Sciences* 4, 515–526.

Putnam, H. (1999). *The Threefold Cord: Mind, Body, and World*. New York: Columbia University Press.

Raffman, D. (1999). "What Autism May Tell Us about Self-Awareness: A Commentary on Frith and Happé." *Mind and Language* 14/1, 23–31.

Rey, G. (1991). "Reasons for Doubting the Existence of Even Epiphenomenal Consciousness." *Behavioral and Brain Sciences* 14/4, 691–692.

Rickert, H. (1922). *Die Philosophie des Lebens: Darstellung und Kritik der philosophischen Modeströmungen unserer Zeit*. Tübingen: Mohr.

Ricoeur, P. (1950). *Philosophie de la volonté I. Le volontaire et l'involontaire*. Paris: Aubier; *Freedom and Nature. The Voluntary and the Involuntary*. Trans. E. V. Kohák. Evanston, Ill.: Northwestern University Press, 1966.

Ricoeur, P. (1985). *Temps et recit III: Le temps raconté*. Paris: Éditions du Seuil; *Time and Narrative III*. Trans. K. Blamey and D. Pellauer. Chicago: Chicago University Press, 1988.

Ricoeur, P. (1990). *Soi-même comme un autre*. Paris: Seuil; *Oneself as Another*. Trans. K. Blamey. Chicago: University of Chicago, 1992.

Rinofner-Kreidl, S. (2001). "Rezension von F.-W. von Herrmanns 'Hermeneutik und Reflexion.'" *Journal Phänomenologie* 16, 90–94.

Rochat, P. (2001). *The Infant's World*. Cambridge, Mass.: Harvard University Press.

Rosenthal, D. M. (1986). "Two Concepts of Consciousness." *Philosophical Studies* 94/3, 329–359.

Rosenthal, D. M. (1993a). "Thinking That One Thinks." In M. Davies and G. W. Humphreys (eds.), *Consciousness: Psychological and Philosophical Essays* (197–223). Oxford: Blackwell.

Rosenthal, D. M. (1993b). "Higher-Order Thoughts and the Appendage Theory of Consciousness." *Philosophical Psychology* 6, 155–166.

Rosenthal, D. M. (1996). "Two Concepts of Consciousness." *Philosophical Studies* 94/3, 329–359.

Rosenthal, D. M. (1997). "A Theory of Consciousness." In N. Block, O. Flanagan, and G. Güzeldere (eds.), *The Nature of Consciousness* (729–753). Cambridge, Mass.: MIT Press.

Rudd, A. (2003). *Expressing the World: Skepticism, Wittgenstein, and Heidegger*. Chicago: Open Court.

Sacks, O. (1995). *An Anthropologist on Mars*. London: Picador.

Sartre, J.-P. (1936). *La transcendance de l'ego*. Paris: Vrin; *The Transcendence of the Ego*. Trans. F. Williams and R. Kirkpatrick. New York: The Noonday Press, 1957.

Sartre, J.-P. (1943/1976). *L'être et le néant*. Paris: Tel Gallimard; *Being and Nothingness*. Trans. H. E. Barnes. New York: Philosophical Library, 1956.

Sartre, J.-P. (1948). "Conscience de soi et connaissance de soi." *Bulletin de la Société Française de Philosophie* 42, 49–91.

Sass, L. A. (1992). *Madness and Modernism: Insanity in the Light of Modern Art, Literature, and Thought*. New York: Basic Books.

Sass, L. A. (1994). *The Paradoxes of Delusion*. London: Cornell University Press.

Sass, L. A. (2000). "Schizophrenia, Self-Experience, and the So-Called 'Negative Symptoms.'" In D. Zahavi (ed.), *Exploring the Self* (149–182). Amsterdam: John Benjamins.

Sass, L. A., and J. Parnas (2003). "Schizophrenia, Consciousness, and the Self." *Schizophrenia Bulletin* 29/3, 427–444.

Sass, L., and J. Parnas (2006). "Explaining Schizophrenia: The Relevance of Phenomenology." In M. Chung, W. Fulford, and G. Graham (eds.), *Reconceiving Schizophrenia* (63–96). Oxford: Oxford University Press.

Scanlon, J. D. (1971). "Consciousness, the Streetcar, and the Ego: Pro Husserl, Contra Sartre." *Philosophical Forum* 2, 332–354.

Scheler, M. (1973). *Wesen und Formen der Sympathie*. Bern/Munich: Francke Verlag; *The Nature of Sympathy*. Trans. P. Heath. London: Routledge and Kegan Paul, 1954.

Searle, J. R. (1998). *Mind, Language, and Society*. New York: Basic Books.

Sheets-Johnstone, M. (1999). *The Primacy of Movement*. Amsterdam: John Benjamins.

Shoemaker, S. (1968). "Self-Reference and Self-Awareness." *Journal of Philosophy* 65, 556–579.

Shoemaker, S. (1984). "Personal Identity: A Materialist's Account." In S. Shoemaker and R. Swinburne, *Personal Identity*. Oxford: Blackwell.

Shoemaker, S. (1996). *The First-Person Perspective and Other Essays*. Cambridge: Cambridge University Press.

Siewert, C. P. (1998). *The Significance of Consciousness*. Princeton: Princeton University Press.

Smith, D. W. (1989). *The Circle of Acquaintance*. Dordrecht: Kluwer Academic.

Smith, A. D. (2003). *Husserl and the Cartesian Meditations*. London: Routledge.

Stawarska, B. (2003). "Facial Embodiment in 'Invisible' Imitation." *Theoria et Historia Scientiarum: International Journal for Interdisciplinary Studies* 7/1, 139–162.

Stephens, G. L., and G. Graham (2000). *When Self-Consciousness Breaks: Alien Voices and Inserted Thoughts*. Cambridge, Mass.: MIT Press.

Stern, D. N. (1983). "The Early Development of Schemas of Self, Other, and 'Self with Other.'" In J. D. Lichtenberg and S. Kaplan (eds.), *Reflections on Self-Psychology* (49–84). Hillsdale, N.J.: Analytical Press.

Stern, D. N. (1985). *The Interpersonal World of the Infant*. New York: Basic Books.

Stolzenberg, J. (1995). *Ursprung und System: Probleme der Begründung systematischer Philosophie im Werk Hermann Cohens, Paul Natorps und beim frühen Martin Heidegger*. Göttingen: Vandenhoeck and Ruprecht.

Strawson, G. (1994). *Mental Reality*. Cambridge, Mass.: MIT Press.

Strawson, G. (1997). "The Self." *Journal of Consciousness Studies* 4, 405–428.

Strawson, G. (1999). "The Self and the SESMET." In S. Gallagher and J. Shear (eds.), *Models of the Self* (483–518). Thorverton: Imprint Academic.

Strawson, G. (2000). "The Phenomenology and Ontology of the Self." In D. Zahavi (ed.), *Exploring the Self* (39–54). Amsterdam: John Benjamins.

Strawson, P. F. (1959). *Individuals*. London: Methuen.

Tatossian, A. (1979/1997). *La phénoménologie des psychoses*. Paris: L'art du comprendre.

Taylor, C. (1989). *Sources of the Self*. Cambridge, Mass.: Harvard University Press.

Thomas, A. (2003). "An Adverbial Theory of Consciousness." *Phenomenology and the Cognitive Sciences* 2, 161–185.

Thomasson, A. L. (2000). "After Brentano: A One-Level Theory of Consciousness." *European Journal of Philosophy* 8/2, 190–209.

Towarnicki, F. D. (1993). *À la rencontre de Heidegger. Souvenirs d'un messager de la Forêt-Noire*. Paris: Éditions Gallimard.

Trevarthen, C. (1979). "Communication and Cooperation in Early Infancy: A Description of Primary Intersubjectivity." In M. Bullowa (ed.), *Before Speech: The Beginning of Interpersonal Communication* (321–347). Cambridge: Cambridge University Press.

Tugendhat, E. (1970). *Der Wahrheitsbegriff bei Husserl und Heidegger*. Berlin: de Gruyter.

Tugendhat, E. (1979). *Selbstbewußtsein und Selbstbestimmung*. Frankfurt am Main: Suhrkamp.

Tye, M. (1995). *Ten Problems of Consciousness*. Cambridge, Mass.: MIT Press.

Van Gulick, R. (1997). "Understanding the Phenomenal Mind: Are We All Just Armadillos?" In N. Block, O. Flanagan, and G. Güzeldere (eds.), *The Nature of Consciousness* (559–566). Cambridge, Mass.: MIT Press.

Van Gulick, R. (2000). "Inward and Upward: Reflection, Introspection, and Self-Awareness." *Philosophical Topics* 28/2, 275–305.

Villela-Petit, M. (2003). "Narrative Identity and Ipseity by Paul Ricoeur." *Online originals*. Available at http://www.onlineoriginals.com/showitem.asp?itemID=287&articleID=11.

Waldenfels, B. (2000). *Das leibliche Selbst. Vorlesungen zur Phänomenologie des Leibes*. Frankfurt am Main: Suhrkamp.

Wegner, D. (2002). *The Illusion of Conscious Will*. Cambridge, Mass.: MIT Press.

Wellman, H. M., D. Cross, and J. Watson (2001). "Meta-analysis of Theory-of-Mind Development: The Truth about False Belief." *Child Development* 72, 655–684.

Wilkes, K. V. (1988). *Real People: Personal Identity without Thought Experiments.* Oxford: Clarendon Press.

Wing, L. (1991). "The Relationship between Asperger's Syndrome and Kanner's Autism." In U. Frith (ed.), *Autism and Asperger Syndrome* (93–121). Cambridge: Cambridge University Press.

Wittgenstein, L. (1953). *Philosophical Investigations.* Oxford: Blackwell.

Wittgenstein, L. (1980). *Remarks on the Philosophy of Psychology II.* Oxford: Blackwell.

Wittgenstein, L. (1982). *Last Writings on the Philosophy of Psychology*, volume I. Oxford: Blackwell.

Wittgenstein, L. (1992). *Last Writings on the Philosophy of Psychology*, volume II. Oxford: Blackwell.

Zahavi, D. (1997). "Horizontal Intentionality and Transcendental Intersubjectivity." *Tijdschrift voor Filosofie* 59/2, 304–321.

Zahavi, D. (1999). *Self-Awareness and Alterity: A Phenomenological Investigation.* Evanston, Ill.: Northwestern University Press.

Zahavi, D. (ed.) (2000). *Exploring the Self:* Amsterdam: John Benjamins.

Zahavi, D. (2001). *Husserl and Transcendental Intersubjectivity.* Athens: Ohio University Press.

Zahavi, D. (2002a). "First-Person Thoughts and Embodied Self-Awareness: Some Reflections on the Relation between Recent Analytical Philosophy and Phenomenology." *Phenomenology and the Cognitive Sciences* 1, 7–26.

Zahavi, D. (2002b). "Merleau-Ponty on Husserl: A Reappraisal." In T. Toadvine and L. Embree (eds.), *Merleau-Ponty's Reading of Husserl* (3–29). Dordrecht: Kluwer Academic.

Zahavi, D. (2003a). "Phenomenology of Self." In T. Kircher and A. David (eds.), *The Self in Neuroscience and Psychiatry* (56–75). Cambridge: Cambridge University Press.

Zahavi, D. (2003b). "Phenomenology and Metaphysics." In D. Zahavi, S. Heinämaa, and H. Ruin (eds.), *Metaphysics, Facticity, Interpretation* (3–22). Dordrecht: Kluwer Academic.

Zahavi, D. (2003c). *Husserl's Phenomenology.* Stanford: Stanford University Press.

Zahavi, D. (ed.) (2004a). *Hidden Resources: Classical Perspectives on Subjectivity.* Special double issue of *Journal of Consciousness Studies* 11/10–11.

Zahavi, D. (2004b). "Back to Brentano?" *Journal of Consciousness Studies* 11/10–11, 66–87.

Zahavi, D. (2004c). "Phenomenology and the Project of Naturalization." *Phenomenology and the Cognitive Sciences* 3/4, 331–347.

Zahavi, D. (2004d). "Time and Consciousness in the Bernau Manuscripts." *Husserl Studies* 20/2, 99–118.

Zahavi, D. (2004e). "Husserl's Noema and the Internalism–Externalism Debate." *Inquiry* 47/1, 42–66.

Zahavi, D. (2004f). "Natural Realism, Anti-Reductionism, and Intentionality: The 'Phenomenology' of Hilary Putnam." In D. Carr and C.-F. Cheung (eds.), *Time, Space, and Culture* (235–251). Dordrecht: Kluwer.

Zahavi, D. (2004g). "Alterity in Self." In S. Gallagher, S. Watson, Ph. Brun, and Ph. Romanski (eds.), *Ipseity and Alterity: Interdisciplinary Approaches to Intersubjectivity* (137–152). Rouen: Presses Universitaires de Rouen.

Zahavi, D. (2006). "The Phenomenological Tradition." In D. Moran (ed.), *Routledge Companion to Twentieth-Century Philosophy*. London: Routledge.

Zaner, R. M. (1964). *The Problem of Embodiment: Some Contributions to a Phenomenology of the Body*. The Hague: Martinus Nijhoff.

Index